Enchanted Wisdom

Enchanted Wisdom

Enduring Ideas of World Religions

Eric Bronson

Rock's Mills Press
Oakville, Ontario
2021

Published by
Rock's Mills Press
www.rocksmillspress.com

Copyright © 2021 by Eric Bronson.
All rights reserved. This book or any portion thereof may not be reproduced or used in any manner whatsoever without the express written permission of the publisher, except for the use of brief quotations in a book review.

Library and Archives Canada Cataloguing in Publication data is available on request.

For information about this book, contact us at customer.service@rocksmillspress.com.

To Asher and Max, my heroes

Contents

Introduction: Our Enchanted World … 13

PART ONE: LETTING GO … 18

1. Hinduism: The Divine Dance … 19
The Dance of Creation … 19
The Discipline of Yoga … 21
Rama and Sita's Unending Love … 22
Bhakti: Krishna's Seductive *Rāsa* Dance … 24
The Goddess Kāli Comes to America … 25
Ahimsa: The Philosophy of Non-Violence … 27
Bollywood's Song and Dance … 28
Discovery Questions … 30
Glossary … 31

BOXES IN THIS CHAPTER: THE *YOGA SUTRA* … 21 • THE *BHAGAVATA PURANA* … 24
SWAMI VIVEKANANDA … 26 • LAWS OF MANU … 27

2. Buddhism: Release from Suffering … 35
The Buddha Awakes … 35
The Community of Nuns, Monks, and Bodhisattvas … 37
Mindful Living and Modern Psychology … 39
Zen Enlightenment … 40
America's Beatnik Buddhism … 42
Tenzing Norgay: A Sherpa Climbs Mount Everest … 43
The Compassionate Dalai Lama … 45
Discovery Questions … 46
Glossary … 47

BOXES IN THIS CHAPTER: THE BUDDHA … 36
THICH NHAT HANH: *CALMING THE FEARFUL HEART* … 38
DAISETZ SUZUKI … 42 • JACK KEROUAC … 43
TENZING NORGAY … 44 • @DALAILAMA … 45

3. Daoism: Embracing Change ... 48
Beyond Words ... 49
Yin and Yang ... 50
Philosophers and Wanderers ... 51
The Seven Sages of the Bamboo Grove ... 54
Relieving the Pressure: Acupuncture and Tai-Chi ... 55
Kung Fu: Bruce Lee's "Way of the Intercepting Fist" ... 58
Blind Abing Plays *The Moon Reflected on the Second Springs* ... 59
Discovery Questions ... 60
Glossary ... 61

BOXES IN THIS CHAPTER: RUAN JI ... 54 • LIU LING ... 55
THE YELLOW EMPEROR'S CLASSIC OF MEDICINE ... 56 • BRUCE LEE ... 59

4. Yoruba: The Rhythm of the Gods ... 63
Olodumare: The Distant God ... 64
Osun: The Protector ... 65
Esu: The Trickster God ... 65
Un-Gendering the Cosmos ... 66
The Slave Trade and Yoruba Diaspora ... 68
Cuba's Batá Drumming ... 68
Brazil's Candomblé Dancing ... 69
Haitian Vodou Resistance ... 70
Wole Soyinka's *Death and the King's Horseman* ... 71
Discovery Questions ... 73
Glossary ... 74

BOXES IN THIS CHAPTER: OSUN PRAISE POETRY ... 65 • OYÈRÓNKẸ́ OYĚWÙMÍ ... 67
BOUKMAN'S PRAYER ... 70 • WOLE SOYINKA ... 72

PART TWO: TWO WORLDS ... 76
5. Judaism: The Oneness of God ... 76
The Limits of Human Knowledge ... 77
Searching for God ... 79
Maimonides and the Mystics ... 79
God's Gender ... 81
Buber's Dialogue with God ... 83
God's Silence ... 83
The Holy Land ... 85
Jewish Humour and the Cosmic Joke ... 87
Discovery Questions ... 89
Glossary ... 90

BOXES IN THIS CHAPTER: THE BOOK OF GENESIS ... 78 • YEHUDA AMICHAI ... 79
MOSES MAIMONIDES ... 80 • LECHA DODI PRAYER ... 82
JUDITH PLASKOW ... 82 • ELIE WIESEL ... 84 • THEODOR HERZL ... 86

6. Christianity: Transcendence ... 93

Mother Mary and the Incarnate God ... 93
Repentance and Forgiveness in Jesus Christ ... 95
Bodies and Souls of the Catholic Saints ... 97
Icons to Another World: Russian Orthodoxy ... 98
The Struggle to Forgive: Lev Tolstoy and Fyodor Dostoyevsky ... 99
Reformation and the Puritan Revolution ... 101
Shouting the Gospel ... 103
Discovery Questions ... 104
Glossary ... 104

BOXES IN THIS CHAPTER: THE BEATITUDES (MATTHEW 5: 2–10) ... 96
NICAEA II (787) ... 98 • LEV TOLSTOY ... 99 • WINTHROP HEADING TO AMERICA ... 102

7. Islam: Strangers Welcome ... 107

Strangers in a Strange Land: The Children of Abraham ... 107
Muhammad: The Lonely Prophet ... 108
Grief and Resistance in Karbala ... 109
Islam's Golden Age ... 110
Sufi Love and Longing ... 112
Naguib Mahfouz's *Cairo Trilogy* ... 114
Malcolm X Walks the Hajj ... 116
Benazir Bhutto and the Challenges of Democracy ... 117
Discovery Questions ... 119
Glossary ... 119

BOXES IN THIS CHAPTER: THE QUR'AN ... 108 • BOX: IMAM MUSA AL-SADR ... 110
MEDIEVAL WAQFA DOCUMENT ... 111 • AL-ARABI ... 113
THE AUTOBIOGRAPHY OF MALCOLM X ... 117

PART THREE: LIVING TOGETHER ... 122

8. Confucianism: Family Harmony ... 122

From Thought to Action ... 123
Living in Harmony ... 125
The Wisdom of our Ancestors ... 126
Filial Piety ... 127
Food for Thought ... 128
The Art of Calligraphy ... 130

The Korean Wave ... 131
Confucian Games ... 132
Discovery Questions ... 134
Glossary ... 134

BOXES IN THIS CHAPTER: XUNZI ... 125 • ANALECTS ... 127 • YUAN MEI ... 129
AMY TAN ... 129 • KHOO SEOW HWA ... 130

9. Sikhism: Resisting Conformity ... 137
Guru Nanak's Multicultural Revolution ... 137
The Gurus and the Khalsa: Building Community ... 139
Kesh (Hair) ... 139
Kirpan (Sword) ... 140
The Lions of Punjab ... 140
Partition: Facts and Fiction ... 142
Defiant Women of the Diaspora ... 144
Bowlers of the Panth: Sikhs and Cricket ... 146
Discovery Questions ... 148
Glossary ... 148

BOXES IN THIS CHAPTER: KIRPAL SINGH ... 142 • AMRITA PRITAM ... 145

10. Navajo: Land of the People ... 151
Blessings of Home ... 151
Roaming Coyote ... 152
Changing Woman and Gender Fluidity ... 154
Monster Slayers: Confronting Colonialism ... 155
Weaving Stories and Rugs ... 157
American Heroes: The Code Talkers ... 158
The Navajo Go Hollywood: Monument Valley in John Ford's Westerns ... 159
Leaving the "Rez" ... 161
Discovery Questions ... 162
Glossary ... 163

BOXES IN THIS CHAPTER: DINÉ BAHANE' (STORY OF THE PEOPLE) ... 152
CHRISTINE MARTIN, NAVAJO WEAVER ... 157 • ESTHER BELIN ... 162

11. Shintoism: One with Nature ... 165
Shrine and State ... 165
Masks of Longing: Zeami's Noh Theatre ... 167
Kurozumi Munetada's Healing Rituals ... 170
Sumo Wrestling: Grappling with the *Kami* ... 171
Mount Fuji: Power and Passion ... 172

Seitō's "New Women" ... 174
Yasunari Kawabata's "Elegies" ... 174
Studio Ghibli and the Wonder of Anime ... 176
Discovery Questions ... 177
Glossary ... 177

BOXES IN THIS CHAPTER: *KOJIKI* ... 166 • KUROZUMI MUNETADA ... 170
YOSANO AKIKO ... 174 • RAICHŌ ... 174 • YASUNARI KAWABATA ... 175

Acknowledgements ... 181
Notes ... 183
Sources for Boxes ... 197
Image Credits ... 199
Index ... 201

Introduction

Our Enchanted World

You're invited to a wedding. That's the good news.

The bad news is that you're already more than 1,600 years late. Worse still, the groom, Mercury, is a Roman god famous for holding a grudge. His ancestor, Hermes, is still used as the symbol for the Greek postal service, so good luck saying your invitation was lost in the mail.

The wedding of Mercury and Philology was a mixed marriage between a god and a human. There were sacred blessings and consecrations, to be sure, but there was more profane dancing, shouting, and partying.

If we are to believe the ~~live tweets~~ detailed impressions faithfully recorded in Martianus Capella's fifth-century "Marriage of Mercury and Philology," the heavenly realms and all the planets were in the wedding band, and they "produced a symphony of the harmonious notes of each, a sweeter song than usually heard."[1] Like the band joining heaven and earth, the marriage proved that enchanted wisdom and earthly intrigues could join together in a "sacred embrace." In Capella's time the message was already spreading faster than Mercury's wings could carry him.

What is the meaning of "enchanted wisdom"? Enchantment is a quality in the world that fires our non-rational imagination. Enchantments trigger in us an elevated sense of excitement, fear, or curiosity. Because these discoveries or experiences are non-rational, we have difficulty understanding or describing them in everyday language. We may be enchanted by sunsets, popular music, or other people, for example. Enchanted experiences are also instructive: they teach us things about ourselves and the world we inhabit. Therefore, "enchanted wisdom" describes many kinds of non-rational knowledge we gain about ourselves and our world.

Nearly a century ago, German sociologist Max Weber famously told his university students, "The fate of our times is characterized by rationalization and intellectualization and, above all, by the 'disenchantment of the world.'"[2] His point wasn't that rational disciplines like science and mathematics were somehow off-base. Clearly, much of our collective wisdom comes directly from these distinctly rational sources. The problem was how to rationally question the foundations of human life without losing our capacities to appreciate the "mysterious incalculable forces that come into play."[3]

Are we losing the capacity to notice and process non-rational experiences? In his epic 2007 book *The Secular Age*, Charles Taylor follows Weber's lead by focusing on modernity's rationally constructed worlds. The 19th-century Industrial Revolution helped usher us into today's age of technology. And according to Taylor, "technology makes it difficult to believe in magic and the enchanted world."[4] When the officially atheist Soviet Union sent the first person into space in 1961, government officials gleefully noted that astronaut Yuri Gagarin saw many things, but he never saw God. Science and technology were shining lights in the darkest places and showing us the world was less mysterious than we once imagined.

But something strange happens when we shine a light in the dark. Yes, we see some things more clearly than we did before. But other things, like the stars in the sky or anything outside the range of the artificial light, become much more difficult to notice. The issue comes back to what parts of life we are hoping to spotlight. If we pay closer attention even the spotlights themselves can reveal ancient enchantments. There's a story of a Japanese Buddhist monk, Soen Nakagawa, who loved to take nighttime walks in New York City and stare up at the lighted skyscrapers. The Buddha spirit, he argued, wasn't chased away by such artificial lights. "Look at the Buddha," Nakagawa used to say, pointing into the lights. "Shining Buddha."[5]

It's easy to forget that so much of today's technology is animated by invisible and sometimes unpredictable electrical surges. In Lagos, Nigeria, a statue of the temperamental, unruly Yoruba god Xango stands outside the National Electric Power Authority. The connections between old and new enchantments have never been so charged. As one philosopher of technology writes, "technology is itself a sacred space ... the place where, like Jacob, we wrestle with the God who comes to engage us."[6]

We've all heard the critique that plugging into our devices can distract us from more meaningful encounters and connections. Instead of going out into nature or meeting new people, we're more content to stay at home in front of our computers or smartphones, surfing online or playing repetitive video games. But modern technology can also bring us closer to ancient enchantments than ever before. PlayStation's wildly popular *God of War*, for example, features a father emotionally struggling to connect with his child while locked in combat with the Norse gods and the monsters that challenge them. Social networks, blogs, and chat rooms have brought diasporic people of Islam, Sikhism, and many other religions closer together. If the internet is devoid of all enchantments, then how do we explain the millions of people clicking on YouTube every day to watch ancient Hindu dance steps reinterpreted and repackaged in the latest blockbuster Bollywood films?

In *The Secular Age*, Taylor reminds us that "something important has happened; there has been a decline in something very significant, which most people recognize under the term 'religion.'"[7] Taylor is partly right. Something important *is* happening. And while there may be a decline "in something very significant," there is also an uptick of interest in something equally significant.

At my university in Toronto, religion classes are fuller than they've ever been. Thousands of students are taking introductory classes on world religions, not because they're interested in memorizing ancient prayers and rituals (though such rituals often come with their own enchantments), but because they feel like something is being left out of their practically organized, goal-oriented and corporatized university experience. We're only slowly reawakening to the ancient understanding that the most meaningful life involves intersecting ways of seeing the world. As the philosopher William James writes, "No account of the universe in its totality can be final which leaves these other forms of consciousness quite disregarded."[8]

Can the sound of a harmonica on a Caribbean Island help us recall "the rosary of archipelagos" and "the amen of calm waters" as they did for Nobel-Prize winning poet Derek Walcott?[9] The connections between ancient religion, nature, and music offer us enchanted ways of understanding our world and richer ways to find our way through it. And yet, there is a danger that such kinds of understanding may go extinct if we don't allow or continue to encourage their possibility.

Money may very well be the root of all evil, as Saint Paul claimed nearly two thousand years ago, but only if the pursuit of riches comes at the expense of other people and richer enchantments. In Gallup, New Mexico, for example, the Navajo and Pueblo Native Americans stand side by side every Saturday, selling corn pollen to entice the gods, lamb, mutton and watermelon juice to strengthen weary grandparents, and second-hand computer video games to dazzle the children. The Hebrew Bible taught us that such forms of enchantments have always been pervasive. "Wisdom cries aloud in the streets," it is written. "In the market she raises her voice."[10] The question again comes down to which slices of life we wish to put under the spotlight.

Enchanting texts are at their most instructive when they point us to real flesh-and-blood people living all around us. Women's stories, for example, have been largely absent from the ways in which public knowledge is traditionally transmitted. In this book, you'll find untapped religious views of gender so far ahead of their time that they were hardly noticed outside their communities. In each chapter you'll also learn of female activists, artists, and warriors whose exploits are still left out of many religion textbooks today. The goal of this book is to help give you the courage and the creativity to put the book down and make richer sense of your interactions with *all* people.

In our time, enchanted wisdom continues to be mined from each of the world religions emphasized below. In this book, stories are told in the third person, as though we are all newcomers to the specific religious traditions. I do so with the understanding that these stories can speak to *all of us*, regardless of our religious backgrounds. Many of the lessons in this book were originally meant for a particular people in a particular religious culture. But these same stories also touch on universal themes that we can all benefit from learning. When contemporary religions are covered in media and social media, the stories are usually centered on violence or hatred. Focusing on enchanted wisdom can give us a fuller picture of these living cultures, helping us see how modern people from these traditions are thoughtfully and peacefully living their lives today.

Can we apply their lessons in our own lives without carelessly appropriating or exploiting the ancient ideas of living, modern people? I think so, but it's a question that should serve as a challenge, and a caution to tread carefully in every chapter. At the end of each chapter are discovery questions meant for students to personally engage with ideas that might fall out of their comfort zone. These chapters are short enough to serve as springboards for further study and, hopefully, a lifetime journey of personal growth.

We'll examine critical ancient texts, but we'll also cast our net wider into popular culture and everyday activities like cooking, weaving, and muscle building. In philosophy, literature, music, and popular culture, the enchanted wisdom of ancient religions continues to be retold and reimagined around the world. The stories remind us of the enchantments that hide out beyond every tree, rock, and concrete building, unpredictably shooting forth between total strangers in our everyday human interactions.

We may have arrived too late for the wedding of Mercury and Philology, but as you pause just a moment before each chapter door in this book, you might still make out "the music of the spheres": the melodies of the worldly and the otherworldly merging as one. The sacred wedding band that rocked Mercury and Philology's wedding is still playing regular gigs all over the world. If we learn how to listen, we may be surprised to hear their faint music in the most ordinary places of our everyday lives.

Enchanted Wisdom

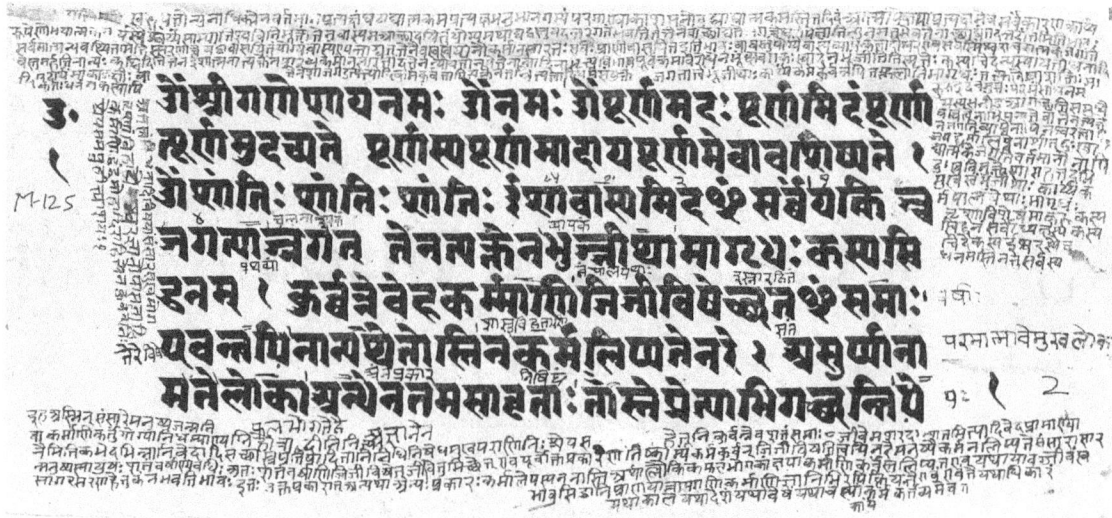

ILLUSTRATION: EARLY MANUSCRIPT, THE UPANISHADS

Part One
LETTING GO

CHAPTER ONE
Hinduism: The Divine Dance

CHAPTER TWO
Buddhism: Release from Suffering

CHAPTER THREE
Daoism: Embracing Change

CHAPTER FOUR
Yoruba: The Rhythm of the Gods

Chapter One
Hinduism
The Divine Dance

The story of the world's oldest grammarian is shrouded in mystery. It's been said that sometime around the sixth or fifth century BCE a man named Pāṇini was struggling to unlock the secrets of the ancient Sanskrit language. At his wits' end, the acclaimed scholar began to meditate day and night. Out from the recesses of the universe Pāṇini heard the beat of the damaru drum, the repeating cycle of fourteen distinct sounds. These sounds, he realized, formed the basis for all Sanskrit grammar.

The ancient story teaches us that the universe speaks in a familiar musical tongue, conveying the blueprints of creation itself. Whether it is the wind whistling through trees, breath blowing through a flute, or language emanating from deep within one's voice box, air makes sounds, and sounds make music. The earliest Hindus believed that when we attune ourselves to the first cosmic sound, the *om*, we connect ourselves to the soundtrack of our existence, ever constant, and yet, still always changing. Though our bodies weaken, die and decay, the *om* of the universe plays on.

The Dance of Creation

The Hindu **Vedas**, some of the earliest recorded religious texts in the world, are written in Sanskrit stanzas meant to be sung to the gods. "The Vedic singers too were aware of the power of music which enchants gods, and pleases them."[11] The Hindu gods of the Vedas appreciated music and often jammed together. When they really got going, they started to dance. Whole worlds were created, destroyed, and recreated through these divine dances. "O Devas," it is written in the *Rigveda*, "when you abide and play together dancing as if joyously in the vast space, then your radiant energy and ecstasy rises high."[12]

Agni, god of fire, **Indra**, ruler of the storms, and **Vishnu**, the protector, were restless, creative, energetic, and always on the move. Unlocking their musical language was the key to **moksha**, or liberating oneself from worldly pain. It has been understood to be the end goal of all human life. "The goal," says one twentieth-century Hindu philosopher, "is not to know the ultimate truth but to *realize* it, to become one with it."[13] For thousands of years Hindus have taught us how singing and dancing can bring us closer to this kind of liberation.

The classic bronze statue of the dancing **Shiva** was created sometime in the tenth century and continues to be the iconic image of Hinduism inside India and around the world. Shiva is portrayed in an aggressive dance pose, his left leg crossed over his right, about to smash down. On his body he carries a skull, a cobra, and the all-important drum to play while he dances. Worship of this particular form of the dancing Shiva can be traced to the city of Cidambaram in the seventh century. The **Cidambaram Temple** continues to be the center of Shiva worship in India today.

The dance highlights a number of significant features of traditional Hinduism. Shiva's dance is both destructive and constructive. The circle of life and death is ever repeating through the dance of life. Hindu texts describe the concept of **reincarnation**, the belief that our souls are constantly moving from body to body in a seemingly infinite process of generation, decay, and regeneration. Shiva's dance shows us how our most creative energies can emerge and re-emerge from seemingly inert matter.

This idea of making something out of nothing has long played an important role in the rise of modern mathematics. **Zero**, for example, was a Babylonian concept that was championed and popularized by Hindu mathematicians. "If you look at zero you see nothing; but look through it and you will see the world."[14] More than a placeholder, zero is a number that stands for everything that isn't there. But because it's still a "real" number, zero tells us that "nothing" is just as real as "something." It's no surprise, then, that "India, as a society that actively explored the void and the infinite, accepted zero."[15]

In modern science, the Hindu concept of zero continues to affect the way we understand (or have trouble understanding) the universe. "Zero is so powerful because it unhinges the laws of physics. It is at the zero hour of the big bang and the ground zero of the black hole that the mathematical equations that describe our world stop making sense."[16] In Hinduism, this ecstatic energy is behind all creation.

A sculpture of the dancing Shiva stands outside the European Organization for Nuclear Research (CERN) in Geneva, Switzerland, linking the two worlds of science and religion. Why would the largest particle physics laboratory in the world feature an iconic image of ancient Hinduism? Like the ancient Hindus, secular Western scientists also see the world as "a continual dance of creation and destruction involving the whole cosmos.... The metaphor of the cosmic dance thus unifies ancient mythology, religious art, and modern physics."[17]

This statue of Shiva stands outside the headquarters of CERN, the European Organization for Nuclear Research, in Geneva, Switzerland.

The Discipline of Yoga

Practices that lead us to *moksha* can help make us happier, less self-centred, and more empowered to live our best selves. The practice of yoga is the centerpiece of this spiritual journey.

In the **Bhagavad Gita**, a preeminent Hindu text, **Arjuna** the archer suffers from fear and insecurity. Through a discussion with the god **Krishna** (disguised as his charioteer), Arjuna learns the ancient art of **yoga** and in the process, develops the courage to achieve heroic feats.

Arjuna questions Krishna about how we can differentiate our friends from our enemies. Krishna quickly corrects him. The only real enemy is the fear and anger we carry inside us, "all consuming, greatly harmful."[18] Yoga, meaning "yoke," teaches us to connect ourselves to something more lasting than our own petty thoughts. Left to our own imperfect devices, we wind up pursuing worldly success, sending us down an endless spiral of always wanting more: more money, more time, more things. We tell ourselves that these rewards are the well-deserved fruits of our actions, but we are deceived.

Krishna cautions us that "the unyoked are bound by desires/ and by attachment to results."[19] In contrast one who "sees clods, stones and gold nuggets/ as one, is said to be a yogi."[20] Resisting attachments to worldly pleasures takes rigorous self-discipline and self-control.

> The man who has abandoned all
> desire moves, free from longing,
> indifferent to "me" and "mine,"
> and without ego, attains peace.[21]

The *Yoga Sutra*

2.15 In other words when through gratification of the thirst for enjoyables, the senses are calmed and do not go after the objects—that is happiness; while restlessness due to thirst for enjoyment is unhappiness.... That is why enjoyment is not the means of attaining spiritual happiness. A seeker of happiness gets into slough of misery through enjoyment of objects and longing for them. This is similar to the suffering of a person who, unable even to stand the sting of a scorpion gets bitten by a serpent.

A variety of yoga disciplines help us pacify and critique harmful desires, freeing ourselves to experience longer lasting pleasures.

Hindus emphasize the need to keep our bodies still in order to retrain our wayward minds. Yoga involves practicing our posture and focusing on our breathing so that we are no longer "looking off distractedly."[22] Once we focus our minds away from the changing things of the world, we can yoke with the all-powerful, creative force behind our existence. We return to our primordial selves, the first sound of creation, the sacred *om*.

Astronaut Sunita Williams in 2004, prior to her 2006 mission to the International Space Station. On a later mission, she served as commander of the station.

The *Yoga Sutra* shows us how practicing yoga not only brings our minds much needed relief, but also helps us notice and repair the suffering of other people. We learn to overlook other people's faults, and develop a "spirit of compassion towards those who are in distress."[23] Turning away from our own selfish desires helps us notice communities of people all around us.

Today, Hindus and non-Hindus alike practice yoga throughout the world. In 2006, Indian-American astronaut **Sunita Williams** packed a copy of the *Bhagavad Gita* on her space shuttle trip to the International Space Station. Whether or not people will one day practice yoga in space is still an open question. But one thing seems clear. "The universal and universalizing potential of yoga makes it one of India's finest contributions to our struggle for self-definition, moral integrity, and spiritual renewal today."[24]

Rama and Sita's Unending Love

The **Ramayana** is one of most popular Hindu stories in India and Southeast Asia today. The version composed by **Valmiki** over two thousand years ago explores philosophical themes like courage, trust, and the mysterious workings of fate. But above all, the story expresses the unbreakable bond between two lovers, **Rama** and **Sita**.

Rama is sent out from the city of Ayodhya, banished to the forest by his father, the King. It is a crushing blow that ultimately leads to his father's death from a broken heart. Rama's young wife, Sita, however, is not broken by despair. Instead she gives up her riches to follow her lover into exile. Confidently and passionately, Sita proclaims:

> I will not tire, my large-eyed lord,
> No, not for a hundred thousand years.
> I do not want heaven
> If that heaven does not have you in it.[25]

When Sita is kidnapped by the **Ravana**, Rama joins up with a monkey army led by the shape-shifting general **Hanuman**. Together they risk life and limb to rescue Sita and return to Ayodhya as the most revered king and queen in Hindu lore.

While the romantic yearnings of the star-crossed lovers dominate the timeless story, Valmiki also explores the philosophy of **dharma** in some depth. *Dharma* is understood as ethical duty, or more simply, doing the right thing. Rama and Sita do right by each other because they bind themselves to an ancient Hindu code of conduct that requires husband and wife to put aside their differences and fight for each other through every danger. As Sita tells the uncomprehending Ravana, "*Dharma* is to me as moonlight to the moon."[26]

Rama, too, never wavers from his respect for *dharma*. He goes willingly into exile so as not to break a son's respect for his father's command. Throughout the story he puts aside his selfish desires to do what is right for others. After he kills the evil Ravana, Rama insists on performing the proper burial rites to show respect for the dead. Valmiki explains how "Rama laid aside his bow and arrows, renounced his righteous rage and re-assumed the face of compassion of lovingkindness."[27]

The story of Rama and Sita has become deeply intertwined with the history of India. The moral resolve of Hindus has often been measured according to how well the people exhibit the lovers' respect for *dharma*.

In 1967, a chemical engineer was watching a quiz show in a Delhi bookstore. The contestants, all children, didn't know the name of Rama's mother (Kaushalya). Horrified, the man changed career paths on the spot and took to writing comic books about Hindu stories of Rama, Sita, Krishna, and many others. **Anant Pai** (better known as "Uncle Pai") became a national sensation with his comic book series *Amar Chitra Katha* (or *Picture Story*). Over fifty years later, the comic books continue to sell over three million copies per year.

"Unless you have continuity with the past, you can't easily be adjusted with the present," Pai said. "The acquaintance with the past is a must. You may not agree with it. You can disagree with it, but be aware of it."[28]

In 1987, the unparalleled popularity of the television show, **Ramayan**, coincided with the rise of Hindu nationalism in India. At the height of the show's popularity, local businesses frequently shut down on Sunday mornings so people could stay home and watch *Ramayan*. It wasn't uncommon for viewers to place their television sets on home altars to emphasize the religious significance of the television viewing experience. Today, in northern Indian cities like **Varanasi**, dance dramas inspired by the *Ramayana* are as popular as ever, particularly around the **Dussera** holiday.

For many Hindus, however, Valmiki's recurring warning to women that they be subordinate to their husbands is outdated. Today, many Hindu artists are looking for ways to update the ancient story with more a contemporary respect for women's equality. In 1990, **Mallika Sarabhai** choreographed the one-person play, *Sita's Daughters*. "As long as the mind is enslaved, you can expect too little in terms of women's emancipation," she said.[29] With its classical **Tamil**-influenced dance numbers, the play's popularity at home and abroad shows how Hinduism's most enduring philosophies continue to be challenged and reinterpreted today. Not surprisingly, in Hinduism the dancer takes the lead.

Bhakti: Krishna's Seductive *Rāsa* Dance

The story of the Hindu god Krishna is most poetically told in **Bhagavata Purana**. As a child, Krishna was a bit of a rake, eating dirt on one occasion and frequently stealing butter from kitchens all over town. Along with Krishna's supernatural powers to destroy evil demons from another world, the blue God is shown to be spontaneous, loyal, and above all, playful.

> **The *Bhagavata Purana***
>
> 33.6 In the rāsa-dance circle with their beloved, the girls' armlets, ankle bells, and waist bells sounded tumultuously.
>
> 33.8 As Krishna's consorts sang his praises, by their dancing steps, gesturing hands, sportive eyebrows and smiles, swaying waists, tightened braids and belts, shifting blouses, ear ornaments swinging against their cheeks and faces perspiring, they shone like streaks of lightning amid a circle of clouds.
>
> 33.9 The world was suffused with their resounding melodic voices as they sang and danced, rapt in amorous pleasure, thrilled by Krishna's touch.

When he grows into adolescence, however, the tone changes. Krishna learns to play the flute, expressing the beauty of his youth, "captivating the hearts of the lovely-eyed *gopīs*."[30] The women are entranced by Krishna's call and leave their homes, whenever possible, to be near his side. "Krishna had stolen the hearts of Vraja's women, and so when they heard his passion-igniting song, they hastened to where their beloved waited, their earrings swaying."[31]

There, in the forest, the *gopīs* danced in a circle around Krishna while he played the melodies of love and longing. The dance is known as a ***rāsa***, from the Sanskrit root word for "emotion." The sensual dance continues to be taught in India today, while the emotions it elicits continue to seduce audiences around the world.

In Hinduism, the story of the *gopīs* is an exemplar of ***bhakti***, complete surrender and devotion to a god. It is not enough to read sacred texts or practice memorized yoga techniques. In the *bhakti* tradition, Hindus must be prepared to stop their worldly activities at a moment's notice, throwing their bodies and minds into the open embrace of the gods.

In the twelfth century, the east Indian poet **Jayadeva** wrote about the love affair between Krishna and **Rādhā**. Jayadeva's wife, a temple dancer, gyrated while he composed the verses of the ***Gita Govinda***. One time when Jayadeva had a case of writer's block, Krishna himself came to the house, ate a prepared meal, and finished the problematic verse before slipping away unnoticed.

The *Gita Govinda* begins with Rādhā, "the story of a lonely cowherdess."[32] Jealous of Krishna's dancing and carryings on with other women, she leaves the party. A repentant Krishna follows her into the woods, suffering the pain of separation. "Sighing incessantly, he pours out his grief."[33]

In the forest, Rādhā waits alone for Krishna, "Her body bristling with longing, / Her breath sucking in words of confusion."[34] At long last they meet and come together: a "tenderness of love" that leaves Krishna and Rādhā forever longing for the other. It is then that Krishna rubs Rādhā's feet, symbolizing the cosmic caress between gods and humans.

For six hundred years, the *Gita Govinda* was sung daily in the Jagannath Temple of Puri, India, where Jayadeva met his wife. The **Odissi** dance that's heavily influenced by the poetry of the *Gita Govinda,* continues to be a revered classical dance style in India today.

Hinduism: The Divine Dance • 25

Mirabai was another medieval poet heavily influenced by Krishna's flute playing. Writing in the sixteenth century, Mirabai was sharply criticized for refusing to conform to the life of the Hindu **householder**. Instead of living in the memory of her dead husband, Mirabai chose to devote her life to the living Krishna. In her poetry she claims not to have much choice. "The song of the flute," Mirabai writes, "is madness."[35] Krishna, "The Dark One," had called her with his music. In response, Mirabai followed the example of the *gopī* women, foregoing custom and worldly gossip to experience the heat of religious ecstasy. She wrote:

> My dancing dress is my faithfulness to him.
> I've stripped off shame and family custom
> To go to the bed of the Dark One.
> Body and mind, Mira wears only the color of God.[36]

Even after participating in Krishna's timeless dance, Mirabai still frequently experienced the pain of separation. At times her longing for Krishna was answered with silence. In those moments, her longing intensified, her emptiness expanded. "Why has the Dark One forgotten his lover?" she asks.[37] It's a religious yearning that still finds frequent expression in the Hindu texts and dance steps of India and Southeast Asia.

The Goddess Kālī Comes to America

In December, Hindus celebrate **Divali** with lanterns and dancing. In the **Bengal** region, a special emphasis is placed on celebrating the goddess **Durga**'s victory over the Buffalo demon. The ***Devi Mahatmya*** describes how Kālī emerged from Durga's forehead to destroy evil and champion the good.

Kālī's ferocity is without compare in the pantheon of Hindu gods. Traditional Hindu stories and images depict her drinking the blood of her victims, getting such a rush from her victories that she dances ecstatically, her blood red tongue lolling from her mouth. Kālī wears a necklace of severed heads, earrings of children's corpses, and bracelets of snakes. Not surprisingly, she is known as the goddess of the cremation ground.

Other stories show more tender sides of Kālī. "Motherly and erotic qualities alternate freely in the descriptions of the goddess."[38] The most iconic image of Kālī and Shiva show the goddess standing triumphantly on top of her happily submissive husband. In the *Mahābhāgavata Purāna*, Shiva says to Kālī, "Worshipping [you], placing your lotus feet on the lotus that is my heart, I will make my heart, which was burnt by separation from you, very cool."[39]

On the banks of the **Ganges River**, Calcutta's **Dakshineswasr Temple** continues to be a pilgrimage site for Kālī worshippers across Southeast Asia and around the world. Singing and dancing, worshippers pay homage to the goddesses' unpredictability, with fierce loyalty and deep love. At the temple, "one can frolic outwardly with the Goddess in her realm of play and rejoice inwardly because of her internal presence."[40]

In 1855, the temple hired **Ramakrishna** as its new priest, tasking him with the job of decorating the Kāli statue. Born into poverty, Ramakrishna arrived at the temple with an "intense restlessness" to get closer to the Hindu gods, Kāli in particular. "All creation is the sport of my mad Mother Kāli," Ramakrishna frequently sang. In Kāli's spirit, Ramakrishna and his students sang and danced every day, encouraging others to realize the goddess' fierce spirit in this world.

One time, Ramakrishna "danced like a mad elephant," pleading with Kāli to "dance about Thy devotees!" and "Dance in all Thy world-bewitching beauty." One of Ramakrishna's disciples describes the religious fervor: "An indescribable scene. The exquisite and celestial dance of a child completely filled with ecstatic love of God and identified heart and soul with the Divine Mother!" Everyone in the room was swept away. "Many of them wept like children, crying, 'Mother! Mother!'"[41]

The idea wasn't to transport oneself to a higher plane, but to see Kāli's eternal play in this everyday world. Ramakrishna frequently cried when attending the theater because he saw no difference between the real world and the world on the stage. It was all a play between gods and humans. This play can give us strength to fulfill our daily responsibilities more enthusiastically. "How can one who is eternally perfect be afraid of the world?" Ramakrishna asks us. "He knows how to play his game."[42]

At the Dakshineswasr Temple today, Hindus still learn to respect all living beings. Ramakrishna never tolerated religious intolerance. Along with a framed portrait of Kāli, a picture of the Christian Christ adorned his bedroom. "There are various paths to reach God," Ramakrishna taught. "Each view is a path. It is like reaching the Kāli temple by different roads."[43]

Seven years after his death, Ramakrishna's greatest disciple Swami **Vivekananda** left Calcutta for America. Only 30 years old, he was tasked with spreading the play of Kāli to people who hadn't even heard of Hinduism. Vivekananda was invited as a distinguished speaker to the 1893 **Parliament of World's Religions** in Chicago. For many of the Westerners in attendance, Vivekenanda's opening address ignited an interest in Eastern religions, and in Hinduism, specifically. Vivekananda began his talk by thanking the 6,000 attendees "in the name of the most ancient order of monks in the world." Hinduism, he argued, was truly "the mother of religions."

Ramakrishna and Vivekananda's brand of Hinduism and Kāli worship continues to impact America and the West over one hundred years later. Feminist thinkers, in particular, are taking a closer look at the Kāli texts to reinvigorate alternate understandings of gender relations. For many Western feminists outside the Hindu religion, the depiction of fiercely caring goddesses like Kāli "seems compelling, provocative, and inspiring."[44] As one Hindu-American philosopher writes, stories of Kāli are "liberating and empowering to all

Swami Vivekananda

If the Parliament of Religions has shown anything to the world it is this: It has proved to the world that holiness, purity and charity are not the exclusive possessions of any church in the world, and that every system has produced men and women of the most exalted character. In the face of this evidence, if anybody dreams of the exclusive survival of his own religion and the destruction of the others, I pity him from the bottom of my heart....

through exposing an essence that goes beyond male and female, beauty and ugliness, life and death, and all forms of alienation and separation.... Her darkness represents those rejected and suppressed parts of female creativity, energy, and power that have not been given a chance to be actualized."[45]

Ahimsa: The Philosophy of Non-Violence

Ahimsa can mean non-aggression or non-violence, compassion, or care. For thousands of years, *ahimsa* has proven to be one of most important and challenging Hindu precepts. According to ancient Hindu texts, it takes an unusually disciplined mind to think compassionately, and a courageous heart to give hope to others. In order to learn non-violence we need to separate our peace of mind from the success or failure of our more selfish efforts. Once we are able to clear our minds, we can learn to perform actions fearlessly, courageously, compassionately.

While studying law in London in 1888, **Mohandas Gandhi** was introduced to the Hindu philosophy of *ahimsa* in the *Bhagavad Gita*. Soon after, he dedicated his life to the practice of non-violence. Convinced that ordinary Hindus could practice the precepts, he turned the religious philosophy into a political movement that helped turn the tide of British colonial rule in India.

"Control over the mind is alone necessary," Gandhi wrote, "and when that is attained, man is free like the king of the forest and his very glance withers the enemy."[46]

By passively resisting English rule through sit-ins and boycotts, Gandhi turned non-violent acts into a devastating force. The British lost their willpower long before they ever ran out of bullets. "This force implied in this may be described as love-force, **soul force**.... This force is indestructible," Gandhi wrote.[47]

> ### Laws of Manu
>
> 5.46 He who does not seek to cause the sufferings of bonds and death to living creatures, (but) desires the good of all, obtains endless bliss.
>
> 5.48 Meat can never be obtained without injury to living creatures, and injury to sentient beings is detrimental to heavenly bliss; let him therefore shun meat.
>
> 5.51 He who permits (the slaughter of an animal), he who cuts it up, he who kills it, he who buys or sells (meat), he who cooks it, he who serves it up, and he who eats it, (must all be considered as) the slayers.

Gandhi believed the force of love was as urgent in the 1940s as it ever was in ancient times. Just as Krishna upholds the world with unceasing action, so can we inject gentler virtues into every dispute we engage in. All it takes is the religious commitment of people who long to put aside their anger and join forces with each other, compassionately and non-violently. "The universe," Gandhi believed, "would disappear without the existence of that force."[48]

Inspired by Gandhi's application of *ahimsa*, Martin Luther King, Jr. launched his own political movement for civil rights in the United States. Calling Gandhi his "guiding light," King traveled to India in 1959 to speak with Gandhi's relatives. Five years before his famous "I Have a Dream" speech, King "left India more convinced than ever before that non-violent resistance is the most potent weapon available to oppressed people in their struggle for freedom."[49]

For Hindus, non-violence and a love for all beings extends beyond human beings to other animal life forms. Over two thousand years ago, one of India's oldest law codes, the *Manusmirti* (or **Laws of Manu**), details the care one should take when taking an animal's life for sacrificing or eating. The casual eating of meat was clearly outlawed because it went against the core Hindu belief of compassion for all living beings. As the Tamil saint **Tiruvalluvar** writes, "Why does one hurt others/ Knowing what it is to be hurt?"[50]

In 1992, **Maneka Gandhi** founded India's largest animal welfare organization, "People for Animals." Along with crusading for women and children, Gandhi has called on the Indian government to ban the use of animals in traveling circuses, and to shut down zoos for their encouragement of "anti-social" behavior.

Like her namesake, Gandhi is an avowed vegetarian. On her People for Animals website, she writes, "I would repeat this invitation to all of you who eat the flesh of animals. Stop killing them, treat them with love and respect as another form of God and see how your happiness increases and the world changes around you."

In many Western countries today, the rise of environmentalism and concern for the non-human is giving vegetarianism an unparalleled boost in popularity. Many new converts to the cause look to the ancient precepts of Hinduism to provide the arguments and endorsements for animal rights. "From India's philosophies that emphasize the interconnectedness of life ... the world can learn a great deal about building an ethic of animal advocacy."[51]

Bollywood's Song and Dance

The growing fascination with Hindu themes today is best seen in the massive popularity of **Bollywood** movies. A typical Bollywood film is marked by six or so dance numbers that feature lush backdrops, modern music, and brightly colored costumes. As prolific as American Hollywood producers, Bollywood studios combine to invest over $3.5 billion on approximately 200 films per year.

While musical films from the Tamil and Punjab regions also enjoy considerable acclaim, the films produced in Mumbai have the most international reach and are enjoyed both by foreign audiences and Indians living abroad. The catchphrase, "first day, first show," has become a point of pride for Indians catching the world premiere of the newest blockbuster film.

As many Indian film critics have noted, "Indian cinema has specific traits that incline it more towards the religious than other cinemas."[52] In the musical dance numbers, especially, Bollywood addresses these Hindu influences with a reverent but playful wink. We can see these influences in three recent Bollywood films that are still popular today.

Hum Dil De Chuke Sanam (Straight from the Heart)
In this 1999 film, Bollywood legend **Ajay Devgn** plays a foreigner, Vanraj, studying classical Hindu music in a plush Gujarat palace in Northwest India. As his character explains to his love interest Nandini, (played by **Aishwarya Rai**), "Music drew me here." Soon after, he passes wind after eating too many lentil beans.

"Do you have songs for every occasion?" Vanraj asks after his digestive troubles subside.

"Yes, every occasion," Nandini explains. "Wedding songs, harvest songs, love songs spring songs..."

"And the one in which you clap?"

"**Garba!**"

In the end, the lovers dance the Garba during the Hindu Navaratri festival, circling the illuminated light of thousands of yellow marigolds. The dance recalls the love story of Rādhā and Krishna, repeating the ancient drum rhythms that reinforce the connections between the Hindu gods and the humans who dance for them.

Lage Raho Munna Bhai (Keep on Going Munna Bhai)
In this 2006 sequel, the comical gangster Munna Bhai (played by **Sanjay Dutt**) sees visions of Mahatma Gandhi in his times of need. Trying to capitalize on his good fortune Bhai helps start a radio show, "Mahatma's Magic." Bhai's first caller has sadly lost his father's savings by gambling it on the stock market. Bhai harnesses Gandhi in order to give the caller sound advice.

"Reduce expenses. Work more. Pay it back penny by penny. Work twice as hard, spend less and save your money."

When the caller says he'd rather commit suicide than face his father's wrath, Bhai persists, invoking Gandhi.

"Why make your father suffer for your mistake? You think your dad will feel joy seeing your dead body? Those shoulders you rode on as a child will now bear the weight of your coffin.... Bloody idiot." In the end the caller confronts his father while "Mumbai is listening," and learns an important lesson about growing up and taking responsibility. In the background, we hear the song, *Bande Mein Tha Dum*, the same song played every year on Gandhi's birthday. In one verse, we hear:

> A brother has become an enemy of his brother
> The storm of hatred is flowing
> O father, please teach love to the cruel hearts
> O father, please come

The lyrics, and the movie, help ensure Gandhi's philosophy of non-violence is kept safely alive for the next generation.

Goliyon Ki Raasleela Ram-Leela (A Play of Bullets: Ram-Leela)
In this 2013 film, classical Hindu themes appear in a Bollywood adaption of William Shakespeare's *Romeo and Juliet*. Ram and Leela rise to the top of two warring clans (the Rajadis and the Saneras). Leela, played by **Deepika Padukone,** dances the Garba. The song's lyrics refer to the *Ramayana*, when Rama refuses to spend the night with another woman while his beloved wife Sita waits at home.

The film's violence reaches its climax on *Dussera* when the parade celebrating Rama and

Sita's victory over evil is sprayed with bullets. Hanuman the monkey god is gunned down on a float. But one young boy who lost his father catches the true spirit of the Hindu holiday. "Uncle Ram says if we forgo revenge, then the barren desert shall bear flowers," he says.

In the end, Ram and Leela meet their deaths as the evil Ravana burns in effigy. It takes the tragic death of the two protagonists for the two families to celebrate *Dussera* together. As the film's narrator concludes, "No longer are houses burned, only lamps are lit. If anger and revenge can turn an ocean into a barren desert, then true love can also make flowers bloom here."

Can Bollywood make flowers bloom in the world's most barren deserts? Some critics point to more dissonant dangers. The feel-good stories can serve to water down the ancient lessons, exploiting sacred themes for easy profits.

Still others point to the celebration of Hindu themes as a way of devaluing or shutting out other religious worldviews. India is home to over 180 million Muslims, but Muslim characters get short shrift in Bollywood films. Although there are a number of popular Muslim actors, they often play Hindus in the films. Shah Rukh Khan (SRK), for example, is one of India's best-known film stars today. Though he identifies as Muslim, his celluloid characters frequently champion traditional Hindu values.

Does Bollywood promote distinctly Hindu codes of conduct at the expense of "other" religious worldviews? Or can the film industry be counted on to help India (and the wider world) usher in a new age of religious tolerance? How Bollywood dances around these issues may go a long way to determining how Hinduism is perceived by a new generation of filmgoers inside and outside of India.

Discovery Questions

1. Find an online translation of the *Bhagavad Gita*. Choose one passage that speaks to a political issue today. How would you develop Krishna's remarks to Arjuna to find the best solution?

2. Attend a yoga class on or near campus. How did you feel? Describe practices that keep alive the spirit of classic Hindu themes. Which features of the class or the room seem more geared for secular customers?

3. Go on YouTube and compare Alia Bhatt's "Rādhā" dance in the 2012 Bollywood film *Student of the Year* with one of Sonal Mansingh's classical Bharatnatyam performances. What Hindu themes do you find in both versions? Describe the different kinds of love Rādhā is capable of expressing in the two videos.

4. Find a quiet place to sit outside one night. What sounds do you hear? Do you hear any repeating rhythms? Describe one thing you heard for the very first time.

5. Research India's controversial 2019 Citizenship Amendment Bill. Does it support or restrict citizenship for religious minorities?

6. Eat a vegetarian diet for 24 hours. Describe what cravings you had and how long they lasted. Did they lead to feelings of anger? Impatience? Dissatisfaction? What can you do to eliminate these cravings, besides eating meat?

7. Watch the 30-minute 1997 interview of master sitar player Ravi Shankar and former Beatle George Harrison on the making of their album, *Chants of India*. Describe Shankar's music. Why do you think it had such an effect on Harrison and the Beatles?

Glossary

Term	Definition
Agni	Element of fire; embodiment of luminous energy
Ahimsa	Harmonized existence; colloquially translated as non-violence
Aishwarya Rai	Popular Indian model and actress
Ajay Devgn	Popular Indian actor
Anant Pai	Renowned comic book author who wrote about characters from Hindu history and mythology
Arjuna	A famed archer and warrior from the Hindu epic *Mahabharat*
Bengal	A region in South Asia that includes the Indian state of West Bengal and the country of Bangladesh
Bhagavad Gita	700 verses of dialogue between Arjuna and his charioteer, the God-head Krishna in the Hindu epic *Mahabharat*
Bhakti	Perseverant devotion and ceaseless dedication
Bollywood	Indian film industry centered in the city of Mumbai
Cidambaram Temple	Hindu temple devoted to the dancing Shiva
Dakshineswasr Temple	Hindu temple dedicated to the divine feminine in the form of Kali
Damaru	A two-headed drum
Deepika Padukone	Contemporary model and actress
Devi Mahatmya	A religious text describing the divine feminine as the creator and sustainer of the cosmos
Dharma	The law of nature which humans are expected to uphold and sustain through thought and action
Divali	Festival of Lights signifying the luminosity of the soul and victory of righteousness over ignorance
Durga	The divine feminine
Dussera	Festival marking the demise of Ravana as depicted in the *Ramayana*
Ganges River	A sacred river that flows from northern India into Bangladesh
Gita Govinda	A poem by Jayadeva that recounts the story of Lord Krishna and Rādhā.
Gopīs	Spiritual companions of the God-head Krishna
Hanuman	A devotee of Lord Rama and central figure of the Hindu epic *Ramayana*
Householder	Head of a household with domestic responsibilities

Indra	Chief of all cosmic beings mentioned in the *Rigveda*; also refers to electricity in the universe and in the human body.
Jayadeva	An east Indian poet of the twelfth century who composed the *Gita Govinda*
Kāli	Embodiment of ferocity and fearlessness of the divine feminine
Krishna	A god-head who was the eighth incarnation of Lord Vishnu
Laws of Manu	Socio-political application of religious themes and philosophies as interpreted by Maharishi Manu
Mahābhāgavata Purāna	Central text of the Vaishnava branch of Hinduism
Mallika Sarabhai	A Gujrati classical dancer and activist
Maneka Gandhi	An animal rights activist who served as India's Minister for Women and Child Development from 2014 to 2019
Mirabai	A sixteenth-century mystic and poet who was part of the Bhakti Movement in India
Mohandas Gandhi	A twentieth-century philosopher and activist who led the Indian independence movement against British rule
Moksha	Spiritual liberation
Odissi	A classical Indian dance style
Om	Primordial vibration
Pāṇini	Ancient Indian grammarian
Parliament of World's Religions	A global interfaith convention held alongside Chicago's 1893 World Columbian Exhibition
Rādhā	Chief goddess of the Vaishnava branch of Hinduism, associated with selfless love.
Rama	The seventh incarnation of Lord Vishnu and key character in the Hindu epic *Ramayana*
Ramakrishna	A nineteenth-century Hindu mystic
Ramayana	A Hindu epic detailing the story of Hindu god-head Rama
Rāsa	A cosmic dance between Krishna and the Gopis of Vrindavan
Ravana	A villainous character in the Hindu epic *Ramayana*, embodying hubris and human ignorance
Reincarnation	A philosophical concept emphasizing the rebirth of the soul
Sanskrit	Ancient language of India in which many Hindu scriptures were recorded
Shiva	Embodiment of the destructive/purifying aspect of nature; the substratum of all living things
"Shiva Tandava Stotram"	A poem recited by Ravana in reverence to Lord Shiva
Sita	Incarnation of Lakshmi and wife of incarnate Lord Rama in the Hindu epic *Ramayana*
Sunita Williams	An Indian-American astronaut
Tamil	A people and language originating in Southern India and Northern Sri Lanka

Tiruvalluvar	An ancient Tamil philosopher and saint
Valmiki	A Hindu saint and scholar; author of the original epic, *Ramayana*
Varanasi	An ancient north Indian city on the banks of the Ganges River
Vedas	Core texts of Hinduism: namely *Rig Veda*, *Yajur Veda*, *Sama Veda* and *Atharva Veda*
Vishnu	"All-pervading," sustainer and preserver of the cosmos
Vivekananda	A disciple of Ramakrishna, famous for introducing Hinduism in the West.
Yoga	"Union" of mind and body with the supreme consciousness
Yoga Sutra	Maharishi Pitanjali's ancient text on practicing yoga

Chapter Two
Buddhism
Release from Suffering

Although the Burke Junction Shopping Mall in Sacramento, California is dedicated to "keeping old things alive," it serves mostly as a tribute to the American West. It therefore may have seemed like an odd place to find Tibetan Buddhist monks practicing a ritual that has been passed down for hundreds of years.

In 2019, surrounded by the happy shrieks of children riding the BuJu Line, a revitalized narrow-gauge railway train, the monks set to work on their **mandala** of the compassionate Buddha, **Avalokiteśvara**. The Tibetan Buddhists come to Sacramento every year to caution Americans about the illusory nature of commercialism and the addictive pursuit of pleasure. Like so many mandala artists before them, after finishing their masterpiece the monks do something extraordinary. After countless hours of meticulous craftmanship, they destroy their intricate sandpainting, giving away their colored grains to anyone who wants it. Closing up shop, they return to India, to their Tibetan community in exile.

In undoing their beautiful artwork, the Buddhist monks are keeping something even older alive and well: a philosophy that nothing lasts. The wheel of creation, destruction, and renewal, what Buddhists call *samsāra*, is constantly spinning. How thoroughly we grasp this cosmology goes a long way to determining how freely and creatively we are able to live our short lives.

Buddhism offers philosophies of hope and compassion, but also one of resistance. In the scriptures that make up the first century **Pāli Canon**, we learn the ancient art of challenging those who so confidently tell us how to live our lives, when deep down, they seem more troubled than we are. Buddhism traces its roots back to one risk-taking human being with the courage to question the so-called experts around him.

The Buddha Awakes

In the fifth century BCE, under the majestic peaks of Himalayan Mountains, **Siddhartha Gautama** seemed to have it all. He was born into luxury, with the promise of financial security and a position of respect in his community. But the young prince had a questioning mind. He wasn't afraid to subject his own privilege to questioning and critique.

The false sense of confidence that fed his friends and family troubled Siddhartha. "The traditional values seemed to be crumbling, a familiar way of life was disappearing, and the order that was taking its place was frightening and alien."[53] In his restlessness, he repeatedly struck out on his own to seek more lasting truths. Siddhartha's wisdom did not come from memorizing formulas or poring over ancient texts. His path was simpler. He observed other people, using empirical evidence to critically evaluate his own unsupported beliefs.

From outside his palace gates, Siddhartha saw sickness, old age, and death. No amount of money or pleasure could change that. What good was all the world's knowledge in the face of such irreversible decay? Siddhartha left the noisy streets of his village to be alone with his thoughts. In the quietest of moments, under a simple banyan tree, the young prince realized that he, too, was driven by his own fears of suffering. By rigorously questioning himself, Siddhartha became awakened to the **Four Noble Truths** and was henceforth called the Buddha, or "the Awakened One."

The Buddha

The Dhammapada

24.338 As long as the roots are unharmed, firm,
A tree, though topped, grows yet again.
Just so, when the latent craving is not rooted out,
This suffering arises again and again.

24.342 Accompanied by craving,
Folk crawl around like a trapped hare,
Being held by fetters and bonds.
They come by suffering again and again, for long.

24.349 For a person having thoughts disturbed,
Acute of passion, looking for the pleasurable,
Craving increases all the more.
That one, indeed, makes the bondage firm.

As the Buddha explained in his first discussion with his fellow monks, suffering is at the core of all birth, life, and death. The Buddha believed that release from suffering comes not from extinguishing life, but from eradicating our "passionate greed" for pleasures and long life. The Buddha declared that "not to receive what one desires is suffering."[54]

Every pleasurable moment carries with it the seeds for inevitable disappointment, if for no other reason than the good times cannot last forever. As the ancient Buddhist commentator **Candrakīrti** explained, "Those who want only to associate with attractive people and do not want to part from them just engage in wishful thinking."[55] Parting with loved ones is made more difficult if we wrongly assume the time may never come.

To emphasize this point, Buddhists return to the story of **Kisa Gotami**. She is best remembered for the intensity of her grief, as she carried her dead child in her arms, pleading with the villagers to help her find a cure. The Buddha took pity on Gotami. He told her to find a home that experienced no pain, and from that home to bring to him grains of mustard seeds. Of course, there was no such home, and therefore, no magic cure. Instead the Buddha taught Gotami a fundamental truth in this world. People suffer, some worse than others, to be sure. But no one escapes this world untouched. *Everybody* suffers.

The news isn't all bad, however. Quite the opposite. Liberating ourselves from our own destructive cravings can free us from the ever-present threat of disappointment. It is possible to break the cycle of suffering and reach the bliss of **nirvana**. The Buddha found a middle way between religious asceticism and secular pleasure. The **Noble Eightfold Path** is a guide for disciplining ourselves to shed our selfish desires and realign our lives with the confusing and changing world in which we live.

Following the path of *dharma*, or truth, requires the help of fellow seekers who have learned to see the emptiness in themselves and others. With compassion and courage, one can learn the ancient path that is as firm and unchanged as the rugged mountains that faithfully guard it.

The Community of Nuns, Monks, and Bodhisattvas

The Buddha might have been content to find lasting happiness and end the story there. The demon **Mara** used all his powers to tempt Siddhartha to enjoy his worldly pleasures and live out his time in blissful ignorance. But the awakened prince was deeply affected by the suffering of others and insisted on helping the rest of us go beyond our self-inflicted limits. The Buddha himself came from a long line of **Bodhisattvas,** enlightened beings who turned away from eternal peace, choosing instead to wander the world to help enlighten others.

Buddhists speak of three jewels that are essential to the religion: the Buddha, the *dharma*, and the *sangha*, or the Buddhist communities of nuns and monks (sometimes extending out to the faithful laity as well). It is said, "The Buddha is like the Himalaya Mountain[s]; the *dharma* is like the healing herbs that are given their being by that mountain; and the *sangha* is like people free from ailment owing to the use of those herbs."[56]

The Buddha gave many outdoor talks that were open to men and women from all walks of life. Liberating oneself from suffering was a topic that interested women and men alike. Over two thousand years ago, many Buddhist women reported the exhilaration of hearing they didn't need to be fettered to a man, a family or their own bodies. After hearing the Buddha's message of hope, **Khama**, one of the first leaders of the community of nuns, freed herself of subservience. "Your desire for sex means nothing to me," she confidently told the demon tempter, Mara. "What you call delight is not delight for me."[57]

The Buddha respected women who stood up for themselves, who refused to be taken advantage of. In many ways, they were encouraged to leave behind the everyday pressures of gender conformity. **Bhadda Kundalakesa**, for example, was about to be killed by a criminal whom she had only just compassionately saved from execution. On top of a mountain she begged the selfish man for one moment of compassion before she died. When it was granted, she hugged her attacker, and then pushed him off the mountain. Such audacious women became famous early teachers of Buddhism.

From the first century CE onward, the Mahāyāna tradition began to emphasize the need to follow the Buddha's lead in helping others escape their suffering. Avalokiteśvara is the Bodhisattva who best represents the spirit of giving. In the *Lotus Sutra*, Avalokiteśvara is described as having "the gaze of great and encompassing wisdom / the gaze of pity, the gaze of compassion."[58] The *Karandavyuha Sutra* relates a story of Avalokiteśvara telling a poor and hungry man that he must give to others. When the man checked his old pots, he was shocked to find Avalokiteśvara had filled them with precious jewels, fancy clothes, and fine foods. The grateful men gave all the pots to Avalokiteśvara, ever thankful to have experienced the joy of giving.

In the Mahāyāna school of Buddhism, wisdom and compassion are always intertwined. From India up through China, Buddhists sensed a "Light constant, inconceivable, light beyond speaking." Such light isn't solely reserved for esoteric priests or exceptional human beings like the **Amida Buddha**. Instead, "The multitudes of beings all receive this radiance."[59] This radiance can give us the light to see ourselves as part of a greater community.

Today, people who practice **Engaged Buddhism** encourage us to seek out the light and resist the forces that pressure us to think and do like everybody else. The Buddha didn't always do what he was told. He stepped away from the rat race and saw how it made other people suffer.

Sulak Sivaraksa is a Buddhist dissident who has been critical of Thailand's military government when it pressures its people into blind faith. But these problems aren't restricted to Southeast Asia. All of us are in danger of letting our light go dim. "Critical (mindful) thinking means deeper understanding of the nature of modern institutions and social structures," Sivaraksa writes. "You should not be hypnotized and misled by the glamorous garbage that media messages convey to you."[60]

Engaged Buddhists remind us that Buddhist enlightenment is no form of escapism. After enlightenment, the Buddha didn't retreat into his own non-judgmental, ethically neutral world. He looked outside his protected world to notice the suffering of others. Then he set about gathering others and encouraging them to do something about it as a concerned community. The Noble Eightfold Path is a guide for fellow resisters to take practical actions that can help ease the suffering of others. Right thinking and right livelihood go hand in hand.

Thich Nhat Hanh

Calming the Fearful Heart

As a soldier you can be compassionate. You can be loving and your gun can be helpful. There are times you may not have to use your gun. It is like that knife that is used to cut vegetables. You can be a bodhisattva as a soldier or as a commander of the army. The question is whether you have understanding and compassion in your heart. That is the question.

Thich Nhat Hanh is an internationally renowned Buddhist monk who was nominated for a Nobel Peace Prize in 1967. Exiled from his home in Vietnam for advocating peace in wartime, Hanh never gave up preaching forgiveness and compassion for others. In his books and his lectures Hanh constantly points out how the anger in our thoughts seeps into our everyday actions and decisions. "To practice Right Livelihood, you have to find a way to earn your living without transgressing your ideals of love and compassion," Hanh writes. "The way you support yourself can be an expression of your deepest self, or it can be a source of suffering for you and others."[61]

How we do our job is almost as important as *what* we do. To be fully engaged in the suffering of others we need awareness, engagement, and especially, **mindfulness**.

Mindful Living and Modern Psychology

For Buddhists around the world, mindful living is the only way to end the cycle of suffering. The *Satipathāna Sutra* (or **Foundations of Mindfulness**) lays out four foundations of mindfulness that lead to nirvana. We need to be mindful of our bodies, our feelings, our minds, and the objects that consume our minds. All four foundations begin with the simple act of **meditation**.

First, we should find a quiet place to sit cross-legged and concentrate on our breath. "Breathing in long, he understands: 'I breathe in long'; or breathing out long, he understands: 'I breathe out long.'"[62] Working on our thoughts takes tremendous discipline and devotion. Most times we are not in control of our thinking. The desires and disappointments we feel so acutely arise from the destructive stories we tell ourselves. All of it is rooted in our habits and thought patterns that were formed in childhood, if not earlier.

Today, Western psychologists are more seriously studying the benefits of mindfully monitoring our thoughts. "The concept of mindfulness is most firmly rooted in Buddhist psychology, but it shares conceptual kinship with ideas advanced by a variety of philosophical and psychological traditions."[63] In cognitive behavioral therapy (CBT), for example, patients are encouraged to notice the harmful thought patterns that govern our lives, in order to change the ways we think and act.

Many Western psychologists focus more on the stories we tell ourselves, rather than the "actual" events we believe we experience. For example, let's say you learn on social media that a friend of yours has gone to a club or party without inviting you. The next day, you are annoyed and deliberately don't respond to their texts. Your first response to seeing the picture of your friend at a party was to feel betrayed. That led you down a carefully curated path of past indiscretions that likely led up to this moment. By only selecting the indiscretions, your mind has clearly shown you that your friend is again in the wrong and passed the tipping point when the friendship can be adequately salvaged.

A good cognitive behavioral therapist might help you see that your first thought was already needlessly discriminating and laced with negative judgment. Because of that, you reached back in the past and pulled out only negative memories to fill out the story arc of a bad friend without hope of redemption. Until you have actually spoken with your friend, there are countless possibilities that you aren't considering. For example, perhaps your friend did try to reach you, thought you were already coming, was caught in a difficult bind that you aren't aware of, made an honest mistake that they will later apologize for, and so on. These are all more positive storylines than the negative one we immediately jump to.

Even if your friend was in the wrong, it still might be considered in a context of more favourable acts performed in friendship. When we monitor our thinking patterns more mindfully, we begin to notice that we don't experience anything neutrally, "but rather through the filters of self-centered thought and prior conditioning, thereby running the risk of furnishing superficial, incomplete, or distorted pictures of reality."[64] If unchecked, such dangerous thinking patterns all too easily lead to confusion, depression, even violence to ourselves or others.

For many psychologists today, the ancient Buddhist practice of meditating on our thinking patterns is a highly effective way of ridding ourselves of the negativity we unknowingly add to our immediate surroundings. We can better look behind the stories we tell ourselves, where we're likely to find "more vulnerable feelings such as uncertainty, sorrow, anger, helplessness, or fear."[65] Rather than running away from such raw emotions we can observe them and even draw strength from them. Once we are empowered to take control of these self-narratives, we will be "less likely to be self-conscious, socially anxious, and … enter absorptive states of consciousness."[66]

If we can stop assuming the worst about other people (and ourselves), we can better overcome the fears and insecurities that too often complicate relationships with strangers, foreigners, and even friends. We become more mentally available to help others overcome their own fears, building stronger relationships based on curiosity and compassion. "It is not that *something different is seen*," renowned psychologist Carl Jung wrote in an introductory book on Buddhism, "but that one *sees differently*."

Zen Enlightenment

The legendary Bodhidharma brought his version of Buddhism from India to China sometime in the fifth or sixth century. His core Buddhist beliefs were smoothly integrated into China's Taoist and Confucian traditions to form the basis of **Chan Buddhism**.

Like Bodhidharma, Chan Buddhists emphasize simple changes in consciousness that can be passed down from one person to another. A famous story from Buddhist lore tells of the Buddha lifting a flower on top of **Vulture Peak**, while giving a talk to his disciples. His best student, Mahākāśyapa, smiled after receiving the unspoken, secret transmission from the Buddha himself. Since that important moment, many different strands of Buddhism promote the idea that release from suffering can be passed on only from teacher to student, through a **mind-to-mind transmission**. The reclusive, temperamental, and mysterious Bodhidharma is believed to be the 28th Buddhist master in a direct line of transmission that traces back to the Buddha and Mahākāśyapa.

In the 12th century Chan Buddhists continued moving east, in time reaching Japan, where their religion was transformed as **Zen Buddhism**. The idea that personal experience is more important than literacy or rule-following had instant appeal. Everything we need to end our suffering is already in our heads. All we have to do is practice mindful living. A meaningful, lasting *satori* (enlightenment) is therefore possible to achieve.

Dogen, the most famous Zen Master of the Middle Ages, exhorted his disciples to let loose the delusions and bad ideas that ruled their minds. Dogen believed we all have the capacity to live more freely. "The mind itself is Buddha," he frequently quoted. But freeing our Buddha minds takes practice and aspiration. Zen training involves leaving behind "the thoughts and awareness of ordinary beings, who have not aroused the aspiration for enlightenment."[67]

Dogen and later Zen Buddhists understood that negativity is born from seemingly rational and logical thinking. The solution isn't to correct the logic, but to abandon such futile grasping altogether. *Satori* comes from seeing things immediately as they are, before one clouds reality with subjective judgements and unhelpful prejudices. It's never too late in our lives to break our destructive thinking habits. When should we start? Dogen answers: "The very moment for this is just now."[68]

Zen Buddhists built on the Chan tradition of master-student transmissions. They documented and pored over earlier dialogues that eschewed rational thinking for more liberated, spontaneous realizations. These ***koans***, or "public documents," became essential components of Buddhist lore.

One famous *koan*, recorded in the 12th-century **Blue Cliff Record**, involves a student asking his master why the Bodhidharma came from the West. In some versions a man is asked the question while hanging by his teeth over a precipice. It doesn't matter if he answers the question rationally or nonsensically. Either way he will surely fall to the death. Dogen confounded himself with this *koan*.

Such riddles draw Buddhist disciples "into the abyss of doubt and intellectual investigation, and lead them to practices that help reach across to the realm of enlightenment."[69] What is the sound of one hand clapping? If there is a good answer it probably won't appear rational. Instead, everything hinges on how freely and easily the students approach their lives, and therefore their responses. Once we are freed from cumbersome and consuming thought patterns, we can begin to see things all around, things we missed when our minds were sadly distracting us.

Zen poets became particularly fond of Chinese **haiku** poets who observed the world around us with profound simplicity. Written in three lines, in a 5–7–5 syllabic form, haiku poets expressed the deepest emotions in the gentle workings of the natural world. Loneliness, nostalgia, and the fragility of life became popular themes of the Zen poetry.

In 1689, the poet **Bashō** set off on a pilgrimage over the mountains and plains of Japan to experience first-hand the famous sights of the Zen tradition. With his mind set free, Bashō was able to see the natural world clearly and directly. In his haiku, Bashō captured the silent spaces that might have otherwise gone unnoticed. He wrote:

Quietness:
Seeping into the rocks,
The cicada's voice.[70]

For Zen poets and philosophers, the person with a clear mind is better able to appreciate the nature that surrounds us all. Perhaps more importantly, we are also more likely to notice the goodness in other people as well. Bashō was especially enamored with a simple and honest innkeeper who gave the poet refuge from the lonely road. The poet wondered "what kind of Buddha manifested himself in this world of mud and dust to help someone like me...."[71]

Zen thinkers frequently remind us that a free mind doesn't shy away from the darkness and meanness of the world. Instead, we are encouraged to see it all and wholly grasp it. The most enlightened poet still has unpleasant experiences. Bashō certainly did. On one particularly dreary day in the mountains, he wrote:

> Fleas and lice:
> a horse pisses
> right near my pillow.[72]

When we are able to fully feel the suffering and sadness in the world, we are in a better position to see the flowers that grow from such fertile soil. Like the Zen precepts that link back to the Buddha, the haiku tradition "is a way of returning to nature, to our moon nature, our cherry-blossom nature, our falling leaf nature, in short, to our Buddha nature."[73] Returning to our Buddha nature takes discipline, creativity, and above all a passion for living a richer life.

America's Beatnik Buddhism

In 1905, **Soyen Shaku** became the first Zen Buddhist **Rōshi** to teach in the United States. Along with his student and translator, **Daisetz Suzuki**, Shaku traveled the country preaching the Buddhist **Middle Way**. His emphasis on how Zen Buddhism helps release us from the tyranny of our thoughts proved to be infectious. Buddhism, he explained, "makes us feel the inmost life that is running through every vein and artery of nature."[74]

For Shaku, freeing ourselves of our attachment to intellectualism can help usher a new form of consciousness, a new kind of religion. "We simply feel," he explained. "And this is what constitutes spiritual enlightenment."[75]

Though Shaku returned to Japan, Suzuki stayed on, writing, teaching, and continuing Shaku's mission to introduce Americans to the simplicity and life-affirming philosophies of Zen Buddhism.

For philosophers like Suzuki, the freedom and innocence of Americans in the 1950s was a fertile ground for planting the seeds of Zen Buddhism. "Zen attempts to take hold of life in its act of living," Suzuki wrote.[76] It was a philosophy that American writers and rabble rousers would take to heart.

In New York City, Suzuki, already more than 80 years old, helped usher in the artistic dynamism of the **Beat Generation**. Led by poets and writers like Jack Kerouac and Allen Ginsberg,

> ### Daisetz Suzuki
>
> *An Introduction to Zen Buddhism*
> Without the attainment of satori, no one can enter into the truth of Zen. Satori is the sudden flashing into consciousness of a new truth hitherto undreamed of. It is a sort of mental catastrophe taking place all at once, after much piling up of matters intellectual and demonstrative. The piling has reached a limit of stability and the whole edifice has come tumbling to the ground... Religiously, it is a new birth; intellectually, it is the acquiring of a new viewpoint.

the Beat Generation lived and wrote rhythmically, gleefully flaunting the bureaucratic rules of a sharply divided America. They wrote of their experiences hitchhiking across the country and experimenting with drugs and alcohol in their never-ending attempts to free their minds. On the dust jacket of his Zen-inspired book, *Dharma Bums*, Kerouac is credited with introducing "an exciting new Way of Life in the midst of modern despair."

The Beat poets would come to learn that their Zen practice offered a more lasting release than the drugs and alcohol they experimented with to alter their consciousness. As West Coast poet **Gary Snyder** wrote to Ginsberg from a Zen monastery in Japan, the "basic central insight, supporting wisdom and understanding, as far as I have little of it, came to me through **zazen** and general Zen practice, not through the mescaline."[77] It was a lesson Suzuki tried to teach Kerouac as well. When the Beat poet showed up at his New York City apartment intoxicated, Suzuki politely refused Kerouac's request to move in together. Instead, Suzuki quietly urged the rambunctious poet to drink more green tea.

Jack Kerouac

Dharma Bums
Because now I am grown so old and neutral… But then I really believed in the reality of charity and kindness and humility and zeal and neutral tranquility and wisdom and ecstasy, and I believed that I was an oldtime bhikku in modern clothes wandering the world (usually the immense triangular arc of New York to Mexico City to San Francisco) in order to turn the wheel of the True Meaning, or Dharma, and gain merit for myself as a future Buddha … at this time I was a perfect religious wanderer.

By the 1960s, Zen monasteries and less formal meditation groups began dotting the country. As the Beats gave way to the Hippies, the transmission of ancient Buddhist precepts would undergo another transformation with a renewed emphasis on love and freedom. As the famous San Francisco Rōshi, **Shunryu Suzuki,** noted, Americans "have a great opportunity to find out the true way of life for human beings. You are quite free from material things and you begin Zen practice with a very pure mind, a beginner's mind. You can understand Buddha's teaching exactly as he meant it."[78]

Thanks to the efforts of so many Japanese masters like Suzuki, Zen continues to be the most popular form of Buddhism practiced in America today.

Tenzing Norgay: A Sherpa Climbs Mount Everest

For people around the world **Mount Everest** represents the ultimate physical and psychological challenge. Hikers and adventure-seekers leave behind their worldly responsibilities, their work and sometimes even their families in order to scale the tallest mountain in the world, standing 8,848 metres (29,029 ft.) above sea level.

Before ascending the mountain, many modern-day thrill seekers stop at **Tengboche Monastery** to receive blessings from the Buddhist lamas. Blessing foreigners who embark on dangerous climbs is a tradition that goes back over one hundred years, since the Sherpas built their first Buddhist monasteries early in the 20th century.

For the Sherpas who live in the Khumbu region of Nepal, in the foothills of the Himalayas, the mountains are linked with Buddhist tenets of freedom, joy, and mental discipline. Their roots can be traced back to Buddhist villages in Tibet. Since the 16th century, Sherpas travel from Eastern Tibet, looking for work in the mountains. They carry with them their gods of their ancient folk religions that meld easily with their Buddhist faith.

The most internationally famous Sherpa, **Tenzing Norgay** was born while his mother was on a pilgrimage to a sacred Buddhist temple, the "Pure God's Palace'" in Tibet's Kama Valley. Before his ascent of Everest brought Norgay international attention, it was his own trip to Tibet that helped transform his life. He spoke lovingly of his Tibetan memories "of the **Dalai Lama** and his blessing; of the shrines and temples on the lonely hillsides; of the pilgrimage I made for my loved ones to the Holy Land of my faith. When the prayer flags flutter, I can still see it. When the prayer wheels tinkle, I can still hear it."[79]

Tenzing Norgay

I am not an educated man—not a lama or scholar who can speak of matters of theology. But I feel that there is room on earth for many faiths, as for many races and nations. It is with God Himself as it is with a great mountain. The important thing is to come to Him not with fear but with love.

But a spiritual yearning would always call Norgay out of the cities and into the mountains. Specifically, he returned to the mountain the Sherpas call *Chomolungma* (Mount Everest), "the Goddess Mother of the Mountains." Six different times he had tried, and failed, to be the first person in the world to summit the great mountain. "I think it is perhaps true that I am more adapted to heights than most men; that I was born not only in, but *for*, the mountains. I climb with rhythm," he explained.[80]

In 1953, Norgay joined the team of British mountaineer John Hunt. In what would be his seventh bid to summit Everest, Norgay was paired with a Christian, New Zealand alpinist Edmund Hillary. The two quickly shared a bond that went beyond mountain climbing. Before their final ascent, Norgay saved Hillary's life, alertly tightening his rope as Hilary fell into a deadly crevasse. Days later, still tied together by their fragile line, Norgay and Hillary became the first mountaineers to successfully summit Mount Everest.

On the summit, "I looked at Tenzing," Hillary later wrote, "and in spite of the balaclava, goggles, and oxygen mask all encrusted with long icicles that concealed his face, there was no disguising this infectious grin of pure delight as he looked all around him."[81] On top of the world, Norgay bowed his head and "thought of God."[82] Then, like a loving parent bringing a gift to his child, he buried candy under the snow as a thank-you present to *Chomolungma*.

On return from the summit, Norgay was met with fame and adulation from all corners of the world. He spent the rest of his life inspiring people to go outside their comfort zones and be open to new experiences. For Norgay, the spirit of Buddhism was always bigger than the tallest mountain. "To travel, to experience and learn: that is to live," he wrote. "The world is wide, and you cannot see all of it even from the top of Everest."[83]

The Compassionate Dalai Lama

In 1935 with the threat of world war creeping ever closer, and internal strife tearing at Tibet's borders, all signs of hope pointed north to the mountains. A rainbow had beckoned the holy lamas out of the suffocating city of **Lhasa**.

As per tradition, the monks gathered at a mountain lake to pray, reflect, and search for signs. The thirteenth Dalai Lama had died two years earlier. The soul of Tibet's holiest Bodhisattva ought to have already been reborn. But where to find such a compassionate being was the question of the day. On the shore of Lake Lhamoi Lhatso, **Palden Lhamo**, the goddess who long ago promised Tibetan Buddhists eternal guidance, blessed a simple lama with a vision. In the glistening water, the goddess showed the lama coded letters and a vision of an old farmhouse with turquoise tiles. Inspired, the subsequent journey would lead the lamas to an unadorned farmhouse deep into hostile Chinese territory, in the village of Takster at the foot of Ami-Chiri, "The Mountain that Pierces the Sky."

There they found a small boy, unusually devout and compassionate for his age. The boy, auspiciously named Lhamo for the goddess of the Lake, passed all the tests, proving himself to be the reincarnated Bodhisattva. He and his family were taken back to Lhasa, away from their idyllic home, where "all wandered unafraid of man."[84]

At the age of 15, the new Dalai Lama became the political and spiritual leader of Tibetan Buddhism. The ceremony, according to tradition, took place at **Potala Palace**, the sacred residence named for the mythical mountain where the Bodhisattva of compassion was said to have lived.

In 1959, the Dalai Lama was forced to leave his palace in Tibet. Insisting that "religion is poison," the Chinese Communist leader Mao Zedong supported the persecution and killing of thousands of Buddhist monks, forcing the Dalai Lama and his band of impoverished but loyal followers to retreat to **Dharamsala** in India. There, the Tibetan Buddhist leaders have lived in exile for over 75 years. In that time, the Dalai Lama became an international symbol of Buddhism and a tireless proponent of compassionate living. He is the author of over 100 books translated into dozens of languages around

The Dalai Lama as a child in the 1940s.

@DalaiLama

March 4, 2019
When the mind is compassionate, it is calm and we're able to use our sense of reason practically, realistically, and with determination.

February 8, 2019
Spiritual practice involves, on the one hand, acting out of concern for others' well-being. On the other, it entails transforming ourselves so that we become more readily disposed to do so.

the world. In his speeches, interviews and written works, the Dalai Lama frequently returns to the core Buddhist themes of changing our thinking patterns.

Our brain "causes a lot of suffering because it is always thinking me, me, me, me," the Dalai Lama explains. Turning our thoughts to others is the real challenge of Buddhist philosophies. "The incredible thing is that when we think of alleviating other people's suffering, our own suffering is reduced," the Dalai Lama claims. "This is the true secret to happiness."[85]

Discovery Questions

1. Go online and find haiku verses written by the 18th-century Zen Buddhist Kobayashi Issa. What essential Buddhist themes can you pick out? Write your own haiku in response.

2. Describe one thing on campus that doesn't move or make any sound. Sit alongside it for a few minutes. Describe all the other things moving or making noise around it.

3. Listen to Krista Tippett's 2003 *On Being* radio interviews with Thich Nhat Hanh and Cheri Maples ("Being Peace in a World of Trauma"). How did Buddhism help Maples become a better police officer?

4. Find a quiet place to sit still for five minutes. Pay attention to your thoughts. Whenever you notice yourself going down one train of thought, stop it and quiet your mind. How many different topics did your mind race to in five minutes? How did you choose which new topics to begin?

5. Go online and watch Sherpa Films' 14-minute film, *Loved by All: The Story of Apa Sherpa*. How does Everest shape the Buddhist Sherpas depicted in the film? Why are so many people attracted to high places like Mt. Everest?

6. Watch the 4-minute BBC video on "The Monk who Ordains Trees." What significance do the trees have inside and outside of traditional Buddhism?

7. Watch part of Roshi Joan Halifax's hour-long 2019 Google Talk, "Standing at the Edge." What does compassion mean to Halifax, and why does she think we have "a deficit of compassion" today? Do you agree?

Glossary

Term	Definition
Amida Buddha	Buddha of infinite light; one of five prominent Buddhas in Tibetan Buddhism
Avalokiteśvara	Bodhisattva of compassion frequently depicted in Buddhist art and literature
Bashō	Zen Buddhist
Beat Generation	20th century American poets and writers who expressed Zen Buddhist themes of freedom and spontaneity
Bhadda Kundalakesa	Buddhist nun converted to Buddhism by the Buddha himself
Bhikku	Buddhist monk; literally, a beggar
Blue Cliff Record	Chan Buddhist collection of essential *koans*
Bodhisattvas	Exceptional and compassionate beings who forgo their own spiritual development to help others find happiness
Candrakīrti	Seventh-century Buddhist scholar
Chan Buddhism	Chinese Buddhist school emphasizing personal enlightenment
Daisetz Suzuki	Zen Buddhist philosopher credited with popularizing Buddhism in the West
Dalai Lama	Spiritual leader of Tibetan Buddhism
Dhammapada	"The Way of Truth"; ancient collection of Buddha's teachings
Dharamsala	City in northwestern India and home of exiled Tibetan Buddhists
Dharma	Foundational teachings of the Buddha
Dogen	13th-century Zen Buddhist philosopher and poet
Engaged Buddhism	Buddhist leaders practically engaged in contemporary social issues
Foundations of Mindfulness	Ancient Buddhist text focusing on the connections and disconnections between the mind and the body
Four Noble Truths	Buddhist path of acknowledging suffering, recognizing its cause, knowing the solution, and practicing the way out
Gary Snyder	Contemporary American poet who converted to Zen Buddhism
Haiku	Japanese short poem that "cuts" to a deeper wisdom
Khama	Converted to Buddhism after hearing the Buddha speak; helped establish first community of Buddhist nuns
Kisa Gotami	Early Buddhist convert who overcame her worldly suffering after speaking with the Buddha
Koans	Zen Buddhist riddles used to help students think outside their ordinary habits and narrow consciousness
Lhasa	Holy city of Tibetan Buddhism in the Himalayan mountains
Lotus Sutra	Ancient foundational text of Mahāyāna Buddhism promoting the attainment of enlightenment
Mahāyāna	"The great vehicle"; popular school of Buddhist thinking that emphasizes how ordinary people can create happiness with others

Mandala	Artistic geometric designs created to help sharpen the mind
Mara	Demon who failed to tempt Siddhartha away from his righteous path
Meditation	A practice or ritual designed to increase mental awareness and focus
Middle Way	A Buddhist path that resists attachment and resistance to pleasure and pain
Mind-to-mind transmission	Buddhist wisdom passed down directly from teacher to student
Mindfulness	Mental state in which one is fully aware, and sometimes in control of their thoughts
Mt. Everest	Tallest mountain in the world; Himalayan mountain on the border of Tibet and Nepal
Nirvana	Ideal Buddhist state in which practitioners are permanently released from their unwanted attachments
Noble Eightfold Path	Buddhist Way, from right thinking to right action, and culminating in peace of mind
Palden Lhamo	Tibetan goddess who protects Lhasa and the Dalai Lamas
Pāli Canon	Oldest collection of classical Buddhist scriptures
Potala Palace	Winter Tibetan residence of the Dalai Lamas until their exile in the 20th century
Rōshi	Zen Buddhist Master
Samsāra	Buddhist cycle of birth, death, and rebirth
Sangha	Buddhist community of nuns or monks
Satori	Zen Buddhist awakened or enlightened state of mind
Shunryu Suzuki	20th century Zen Buddhist monk who founded the San Francisco Zen Center and helped popularize Buddhism in North America
Siddhartha Gautama	Indian Prince who became the Buddha after becoming enlightened
Soyen Shaku	First Zen Buddhist Rōshi to teach in the United States
Sulak Sivaraksa	20th century Buddhist, and social activist in modern Thailand
Tengboche Monastery	Tibetan Buddhist monastery on one of the routes to Everest base camp
Tenzing Norgay	Sherpa guide who was on the first team to ever successfully summit Mount Everest
Thich Nhat Hanh	Vietnamese Buddhist monk who was an early proponent of "Engaged Buddhism"
Vulture Peak	Mountain retreat in northeast India where Buddha discussed his most cherished teachings
Zazen	Seated meditation in the Zen Buddhist tradition
Zen Buddhism	Japanese Buddhist school heavily influenced by China's Chan Buddhism

Chapter Three

Daoism
Embracing Change

For most Chinese tourists, the Daoist Temple on Jade Maiden Peak is a long way to journey for a hot cup of tea. It likely involves taking a high-speed train from the city of Xi'an in central China, then a local bus to the base of **Huashan Mountain**, perhaps a cable car ride, followed by a treacherous hike across narrow passes over precipitous drops.

The five peaks promise spectacular vistas, majestic sunrises, and something else that is noticeably lacking from our everyday world: "As a sacred site, Huashan is associated with dense strands of history, memory, and experiences of power."[86]

One of the earliest known residents was a flute player who lived in a cave thousands of years ago. He played so beautifully his music filtered into the dreams of the musical **Nong Yu** ("Plays with Jade"), the daughter of a powerful duke. Disenchanted with the trappings of life in a royal court, the Jade Maiden left it all behind to make music with the cave hermit for the rest of her days. They attracted all kinds of supernatural beings with their celestial music, until they were finally carried off to heaven by a phoenix, never to walk the mountain pass again.

If we are to understand the spirit of this ancient Chinese religion, we might start with appreciating the Daoist temple that stands on Jade Maiden Peak. The temple, like the religion it serves, pays tribute to those like Nong Yu who walk away from their inherited riches, dedicating their entire lives to the spontaneous expression of their creativity.

Beyond Words

Daoism contains a canon of seminal texts that explains (in words) why the *Dao*, or Way, cannot be explained with words. It's a paradox that lies at the heart of this ancient religion. How do we say the unsayable?

Dao is underneath all words, invisible and indivisible. In Daoism's seminal text, the ***Laozi***, we learn from the very first line that "[i]f the Way can be spoken of it is not the constant Way." We need to look beyond the everyday world of words because "the nameless is the beginning of the myriad things."[87] One of the oldest texts in the world, the ***Book of Changes*** (*I Ching*), isn't even written in words. It's written in 64 **hexagrams**, each with six lines, broken and unbroken, that point to a deeper significance, predicting a future we can't fully grasp.

We all know that words and names help us learn about the world by teaching us to differentiate between things. From an early age we learn that a table is for eating on, a chair is for sitting on. But words also fix the meanings so that we have trouble seeing the world more creatively. Can't we sometimes eat on a chair, or sit on a table? Or turn them both into firewood to stay warm in an emergency? Don't the most creative artists, poets, and scientists constantly challenge us to see things in new ways? Words are helpful, Daoists concede, but only when we resist overly rigid definitions and interpretations.

Words can describe the world, but if we want to discover what comes before the world of words, then it's better to keep our mouths closed. Of course, if words are so problematic, we might question the value of reading so many Daoist texts. The *Laozi* is composed of roughly 5,000 characters, a fair number of words to translate in any language. Once we decode their meaning, we're probably going to have to leave the words behind. That's just what **Laozi** did, after all.

Sometime in the sixth century BCE, the Old Master went on a one-way journey, leaving his practical life behind. Following his precept, "A good traveler leaves no tracks," he headed west over the mountains. When the border guard recognized Laozi and realized he wasn't planning to ever come back, he blocked the way, insisting that the great sage leave something of himself in return. Agreeing, the philosopher composed the *Laozi* on the spot to help others do just as he did: learn the lessons from the past, adjust to the unknowable and ever-changing present, and leave all the other junk behind.

Yin and *Yang*

While it may not be possible to fully capture the Dao in words, there are ways of getting closer to its power. Understanding the cosmic interplay between the **yin** and **yang** is a useful first step.

The *yin* and *yang* are first described in commentaries on the *Book of Changes*. Over 3,000 years ago, the universe was believed to be composed of two opposing forces, each constantly fighting for supremacy over the other. Hot and cold, light and darkness, heaven and earth, male and female: the *yin* and *yang* came to represent the constant tension and striving in the universe. "The successive movement of yin and yang constitutes the Way (Tao).... And the common people act according to it daily without knowing it."[88] According to the *Book of Changes*, the *yin* and *yang* are always at play, whether we acknowledge it or not.

The symbol of the *yin* and *yang* is shown with a curved line between the two emphasizing how neither side is fixed but, rather, are constantly shifting. Each side also contains a piece of the other embedded inside itself. Cosmologically, Daoists see themselves as hard *and* soft, black *and* white, male *and* female. While the Daoist *yin* and *yang* can sometimes serve to reinforce old-fashioned gender binaries, the ancient cosmology can also help us see how "masculine" and "feminine" traits are intertwined in all of us.

Some Daoist scholars have noted how the yin is "necessary for the working of the universe, equal and for some schools even superior to the yang."[89] In the *Laozi*, the characteristics associated with the yin are championed as nature's ways that are worthy of emulation. Philosophies based on this "accentuation of femininity"[90] have attracted spiritual seekers for thousands of years. In the *Laozi* it is written, "The soft overcomes the hard ... the weak overcomes the strong."[91] Learning how to harness the "softer" sides of humanity helps restore balance and conquer the enemies within and without.

The *Laozi* was originally meant as a handbook for politicians. Traditionally, the common belief was that rulers needed to show strength if they wanted to succeed. The *Laozi* countered that erroneous thinking by showing how strength in weakness could ultimately prove to be more successful. In the *Laozi* it is written:

> Do not domineer over all under heaven with weapons.
> Such deeds will deeply receive retribution;
> In places where armies have stationed, thorns and brambles will grow.
> Those who are good [at fighting] just gain a victory, but do not seize strength from it.[92]

Daoists believe that victory in battle brings only temporary relief. True strength comes from being so well balanced that other people will seek to emulate us, not fight us.

Learning how to balance the tensions inside each of us is no easy task. "There must be individuals who, recognizing the difficulties, still dare act toward surmounting the opposites."[93] Through discipline and practice, Daoism teaches us it is possible to abide by this Way. Its history is rich with stories of ordinary people who cultivated inner peace and therefore went on to do extraordinary things.

Philosophers and Wanderers

Once we learn to resolve our suffering by accepting inner conflict, we are freed from the negative consequences of our stressed and overworked mind (and body). No longer constrained by external forces, we can live more spontaneously and meaningfully. We move lighter, but forcefully; swifter, but at rest. Looking outside, we see nature does this all the time.

Take water, for example. "Nothing under heaven is softer and weaker than water," Lao Tzu writes. "Yet nothing is better for attacking the stiff and the strong."[94] Water is most effective when it keeps moving, never getting stuck in any one place, never turning back. This constant motion is a key characteristic of the *Dao*, and why it's so difficult to pin down. Humans are in constant motion, too. But sometimes we are unnaturally fraught with anxiety. **Zhuangzi**, the ancient Daoist philosopher, observed, "Is it not sad how we and other things go on stroking or jostling each other, in a race ahead, a gallop which nothing can stop?" Disbelievingly, he asked more pointedly, "Is man's life really as stupid as this?"[95]

The Daoist ideal is to have a quiet mind that moves freely. For Zhuangzi, to be fully free means unlearning some of the practical, worldly advice that slows us down. If we pull out that giant tree of accumulated wisdom, "why not plant it in the realm of Nothingwhatever, in the wilds which spread out into nowhere, and go roaming away to do nothing at its side, ramble and fall asleep in its shade?"[96] True wisdom, he argued, is something more than collecting pointless trivia or memorizing facts.

A calm mind gives birth to free thinking and spontaneous living. It also leads us closer to the Dao and therefore helps us get in touch with ourselves. As the famous Daoist master of the **Quanzhen School**, Wang Zhe, wrote, "When calmness arrives with the calmness, you shall definitely unite with the mysterious." When our mind is still, only then can we "act with free abandon, and know what it is to be relaxed and content."[97]

To encourage free thinking, Daoist monks have long been encouraged to stay on the move, **cloud wandering** from temple to temple, finding meaning in new experiences. Living life meaningfully and adventurously means not looking to capture every moment for posterity. "To remain neither in motion or still is a fundamental principle," wrote **Cao Wenyi**, a 12th-century Daoist nun. "To be neither square nor round is the Great Dao."[98] Keeping still while staying on the move, constantly adjusting to one's surroundings, seeking the lowest places where no one else will go, that's what water does, too.

Wandering from place to place helps free the seeker from getting mired in bad habits and sluggish thinking. But a life without lasting relationships inevitably comes with loneliness. Daoism is filled with such stories of spiritually sorrowful longing. The eighth-century poet **Li Po** is still revered in China today for expressing the sometimes painful journey through a beautiful natural world that constantly reminds us of our own impermanence. He drowned, some say, when he fell out of his boat desperately trying to embrace the moon reflected on the water. In his poem, *Long Yearning*, Li writes:

The crater taking up the lower two-thirds of this photograph was discovered on the planet Mercury when the space probe Mariner 10 carried out a series of surveys in 1974–75, and named after the Chinese poet Li Po. It is about 120 kilometres wide.

The sky is long, the road is far, bitter flies my
   spirit;
The spirit I dream can't get through, the mountain
   pass is hard.
Long yearning,
Breaks my heart.[99]

In the 12th century, **Sun Buer** was at a crossroads. She had studied the ancient texts, practiced Daoist rituals, and sought to integrate a Daoist lifestyle amidst the daily pressures of her family life. But after her children had grown, she felt no closer to achieving inner peace or lasting happiness. Her husband attributed Sun Buer's melancholy to too much *yang*, not enough *yin*. She had gotten herself out of balance, "analyzing too much at the expense of intuition."[100] Sun Buer's teacher pointed out that she could never become "one with the sun and moon" while she stayed at home, ensnared in gender stereotypes. She would need to transform herself, to change her life and embark on a perilous journey. But such options were not realistic for Chinese women in the 12th century. Remarkably, Sun Buer's response was to douse herself in scalding oil, permanently disfiguring her face and thereby transforming the way other people looked at her. Later she feigned madness so her husband would let her alone to cultivate her inner strength until she was ready to leave home. Over one thousand miles away, she began her new life as a Daoist poet and nun, living in ascetic squalor.

When Sun Buer returned home twelve years later, she was dispirited to hear about her husband's newly discovered ability to turn stones into silver. She reminded him that "gold and silver are material things that we must leave behind."[101] Already in her early sixties, Sun Buer's Daoist training had invested her with new powers. Her story shows how we can transform ourselves at any age, so long as we commit ourselves to opening our minds and changing our daily habits.

Today, Sun Buer is remembered as one of the **Seven Realized Ones**. Even in death, Sun Buer was "fully in control of her body and her life, and realized her original destiny by returning in glamour to the realm of the immortals."[102]

Physical and spiritual wandering has long been encouraged in the legends and stories of Daoist lore. ***The Journey to the West***, for example, is one of the most beloved tales of philosophical wandering in Chinese literature. The sprawling 16th-century story pulls from a wide range of traditional Daoist sources (along with Buddhist and Confucian texts as well). The book opens with a **Handsome Monkey King** who leaves his familiar, comfortable world behind for an uncertain future of infinite possibilities.

> The heaven-born monkey, strong in magic might,
> Rode the raft and caught the fair wind;
> He drifted across the sea in search of immortals' way,
> Determined in heart and mind to achieve great things.[103]

Having "drifted across the oceans and trudged through many regions for more than ten years,"[104] the Monkey King meets a Daoist Master who teaches him the secret of avoiding the calamities that befall us all. Carelessly, the Monkey King uses the magic to turn himself into a pine tree just so he can impress his friends.

Even when he becomes known as "the Great Sage, Equal to Heaven," the Monkey King can't stop making mischief. He eats the **Queen Mother**'s immortal peaches, drinks the **Jade Emperor**'s wine, and even sneaks into Laozi's palace to steal magic elixir while the Old Master is out giving a lecture.

Are these satirical tales meant to poke fun at the age-old Daoist tradition? Or do the sometimes absurd stories carry words of wisdom about the need to walk lightly, naturally and freely through this changing world? *The Journey to the West* has taken a central place in the Daoist canon, retold and reinterpreted in stories, films, dances, operas, and **shadow puppet shows** throughout China today. Contemporary audiences relate to the ways such stories balance ancient philosophies with superficial pleasures. Like the *yin* and *yang*, the distinctions between profound wisdom and profane living are porous and always shifting.

The Seven Sages of the Bamboo Grove

In the third century, seven loosely connected Daoist literati left their government posts and retreated to a bamboo grove to drink wine, play music, and engage in "pure conversation."

The Seven Sages of the Bamboo Grove as depicted in a painting in the Long Corridor, a covered walkway more than 725 metres long in the Summer Palace in Beijing.

The fourth-century collection *A New Account of Tales of the World* relates how the Seven Sages turned their backs on political intrigue and corruption. The romanticized stories quickly became lasting symbols of Daoist spontaneity and gleeful resistance. Paintings of their exploits have been found on brick walls in Nanking tombs. Exaggerated, ribald accounts of the men soaking in pleasurable activities go a long way in establishing a kind of lighthearted humor that differentiates Daoism from other religions.

If there could be said to be a representative of the reclusive forest Daoists it would be **Ruan Ji**, an infantry colonel, poet, and expert whistler. He once stayed drunk for 60 days in a successful bid to derail a bad marriage. The whole Ruan family is said to have drunk wine out of a communal vat. "One time a herd of pigs came to drink and went directly up to the vat, whereupon pigs and men all proceeded to drink together."[105]

> ## Ruan Ji
>
> *Songs of my Heart*
>
> Fragrant trees, heavy with bright leaves,
> blue clouds, wandering across the sky ...
>
> I long in the end for happiness, and harmony,
> not pain, not separation.

Liu Ling was another free-spirited Daoist poet of the bamboo grove. There are many stories that feature him drunk and naked in his home. One time, when friends came to visit, they lectured him on his irresolute lifestyle. He explained, cryptically, that the universe was his home and his house served as his pants. Then he asked them, "What are you, gentlemen, doing in my pants?"

In the annals of Daoist literature such light-hearted stories make a serious point. Stepping outside the rat race comes with the inevitable shunning from uncomprehending family and friends. Consider **Xi Kang** as an example. Reading Laozi and Zhuangzi awoke inside him an independence so fierce that "any desire for fame or success grew daily weaker."[106]

> **Liu Ling**
>
> *Hymn to the Virtue of Wine*
>
> Without a thought, without anxiety,
> His happiness lighthearted and carefree.
> Now utterly bemused with wine,
> Now absently awake,
> He calmly listened, deaf to thunder's crashing roar ...

Xi Kang was executed, in part for his standoffish behavior that was perceived as disrespectful and rude. A true Daoist, he never defended himself, even as his supporters desperately appealed for clemency. Instead, the night before he died, Xi Kang played on the **zither** a melody that he had never taught to anyone. Thus, after he died, it would never be played again. Such commitment to throwing himself into the moment took him years of disciplined training.

The Seven Sages are often heralded as men who realized and enacted the Dao in their shockingly free lifestyles. The *Zuanghi* long ago championed the merits of such good-timing rabble rousers. "The decencies of conduct are nothing to them.... They are the sort that roams beyond the guidelines."[107] As the bawdy stories of the Seven Sages teach us, such training can lead to a life without restrictions, in spite of the dangers amassing outside the gate.

Relieving the Pressure: Acupuncture and Tai-Chi

According to *The Book of Changes* and the *Laozi*, the universe requires both *yin* and *yang* to continue creating and recreating life. Because we are creations in/of this cosmos, human beings also contain these opposing forces. Daoist healers examine how the *yin* and *yang* interact inside each of us and how they can help us better adjust to the changes we encounter every day.

Traditional Chinese medicine is founded on this intimate connection between the human being and the cosmos. Our bodies are "a miniature version of this enormous system—a miniature universe. Each person thus represents a unity of opposing parts."[108]

The basic material substances of these energetic forces are known as *qi*. Like the universe itself, our bodies are maintained by *qi* circulating throughout our passageways, giving us our life and vitality. *Qi* is constantly transforming itself and us, setting the forces of *yin* and *yang* in motion. "The entire process in the universe—the emergence of new things to replace old things—is the result of the motion and transformation of Qi."[109] The ever-changing *qi* cannot be isolated and scientifically examined, but it can be revealed in its tangible effects on our moods and even our organs.

The Yellow Emperor's Classic of Medicine

In the past, people practiced the Tao, the Way of Life. They understood the principle of balance, of yin and yang as represented by the transformation of the energies of the universe... They maintained well-being of body and mind; thus, it is not surprising that they lived over one hundred years.

These days people have changed their way of life.... Seeking emotional excitement and momentary pleasures, people disregard the natural rhythm and order of the universe. They fail to regulate their lifestyle and diet, and sleep improperly. So it is not surprising that they look old at fifty and die soon after.

The *qi* in our bodies should match the *qi* of the universe. When our *qi* is unnaturally impeded or blocked, our *yin* and *yang* get out of balance. We might feel afraid, stressed out, or unusually tired. We might also feel physical sensations like upset stomachs, headaches, or shortness of breath. These physical manifestations serve as warnings that some of our *qi* need to be set free. "The aim of treatment is to adjust and help sustain the body's own balancing system to reestablish the normal equilibrium."[110]

Traditional Chinese medicine based on Daoist precepts advocates a **holistic** understanding of the human body that looks at particular aches and pains in a larger context. Emotions and psychological states must be taken into account. Weather, geography, and astronomy also play important roles in our sicknesses and our holistic healing.

Today, more people outside of China are looking towards traditional Chinese medicine for forms of **alternative medicine** that help ease pain and anxieties by looking at the bigger picture without the side effects or addictive properties of some drugs. Daoism has promoted such holistic medical practices for over 2,000 years.

Daoists believe that *qi* moves with blood through the body along twelve major channels or **meridians**. "The meridian system provides the pathways for the movement of *qi* and blood, for the regulation of Yin–Yang, and for the various organs to influence one another."[111] The Daoist solution is not to treat the place where one feels the pain, but to open the place where the *qi* may be blocked.

In the ancient practice of **acupuncture**, the doctor locates pressure points where nerve endings send messages to the spinal cord, brain, or pituitary gland. Sticking small needles into the skin at just the right places releases or changes the flow of the pain recep-

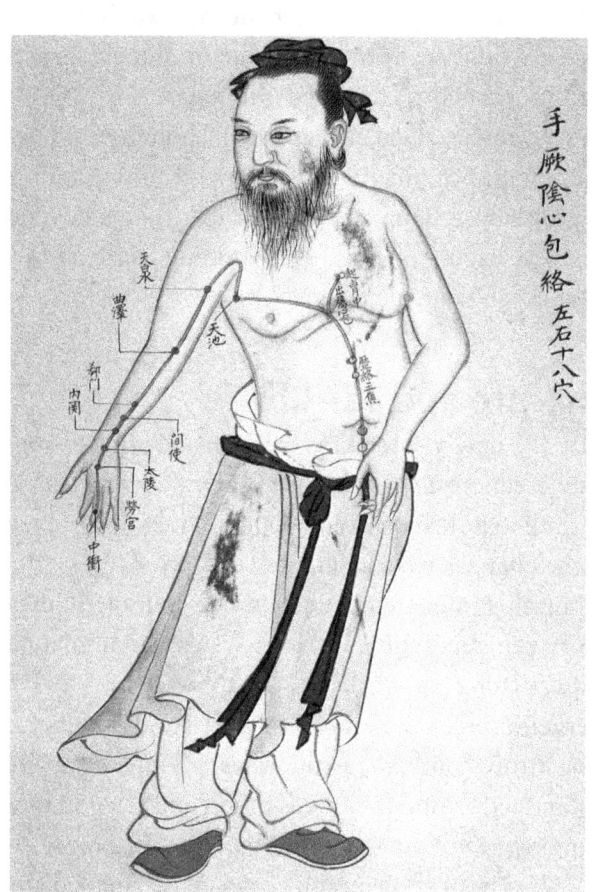

This 18th-century Chinese acupuncture chart shows the location of acupuncture points to control diseases of the heart and sexual organs.

tors through the central nervous system. When performed accurately and effectively, acupuncture can lead to pain relief for headaches, muscle damage, and nausea. This holistic approach locates the origin of pain in parts of the body where Western doctors may not focus their attention. For that reason, over one million Americans use acupuncture as an alternative or complementary means to treat their ailments. American athletes like basketball player Kobe Bryant, tennis star Serena Williams, and football player Aaron Rodgers all used acupuncture to help keep their bodies in superior condition.

The Daoist practice of *Tai-Chi* also focuses on both the physical and mental steps we can take to restore our balance and build our strength. Physically, we can do exercises that open our channels and release our *qi*. Practicing *Tai-Chi* helps us better adjust to our constantly changing *qi* so we don't try to hold it still, or mentally block it from transforming us in unexpected ways.

There is a range of stretching exercises we can take to help the flow of blood that contain our *qi*. "Regulating the body is adjusting your body until it is relaxed, centred, balanced, and rooted. For example, when you practice a pushing movement, the muscles should be relaxed to such a deep level that you can feel your arms relax all the way to the marrow."[112] Such stretching exercises develop our physical coordination by restoring balance, both physically and mentally.

In *Tai-Chi*, there is no perfect exercise or ideal form that will bring any kind of permanent healing. Because the *qi* inside our bodies is constantly changing, Daoism preaches a lifetime of adjusting and re-adjusting ourselves to changes inside and outside our bodies. "In playing Tai-Chi, our aim must be to change again and again; to play with variations in order to make progress each time in our understanding of the principles we are attempting to embody."[113]

Chang San-Feng is considered the founder of modern *Tai-Chi*. Born in 1247, he didn't learn how to live a Daoist life until he turned 67 years old. Living on China's Wu-Tang Mountain for nine years, Chang San-Feng was known as the "sloppy Taoist" because he often pretended he was mad to avoid being called back to the city by the royal court. On windy nights he went on hikes to improve his breathing. On rainy nights he read classic Daoist texts like the *Laozi* and *Zhuangzi* to purify his mind.

In one story, Chang San-Feng got the idea of *Tai-Chi* while watching a magpie attack a python on Wu-Tang Mountain. The snake remained balanced and still, successfully evading the danger whenever the magpie went in for the kill. Both the magpie and the python dispersed when Chang San-Feng got closer to the action. True power, he learned, comes not from angry attacks but from knowing how to overcome obstacles with quieter, inner strength.

Chang San-Feng is alleged to have lived over two hundred years. Stories tell of how he tamed and befriended a wild ape, killed ferocious tigers with his bare hands, and melted snow with his inner heat. The medieval legends of Chang San-Feng attest to the Daoist philosophy of balancing the opposing forces of *yin* and *yang*, staying still and taking action, blending mental discipline with physical strength. "The Tai-Chi master can choose how to respond to any situation. In response to an attack, he or she can disappear like the fog, resist like a mountain, or fight back like a tiger."[114]

Kung Fu: Bruce Lee's "Way of the Intercepting Fist"

In the *Laozi* it is written, "Those who act on it will fail. Those who try to grasp it will lose."[115] The Daoist conception of **wu-wei**, or "action without effort," is a central component of the Chinese martial arts. While training in **kung fu**, a fighter learns to conserve energy, relaxing one's muscles, waiting for the opponent to show weakness before swiftly and decisively striking.

Since every fight is unique, every fighter different, successful *kung fu* fighters learn to adapt their style on the move, turning their opponents' strength against them. In that way the weak overcomes the strong, as Daoists have persistently proclaimed. To act without effort, fighters need to cultivate hardness and softness, brute force and gentle patience.

In 1959, an 18-year-old Bruce Lee, already a cha-cha dance champion and budding *kung fu* expert, left his home in Hong Kong and sailed to America, making his way to San Francisco's Chinatown. Across the bay in Oakland he would meet other Chinese-Americans who were also schooled in Daoist-infused martial arts like *kung fu*.

But soon Lee tired of the different schools of *kung fu*, each teacher passing on a tradition unchanged and unchanging. Lee understood that like the Daoist *yin* and *yang*, people are

This statue of actor and martial artist Bruce Lee was erected on the Avenue of Stars in Hong Kong.

constantly changing. He believed that "we are always in a learning process, whereas a 'style' is a concluded, established, solidified something. You cannot do that, because you learn every day as you grow older."[116]

Departing from the traditional "ten thousand elephants technique," Lee endorsed his "one-inch punch." One day he asked one of his students to hold a thick Oakland telephone book over his chest. From the distance of one finger away, Lee used muscles in his core to give his punch its power. And it did carry unexpected power. "Bruce knocked him into the couch," said one witness, noting how the student's legs "went straight up and over. I thought he'd go through the living room window."[117] Relaxed muscles generate more power, Lee explained. It comes back to action without effort.

With his lightning-quick punches and kicks and his infectious charisma, Lee made an easy transition into the movies, twice breaking Hong Kong box-office records before taking Hollywood by storm. The films **Way of the Dragon** (1972) and **Enter the Dragon** (1973) feature Lee at the prime of his *kung fu* career.

But the philosophy behind his "**Way of the Intercepting Fist**" (*Jeet Kune Do*) was best expressed in the four episodes he helped write for the 1971–72 television show **Longstreet**. In the show Lee teaches a blind man how to clear his mind and conserve his strength to defeat criminals targeting him on the docks. Lee invokes and popularizes ancient Daoist precepts, imploring his pupil to stop thinking and be more like water. The blind man overcomes his initial skepticism and begins to feel his body and mind working as one. "It's funny," he

> ## Bruce Lee
> *Tao of Jeet Kune Do*
>
> Truth has no path. Truth is living and, therefore, changing. It has no resting place, no form, no organized institution, no philosophy. When you see that, you will understand that this living thing is also what you are.

says to Bruce Lee's on-screen character, "that out of a martial art, out of combat, I feel something ... something peaceful. Something without hostility."

Posthumously, through his films and philosophies, Lee continues to introduce the martial arts to audiences around the world, and in the process, teaches the fundamental principles of Daoist *wu-wei*.

Blind Abing Plays *The Moon Reflected on the Second Springs*

One of the most revered pieces of Chinese classical music today is the transcendent *erhu* song, ***The Moon Reflected on the Second Springs***. It is "the sound of a lost soul in a time of turmoil," as one Chinese critic writes.[118] Composed by a blind, "illegitimate" son of a Daoist priest in China's Wuxi region, the famed musician's biography is as mysterious as the music itself. The musician, known colloquially as Abing, has been the subject of at least one documentary film and a popular eight-episode China Central Television show.

Growing up at the turn of the 20th century, Abing was encouraged to become a Daoist master, but eventually he was kicked out of his temple ensemble for playing secular music with other bands around town. After losing his eyesight, Abing took to the streets to play for money. He practiced merging his traditional Daoist music with the bawdy pop songs blaring from the Wuxi opium dens he frequented. Because of his unique compositions, Abing became something of a street corner legend, singing out the news of the day to his otherworldly *erhu* and *pipa* playing.

The only known photo of Abing is from his identity card issued during the Japanese army's occupation of the eastern Chinese city of Wuxi in the late 1930s.

In 1950, musicologists from Shanghai College came to Wuxi to record the best classical music from the region. They stumbled on the wandering blind musician somewhat by accident, and recorded his music in a local school near his home. By that time, Abing had lost his instruments and was clearly dying from syphilis. Though he hadn't played in years, that rough recording, named for an unspecified Wuxi spring, continues to inspire classical orchestras around the world.

On a much publicized tour of China with his Boston Symphony Orchestra, the renowned conductor Ozawa Seiji heard Abing's song for the first time and was deeply moved. Getting out of his chair for the performance, he explained, "People should listen to this kind of music on their knees."

Throughout his life, Abing lived with contradictions, continuously improvising his music according to his shifting circumstances. But Abing is a controversial figure in Daoist lore. Did his seemingly dissolute lifestyle demean the music of religious longing he composed on the streets? Or, does his ethereal music show us how the Daoist religion continues to lift up the noisy sights and sounds that surround us every day?

Today, a clock tower atop the library in a Wuxi square chimes *The Moon Reflected on the Second Springs* every hour. It reminds us that in our own constantly changing days, the ancient tenets of Daoism still strike as steadily and serenely as ever.

Discovery Questions

1. Find an online translation of the *Laozi*. Choose one passage that speaks to a political issue today. How would you develop Laozi's answer to find the best solution?

2. Take a walk in or around campus for one hour, without stopping. What did you see that you never noticed before? Did anybody notice you? Did it feel weird in any way? What are some of the topics your thoughts returned to? What did you achieve?

3. Describe a busker you've seen playing music in the street for money. Are they working the crowd or are they lost in their own music? What are they thinking about while they're playing?

4. Describe "hard" and "soft" character traits in yourself. Do they co-exist peacefully or in conflict? Which ones are currently out of balance? What can you do about it?

5. Watch the short online UNESCO Heritage documentary, "Chinese Shadow Puppetry." Why are people still attracted to such "folk arts"? How would you describe the music? If you were to write a shadow puppet play which folk characters would you include? Why?

6. Find an article about a recent music or sports event on campus. In which ways to the words help you picture what happened? What wasn't described in words? Why not?

7. Watch Bruce Lee's daughter Shannon Lee give her 2015 TEDx talk, "Be an Action Hero: The Philosophy of Bruce Lee." Which aspects of Bruce Lee's philosophy coincide with Daoist beliefs? How do they differ?

Glossary

Terms	Definitions
A New Account of Tales of the World	Fifth-century collection of lighthearted observations promoting Daoist customs and mores
Acupuncture	A form of medical healing that relies on thin needles placed along the body's pressure points
Alternative medicine	Holistic approaches to addressing the body and mind through natural practices and herbal medicines
Book of Changes	*The I-Ching*; ancient text of hexagrams that can be decoded to prophesy the future and clarify deeper meanings
Cao Wenyi	11th-century Daoist philosopher and writer praised by the Emperor
Chang San-Feng	12th-century martial arts expert who discovered and popularized Tai-Chi
Cloud wandering	Daoist practice of traveling from temple to temple, often across difficult mountain terrain
Enter the Dragon	1973 film featuring Bruce Lee using martial arts to avenge the death of his on-screen sister
Erhu	Two-stringed musical instrument played with a bow
Handsome Monkey King	Mythical literary character with supernatural strength
Hexagram	Series of symbolic broken and unbroken lines read from the bottom up
Holistic	The view that the different parts of the body work together and are not independent of the larger natural world
Huashan Mountain	Sacred mountain in Northwest China with Taoist temples built into its rugged terrain
Jade Emperor	"Heavenly Grandfather"; one of the most powerful and popular gods in the ancient Daoist cosmology
Kung fu	Physically demanding body movements that highlight and strengthen one's balance and inner calm
Laozi	The "Old Master"; founder of Daoism in the sixth century BCE
Laozi	Foundational collection of poems covering core Daoist precepts of ethics, character development, and political action
Li Po	Eighth-century poet who writes nostalgically of nature and the passing of time
Liu Ling	Third-century poet more popularly remembered for his love of wine
Longstreet	1971–72 television series featuring Bruce Lee's philosophy of kung fu
Meridians	Channels inside the body through which our vital energy travels
Nong Yu	Woman of ancient literature who heroically forgoes worldly responsibilities for heavenly creativity
Pipa	Four-stringed instrument played by plucking
Qi	Energy sources that flow through the body affecting our moods, vitality, and overall life force

Quanzhen School	Monastic community founded in the 12th century, dedicated to the "Way of Perfection"
Queen Mother	Ancient deity who grows peaches bestowing immortality
Ruan Ji	Third-century poet known for promoting Daoist freedom while dismissing its stricter rules and rituals
Seven Realized Ones	12th-century scholars and promoters of the Quanzhen School's teachings
Shadow puppet shows	Ancient art form using cut-out puppets to tell old stories with modern lessons
Sun Buer	One of the Quanzhen School's "Seven Realized Ones"; emphasized spiritual progress over physical beauty
Tai-Chi	School of martial arts that emphasizes stretching the muscles and practicing breathing techniques
The Journey to the West	Rollicking novel blending animal folktales and Buddhist beliefs with classical Daoist philosophies
"The Moon Reflected on the Second Springs"	"*Erquan Yingyue*"; 20th century ehru composition written by Blind Abing
Traditional Chinese medicine	Forms of alternative medicine utilizing Daoist principles of harmony, balance, and energy sources
Way of the Dragon	1972 film featuring Bruce Lee using marital arts to protect a local restaurant against a violent crime syndicate
"Way of the Intercepting Fist"	Bruce Lee's martial arts philosophy influenced by his studies of Daoist *kung fu*
Wu-wei	Action by non-action; fundamental Daoist precept
Xi Kang	Daoist poet and scholar who wrote extensively on music theory
Yang	Hard, warm, actively creative primordial stuff of all life
Yin	Soft, cool, passively creative primordial stuff of all life
Zhuangzi	Renowned Daoist scholar of the fourth-century BCE; his most famous stories and interpretations are compiled in the *Zhuangzi*

Chapter Four
Yoruba
The Rhythm of the Gods

The Yoruba tell a story about Ijapa, a trickster tortoise who snuck into heaven and stole a hollowed-out dried gourd full of all the world's wisdom. Back home in the forest, he found that the stolen calabash of wisdom dangling from his neck prevented him from crossing over a fallen tree. Disgusted, Ijapa smashed the calabash and scattered the accumulation of wisdom all around the world. The story reminds us that wisdom is for everyone, not meant exclusively for tricksters, kings, holy men, or even gods.

"Yoruba" is a designation that encompasses a culture, language, and religion. Over 100 million people can trace their Yoruba roots back to a region in southwestern Nigeria, Benin, and Togo known as **Yorubaland**.

Ile-Ife is Yorubaland's most sacred city because it marks the place where the first human beings were created. The origin stories bind the city to the people who live in its vicinity. In music, poetry, and stories, Ile-Ife offers a still more spiritual connection to people across the ocean, whose personal histories and family trees were irrevocably uprooted. "To the Yoruba people, Ile-Ife is the place where the Yoruba connect to a historical and mythic lineage that defines, creates, and promotes an understanding of the world and a source of identity throughout West Africa and the diaspora."[119]

Known as the **Orisa**, the gods of the Yoruba are social by nature, cavorting with each other and with the humans who came later. There are at least 401 *Orisa* in the Yoruba pantheon. The numeral "1" is always added to the total on the understanding that new *Orisa* are created according to changing circumstances. The life-giving care of the *Orisa* is one constant in the lives of people separated by time and place. To reciprocate, the Yoruba traditionally appease the *Orisa* with food and gift sacrifices, inviting them into the human world through singing and dancing to ritualistic drum beats.

The *Orisa* move between the worlds of the living and the dead and attempt to keep the balance between them both. In the Yoruba cosmology all human actions directly influence the three realms, and the unseen worlds equally impact our day-to-day decisions. "To the Yoruba, while particular persons (or entities) appear outwardly different, behind surface appearances they are only manifestations of an underlying power which unifies all creation."[120] Acting in accordance with the will of the underlying powers goes a long way to living a satisfying and fulfilling life.

There are few divine laws or absolute commandments in the Yoruba tradition. Instead, there are stories and divinations meant to guide followers through the vagaries of daily life. The practical lessons teach us what works, rather than what's expected. Perhaps it is because "the Yoruba people, while appearing to be very deeply religious, never lose sight of the purpose of religiosity—the enhancement of human existence."[121]

Olodumare: The Distant God

In the Yoruba origin story, **Olodumare,** the "hidden or distant controller of the universe,"[122] commanded an *Orisa* to climb down a celestial chain to a world of water. This god got waylaid by a drinking party along the way and never made it down. Instead, another *Orisa,* **Oduduwa**, stepped in, carrying a shell filled with dirt and a guinea fowl to spread the earth over the water, thereby creating the sacred land where humans and *Orisa* could reside. Valleys and mountains sprouted between the guinea fowl's giant claws.

A sculpture of Oduduwa.

The story, told in many different forms, teaches us more than the history of creation. It shows that gods, like humans, can get distracted in moments of weakness and make mistakes. This injection of fallibility at the beginning of creation is a central theme in the Yoruba religion. Even Olodumare has limits. "Olodumare never pretends to have endless, total, incorrigible knowledge … this makes meaningful the various paradoxes, dilemmas, incongruities, and dissonances in the world."[123]

Because Olodumare is not infallible, the highest god relies on a divination system called ***Ifá*** to help find the wisest path forward. There are 256 chapters of *Ifá* poetry that are "believed to be ageless and all-embracing."[124] *Ifá* divination is passed on to **babalawos** who are trained in using the divination to help people achieve their personal goals, overcoming material and spiritual obstacles along the way. The Yoruba remind us that nobody successfully negotiates this world entirely on their own. "They know that life is full of paradoxes and contradictions and do not seek cleverly to blink at the truth."[125] Even the highest God requires constant counsel and correction.

Because we all err at sometimes critical junctures, the relationship between gods and humans is always tenuous. The "breach or imbalance within or among those realms violates the Yoruba concept of order."[126] Understandably, we all inevitably fall short of this sacred charge. It is the role of the *Orisa*, then, to help us keep the balance when mistakes are made. Humans and gods make mistakes, and when we do, understanding and redemption are essential building blocks for the daily upkeep of our ancient and delicate world.

Ọṣun: The Protector

After the earthly realm was established, Olodumare sent seventeen *Orisa* to populate the earth with new life. Sixteen deities failed. Desperate, they appealed to **Ọṣun**, a female goddess. She agreed to help them with her bountiful, life-nourishing waters. "What emerges is the picture of an exceptional goddess whose presence at the organization of the world placed her in a pivotal position as a woman of power."[127]

Ọṣun is known primarily as a river goddess, representing birth, creative nourishment, and the rushing constancy of constant change. Like the mighty rivers cutting across the African continent, Ọṣun can be volatile and destructive. But Ọṣun also reminds us of the river's distant calm, and the "audibly soothing sound of its journey over rocks and riverbeds."[128]

In more troubled times, the Yoruba women all moved to the top of a mountain to escape their men. Without women, the villages were on the verge of imminent collapse. Death and decay quickly replaced the promise of a creatively dynamic future. One by one the Yoruba gods were called in to violently attack the town and force the women back into society. One by one the gods were defeated by the women on the mountain. Finally, Ọṣun agreed to have a go at it. She convinced the women to return by sweetly and gently singing compassionate songs about the villages' difficult plight. Because of Ọṣun's empathy, the women agreed to follow her back to their towns, ending "the threat to human and divine existence."[129]

> ### Osun Praise Poetry
>
> She beckons at the palm wine seller to bring her wine
> The palm wine sells at an exorbitant price;
> But my mother does not buy overpriced goods
> The mighty water is rushing past
> It is flowing to eternity.

The two-week **Ọṣun-Osogbo Festival** celebrates Ọṣun's relationship to Nigeria's commercial city, Osogbo. Like Ọṣun, the Yoruba people of the Osogbo Market are expert at making colorful dyes and tasty bean cakes for travelers to enjoy. Held in August, the festival features singing, dancing, and giving thanks to the goddess of the river that still bears her name. Mothers, or women who hope to become mothers, bathe in Ọṣun's waters in hopes of a blessing from the goddess. Overseeing the birth of Yoruba children, Ọṣun serves as "the mysterious force in the protective waters of the womb,"[130] reminding us that our "lives should be as cool and clear as water drawn from rivers early in the morning."[131]

Esu: The Trickster God

Over the New Year's holiday, the Nigerian city of **Ila-Orangun** is taken over by bawdy music and late-night dancing in honor of the most coy and challenging *Orisa* in Yoruba stories. **Esu** is described as the gatekeeper to the land of the gods, moving easily between the two worlds of *Orisa* and humans. Serving as Olodumare's eyes and ears, Esu helps ensure the other *Orisa* stay in their proper places.

On earth, and in the world of the gods, Esu cannot be trusted. The god plays the role of the trickster, a concept possibly borrowed from the nearby Fon people in Nigeria and Benin. The trickster wreaks havoc on orderly society, testing relationships, instigating wars, and inflicting suffering for seemingly whimsical reasons. One Yoruba story tells of Esu wearing a hat with a different color on either side. When Esu walks in between two friends, they immediately start quarreling about what color the hat is. Then Esu walks back between them, showing them the other color of his hat. They take to arguing still more intensely. When they come to blows, Esu laughs and sets fire to the village. The trickster god does not apologize or regret the acts, saying only that "sowing dissension is my great delight."[132]

Esu is loved and feared, especially in Nigeria's open markets where success in business is never predictable and always volatile. "For the Yoruba, the world is likened, in its dynamic and interactive unpredictability, to the marketplace with its myriad of arrivals and departures."[133] Statues of Esu are often garlanded in sea shells that traditionally represent Yoruba commerce.

But while tricksters like Esu seem to destroy more than they create, they help us pay closer attention to our relationships with each other. Esu serves "as an antagonist, creating the critical doubts that are necessary to prevent complacency, false certainty, or peremptory acceptance of any appearance of truth without having exhausted all the possible relevant evidence."[134] Without tricksters like Esu, without discord and dissent, societies and religions go stagnant and too often tear themselves apart from the inside out.

Osun-Osogbo Sacred Grove in Nigeria is one of the few remaining Yoruba sacred groves. Such groves, which at one time were located near almost all Yoruba cities, have fallen victim to urban sprawl. This particular grove has now been declared a UNESCO world heritage site.

The trickster Esu also introduces an important philosophical component to the Yoruba cosmos. Thousands of years ago, Yoruba elders understood that chaos played a critical role in the formation of the universe. But because Esu is a god who cares, we are not left alone with meaninglessness or ethical passivity. Instead, Esu "demands that humans deal actively with those aspects of the universe that are random and without explanation. Esu does not show a person the way—he creates a situation in which an individual must find it on his or her own."[135]

Un-Gendering the Cosmos

The Yoruba *Orisa* take on many different forms, shapes, and bodies. In sculptures and paintings, the same *Orisa* can look very different. One reason for the inconstancy is that Yoruba language does not have gendered pronouns like "he" or "she." Yoruba speakers are far more likely to use nouns like "child" or "person" instead of "boy" or "girl." In the Romance languages spoken in many Western countries—for example, French or Italian—one must make an extraordinary effort to avoid using gendered pronouns. In Yorubaland it is the opposite: one must take pains to emphasize a person's gender, and will do so only if such gendering is clearly relevant to the story. In Yoruba, "It is possible to hold a long and detailed conversation about a person without indicating the gender of that person."[136] There may still be social hierarchies and divisions between the rich and poor, but the role of gender may be less important than seniority or family lineage.

Without gendered pronouns, it is nearly impossible to determine the gender of many of the original *Orisa*. In the ancient art of Yorubaland, for example, Esu is sometimes depicted as a man with a phallic head. More often, Esu is shown to be a pregnant woman on her knees in a pose symbolizing creativity and fertility.

Since the gender stereotypes that plagued the West were largely absent from the Yoruba language and culture, it was not unusual for women to have leadership roles. For thousands of years Yoruba women have been in charge of family finances, buying and selling goods in marketplaces across southwestern Nigeria. The marketplace is also a central public sphere, a crossroads for ideas, royal proclamations, and festivals.

In the 20th century, Yoruba-born **Alimotu Pelewura** rose to the leadership of the **Lagos Market Women's Association**, a post which was one of the most powerful political positions in Yorubaland. In 1940, Pelewura closed the markets to lead successful protests against wartime taxes that unfairly singled out women. In a fiery December meeting, Pelewura insisted on no taxation without representation. Her speech, which ended, in her native Yoruba dialect, catapulted her into national politics at a critical time in the Nigerian independence movement.

Such examples don't prove that Yoruba women were the political equals of men, but do help us see that historically women of Yorubaland "wielded influence in policy-making and possessed institutional mechanisms for making that influence felt."[137] There is a famous Yoruba proverb that emphasizes the fundamentally equivalent

Oyèrónkẹ́ Oyèwùmí

Invention of Women

As the work and my thinking progressed, I came to realize that the fundamental category "woman"—which is foundational in Western gender discourses—simply did not exist in Yorùbáland prior to its sustained contact with the West. There was no such pre-existing group characterized by shared interests, desires, or social position.

roles that men and women play in their communities: "Washing the left and right hand each with the other ensures clean hands." The proverb implies that "male and female principles are crucial to a smooth living experience."[138]

As Nigerian playwright **'Zulu Sọfọla** has repeatedly pointed out, traditional Yoruba culture contains both the malady and the cure. Her play *The Sweet Trap*, for example, opens with men crassly insulting women as part of a longstanding tradition during the **Oke'badan Festival** that was originally meant to celebrate fertility. In the first scene of Sọfọla's play, one disgruntled wife discusses how "this festival degenerated into a rowdy display where men could take revenge for their bruised egos." The female characters struggle to balance their modern sensibilities with their religious roots. The play ends with the fiercely independent main character on her knees, submissively weeping for her husband's forgiveness.

For many Yoruba women, throwing themselves blindly into Westernization or obediently retreating into a distant past both come with their own complications. The solution for many playwrights and intellectuals since Sọfọla comes from mining traditional Yoruba culture for modern interpretations that can challenge inequalities while still honoring the *Orisas* who have long looked after their communities.

The Slave Trade and Yoruba Diaspora

From the 16th to the 19th century, over three million people from Yorubaland and the surrounding regions were captured, shackled, and taken aboard transatlantic ships on the **Middle Passage**, to be sold as slaves in the Americas and West Indies. Permanently cut off from their family, friends, and larger Yoruba communities, many slaves turned to religion as a means to help repair the damage triggered by the cruelty and moral depravity of their African captors, European traders, and American slave owners. During the slave trade, the Yoruba tradition was passed on (sometimes secretly) from generation to generation, in modern-day countries as diverse as Cuba, Brazil, and Haiti.

In such places, far from Yorubaland, the ancient stories are still told today, interpreted in a modern context through the rhythm of the drums and the movements of the body. Though they speak Spanish in Cuba, Portuguese in Brazil, French-based Creole in Haiti, and English in Nigeria, the rhythm of the *Orisa* bind the people of the Yoruba **diaspora** together, heavily contributing to each country's unique political and cultural life to this day.

Cuba's *Batá* Drumming

In 1789, Cuba entered the slave trade to buy West African laborers for its booming coffee and sugar plantations. The majority of the slaves were taken from Yorubaland and the Congo. Separated from their families, communities, and material possessions, the Yoruba arrived in a foreign land isolated and homesick. For these new Cuban slaves, "Religion was the vehicle for the transmission of the beliefs, moral ideas, and aspects of the worldview of Africa, as well as a means of preserving as much of their way of life as was possible."[139]

In Cuba, the displaced Yoruba founded a religion called **Santería**, blending Yoruba traditions with Colonial Spanish Catholicism already rooted on the Caribbean island. Though the African transplants arrived empty-handed, their connections to their homeland "were held in the melodies produced in their throats and in the complex rhythms of their hands."[140]

In the provinces of **Havana** and **Matanzas**, the Yoruba rebuilt their sacred *Batá* **drums** by carving out hollow spaces inside wood, collecting sacred herbs, seeds, and blood and mixing them into a paste, covering them with tightly stretched animal skin dipped in Ọsun's purifying water. The Orisa Àyàn resided inside a properly consecrated *Batá* drum, adorned with bells. For the Yoruba people, consecrated musical instruments, and *Batá* drums specifically, "cease being representation of the orisas; they become the orisas."[141]

In a Santerían **tambor**, or "drumming ceremony," *Àyàn* summons the *Orisas* to come out and take possession of the congregants. The three *Batá* drums must be struck in perfect rhythm, led by the *Iyá*, or mother drum. "*Àyàn*'s voice is vibrating skins, bells, and vessels that push around invisible air."[142] When played correctly, the Yoruba drumming patterns can lead to an ecstatic union between *Orisas* and humans.

This joining of the sacred and the profane continues to be a central theme of Yoruba-influenced Cuban music. In the 1950s, the Cuban folk band **AfroCuba de Matanzas** invented the *Batárumba*, incorporating Yoruba drum rhythms into secular Latin dance music. Today, internationally renowned Cuban bands like **Yoruba Andabo** are known for injecting Yoruba chants and rhythms into their popular recorded music. As the 2015 Juno award-winner **Daymé Arocena** said, "Santería came to my life through music. I fell in love with religious music, because it has an impressive rhythmic and melodic richness."[143]

Today we still hear the five-stroke percussion pattern of rumba or salsa music in dance halls or public squares across the Americas. The sensual, rhythmic strains conjure the not-so-distant sounds of the ecstatic Yoruba drummers calling the *Orisas* to energize and fire up the faithful crowd.

Brazil's Candomblé Dancing

Yoruba people traveling from the inland regions to the coast of Benin were known as the *Nago*. In the 19th century, thousands of *Nago* were captured, shipped across the ocean, and sold as slaves in the Bahia region of Brazil. In 1888, Brazil formally ended slavery, but without money or formal education, the transplanted Yoruba went from the poverty of slavery to the destitute shanty towns known as *favelas*. There they established **terreiros**, spaces where the ex-slaves could perform religious rituals recalling Yoruba *Orisas* like **Xango**.

The *Nago* revered Xango, the *Orisa* of thunder and lightning, fourth ruler of the Oyo Empire (Oduduwa was first), and the bearer of a deadly double-sided axe. "In this light, the justice-seeking character of Xango, with his warrior nature, would have contributed to transform him into a popular emblem of resistance and an allied spiritual force in the struggle against slavery."[144]

The adaptation of Yoruba rituals in Bahia became known as **Candomblé**. Such rituals pass on important knowledge about race, culture, and history, not through textbooks or superhuman feats of strength, but through intensely social and participatory singing and dancing. Candomblé "is an ancient, complex, and powerfully beautiful belief system in which spirituality is expressed through sophisticated rhythmic structures and divinity makes itself present in the bodies of dancers."[145]

As many anthropologists have pointed out, such rituals do more than call forth the gods. "The dancing bodies accumulate spirit, display power, and enact as well as disseminate knowledge."[146] Knowledge is disseminated by participating in the ritualistic dances, improvising ancient themes with bodily movements that resist and challenge the hierarchies the Yoruba are forced to confront every day.

In the crowded Bahian *favelas*, Yoruba dance ceremonies mixed with Congolese and Indigenous dance movements, giving rise to more secular dances like the **samba**, now the national dance of Brazil. One still finds echoes of Yoruba dance steps in samba, and conversely, one can also find samba dances as part of Yoruba rituals. The dancing communicates a complex history of worldly suffering and ecstatic, otherworldly faith.

In Rio de Janeiro, the largest Carnival celebration in the world celebrates the Christian Lent with Yoruba dance steps and secular rhythms. Yoruba rituals are always improvising according to time and place. While Brazilians have taken samba dancing to new elite levels, it's important to recall a time not too long ago when such dancing was the nourishment for survival in a cruel and racist New World. Even today, the Yoruba of Brazil "dance and play music in order to save and protect their individual spirits, their dignity as humans, and their sense of a cosmic family."[147]

Haitian Vodou Resistance

The majority of slaves who arrived in Haiti in the 16th to the 18th century came from Dahomey (now Benin) and further inland. Outside Nigeria, the Yoruba constituted a smaller minority. But their presence in Dahomey helped influence the **Vodou** religion that the slaves brought with them on the Middle Passage from the Dahomean port city of **Ouidah**.

The pantheon of Yoruba gods blended with the gods of neighboring African religions to form a Creole culture that met the needs of the new Afro-Haitian population. Esu the trickster became **Papa Legba**. The Yoruba *Orisa* **Ogun** morphed into **Ogou Ferrai** whose symbol still figures prominently on Haiti's national flag.

As in Brazil and Cuba, the Yoruba slaves of Haiti used their music to call out to the *Orisa* in times of trouble. "Vodou is, in great part, a religion of the body. The arms, legs and heart dance to draw and praise the spirits. Ears hear the rhythm of the drums and the voice is used to sing praises and plead for intercession."[148]

In 1697, France colonized Haiti (called Saint-Domingue at the time). They exploited West African labor to work the sugar plantations that quickly became the most profitable in all the world.

On August 14, 1791, Vodou music and dancing melded with politics to provide the soundtrack for the most successful slave revolt in the modern era. On a forested hilltop in **Bois Caiman**, **Boukman Dutty** and a Vodou priestess led a religious ceremony appealing to Ogun, the *Orisa* of justice. After sacrificing a pig, Boukman (whose nickname refers to his love of books) and the congregants took a blood oath to resist the colonial slave owners.

> ### Boukman's Prayer
> The god who created the earth; who created the sun that gives us light. The god who holds up the ocean; who makes the thunder roar. Our God who has ears to hear. You who are hidden in the clouds; who watch us from where you are... Listen to the voice for liberty that sings in all our hearts.

Thirteen years later, the Haitian slaves defeated Napoleon's army (much to the surprise of the French) and declared themselves a fully independent country. The successful slave revolution is unprecedented in the history of the African slave trade. The Yoruba *Orisa* helped the exploited mill workers fight for their freedom and restore the balance that was smashed by the colonists' greed.

After the revolution, thousands of disgruntled slave owners and their Afro-Haitians slaves began migrating to cities on the North American coast of the Gulf of Mexico. Haitian migration doubled the population of New Orleans, Louisiana in just one year.

Features of Voodoo (as it is more commonly spelled in North America) like zombies, gris-gris, and dolls with pins excited an American gothic imaginary. The dangers of racism and stigmatization are always prevalent in such forms of cultural appropriation. Today, tourists in New Orleans buy souvenirs in Voodoo temples and dance to Western funk music with unrecognized traces of once sacred Yoruba rhythms.

However, as new generations of Afro-Haitians emigrate for new opportunities, the roots of Yoruba culture continue to be expressed and exposed in their art and culture. **Ulrick Jean-Pierre**, for example, is a Haitian-born artist, now living in New Orleans. In his "Cayman Wood Ceremony," a painting that honors Boukman, "we can hear the Vodou drums pulsating in the night, the lament of the slaves calling on the African spirits to come and help them in combat, while their vociferous and angry voices explode in the night sky and roll like a rising wave."[149]

Since Haitian independence was formally declared in 1804, Vodou continues to draw on ancient Yoruba deities and practices to respond to modern day concerns, from unemployment to the 2010 earthquake. "In the painful conditions of life in Haiti, Vodou enables its followers to deal with historical and contemporary realities of Haitian society by relating the sacred and the profane to their difficult dance of life."[150]

Wole Soyinka's *Death and the King's Horseman*

Because of their exposure to outside influences, the people of the Yoruba diaspora were forced to make changes to their rituals in order to keep the fundamental spirit alive and flourishing. Back home in Yorubaland, the religion also underwent dynamic changes. After the slave trade was disbanded in the 19th century, the British increased their presence on the African coast. Missionaries brought Christianity to the Yoruba, elements of which which found their way into Yoruba prayers and practices.

In the waning years of the slave trade, Western powers sensed easy profit in Yorubaland and throughout the African continent. The British attacked the city of **Lagos** in 1851 and annexed it outright 10 years later. Interactions between European Christians and Middle Eastern Muslims had a strong influence on the Yoruba. This blending of two or more religions is known as **syncretism**.

In this syncretic environment, **Wole Soyinka** was born in 1934. Soyinka considers himself a Yoruba writer, but he writes primarily in English, having attended university in England. By the time Soyinka won a Nobel Prize for Literature in 1986, he was considered "one of the finest poetical playwrights that have written in English."[151]

True to his Yoruba roots, Soyinka was critical of corrupt leaders throughout his life. In 1967, he was imprisoned and placed in solitary confinement for his dissenting role in Nigeria's civil war.

In many of his plays and poems, Soyinka defends the poor and downtrodden left behind by Nigeria's Westernization. In his play *Death and the King's Horseman*, he presents "a stout defense of the Yoruba culture and the particular animist cosmology that underlies it."[152] The play is based on a Yoruba tradition: when a king dies, his horse and horseman must also die in a sacred ritual so the king can be properly escorted to his new life in the underworld. The horsemen consider it an honour to accompany their king and they therefore plan for the day throughout their lives. This honour is passed down from father to son across the centuries.

Wole Soyinka

Death and the King's Horseman

There is only one home to the life of a river-mussel; there is only one home to the life of a tortoise; there is only shell to the soul of man; there is only one world to the spirit of our race. If that world leaves its course and smashes on boulders of the great void, whose world will give us shelter?

In Soyinka's play, the British colonial officer does not want to compound the death of the king with the death of his horseman. To the Western official, saving individual lives and keeping the peace is more important that perpetuating an ancient religious ritual.

The play begins with the horseman Elesin dancing and singing besides a Yoruba drummer on his way to meet women at the market. He hedonistically enjoys himself with food and sex before preparing himself for his ritualistic death. While the town is preparing for Elesin's journey to join his king in the underworld, Elesin's son, Olunde, returns home from his studies abroad in England. He has briefly postponed his training to be a Western-style doctor so that he can be in town to bury his father.

The district officer is touched by Olunde's family loyalty but also believes the horseman's son is "much too sensitive.... The kind of person you feel should be a poet munching rose petals in Bloomsbury [in England]."[153] The officer's wife pleads with Olunde to help put an end to the seemingly outdated ritual and save his father's life. Olunde is not convinced. "What can you offer him in place of his peace of mind, in place of the honour and veneration of his people?" he asks the British officer's wife. "You white races know how survive; I've seen proof of that.... But at least have the humility to let others survive in their own way."[154]

Meanwhile on the streets, the drums beat a more somber rhythm as Elesin prepares for his final moments in the world of the living. He looks to the moon and waits for a sign that the gateway to the underworld is opening. "Is there now a streak of light at the end of the passage, a light I dare not look upon?" Elesin wonders. "Does it reveal whose voices we often heard, whose touches we often felt, whose wisdoms come suddenly in the mind when the wisest have shaken their heads and murmured, it cannot be done?"[155]

At the critical moment, Elesin is handcuffed, arrested, and placed in a cellar that once housed slaves before their fateful journey to the Americas. The district officer, thinking he has saved Elesin's life, has instead destroyed a critical link between the Yoruba and the *Orisa*. "The world is set adrift and its inhabitants are lost," Elesin bemoans. "Around them is nothing but emptiness."[156]

Realizing his father has failed in his sacred mission, Olunde swiftly takes his own life so someone can still accompany the king before it's too late. Elesin is portrayed as a coward, hungrily enjoying the leftovers of the world, unable to take decisive action when his sacred duty is called upon. If he had only been more courageous, he could have fulfilled his religious responsibility before getting himself arrested. As a disgusted townswoman says to Elesin, "You sat with folded arms while evil strangers tilted the world from its course and crashed it beyond the edge of emptiness—you muttered there is little that one man can do, you left us floundering in a blind future."[157]

Too late, Elesin strangles himself with the prisoners' chains and dies in shame. "With both Olunde and Elesin dead, the horseman ritual itself dies because nobody else knows the sacred message."[158] In Soyinka's play, everybody loses: the British colonists are dismayed, the Yoruba villagers are broken. In a rapidly globalizing world, the Yoruba must struggle to maintain their religion, their culture, and their art.

In the final line of the play, Soyinka offers a loaded message to the Yoruba people who feel powerless after the tragedy of the slave trade and the seemingly insurmountable ruptures caused by English colonialism. "Now forget the dead," the townswoman says, "forget even the living. Turn your mind only to the unborn."[159]

As artists like Soyinka remind us, although the future might look very different than the past, Yoruba culture thrives in unforeseen ways from Western Africa to the Americas. The Yoruba worldview continues to be retold and refreshed in the stories of a people and the rhythmic, steady beating of the sacred drums.

Discovery Questions

1. Go to YouTube and scroll through the winning Samba school performances in recent Rio de Janeiro Carnival parades. Which features of Yoruba religion can you find? Would you call the dancing religious, secular, or both?

2. Go to a dance club off-campus one evening and observe the dancers. Are some people more "lost" in the music than others? How so? Do you notice a difference in your own body immediately after leaving the club and stepping onto the pavement?

3. Go to a pool, lake, or beach and immerse yourself in water. What goes through your mind? Do you notice a difference in how you felt before and after the immersion?

4. Have you ever been homesick? Describe your feelings. Have you ever felt out-of-place even when you were at home? Are the two feelings similar or different?

5. Go onto Amnesty International's website and read their Modern Slavery Act Transparency Statement. What forms of slavery exist in North America today? What can you do about it?

6. Go onto the @AfriFeminists Twitter page and describe some of the issues being raised. Which religious ideals are they challenging or endorsing?

7. Watch the 14-minute Broadly documentary on Manbo Katy, "Meet the Vodou Priestess Summoning Healing Spirits in Post-Earthquake Haiti." How does Vodou "liberate" the survivors of the 2010 earthquake?

Glossary

Terms	Definitions
Afrocuba de Matanzas	A contemporary Afro-Cuban Jazz band famous for inventing the *Batárumba*, which incorporates Yoruba drum rhythms into Latin dance music
Alimotu Pelewura	20th century women's advocate and leader of the powerful Lagos Market Women's Association
Àyàn	Orisa associated with the *Batá* drum; name given to drummers and children of drummers
Babalawos	High priests of the *Ifa* divination system
Batá drums	A double-headed drum used primarily in religious functions
Bois Caiman	Haitian forest where congregants used a Vodou ceremony as a platform for resisting colonial rule in the late 18th century
Boukman Dutty	Beloved leader of the 19th-century Haitian revolution
Candomblé	Religious adaption of Yoruba rituals in Bahia, Brazil, in which divine spirits inhabit the bodies of rhythmic dancers
Daymé Arocena	A contemporary Afro-Cuban jazz vocalist
Diaspora	A population that is scattered beyond its own homeland
Esu	Trickster god and gatekeeper to the world of the Orisa
Havana	One of two provinces in Cuba where the Yoruba resettled and rebuilt their sacred Batá drums
Ifá	An ancient Yoruba divination system used by the Orisa and humans alike
Ila-Orangun	An ancient Nigerian city in the Osun district
Ile-Ife	The most sacred city in Yorubaland where the Orisa first arrived and created human beings
Iyá	The lead drum in Yoruba religious rituals
Lagos	The most populous city in Nigeria
Lagos Market Women's Association	A women's rights and business advocacy group
Matanzas	Capital city of the province of Matanzas, Cuba
Middle Passage	A path of the transatlantic slave trade in which African people were dispossessed of their land and forcibly transported across the Atlantic Ocean
Nago	Refers to the Yoruba people that traveled from the inlands to the coast of Benin in Western Africa
Oduduwa	Favored *Orisa* and first ruler of Oyo Empire
Ogun	The *Orisa* of iron and justice

Ogou Ferrai	Haitian adaptation of Yoruba Ogun; protector spirit
Oke'badan Festival	A celebration of life and fertility
Olodumare	Chief *Orisa* of the Yoruba pantheon
Orisa	Spirits or divine beings that possess the power to influence human actions and intentions
Ọsun	*Orisa* of birth and creative nourishment; traces origin to Osun River in Nigeria
Osun-Osogbo Festival	A celebration that commemorates Osun's relationship to Nigeria's commercial city, Osogbo
Ouidah	West African city located in southern Benin which served as a central port for the Slave Trade
Papa Legba	Vodou adaption of Esu in Haiti; intermediary *Orisa* between the world of spirits and humans
Samba	The national dance of Brazil
Santería	An Afro-Cuban religion that was developed by Yoruba slaves
Slave Trade	The capture, forced migration, and enslavement of African people in the Americas
Syncretism	Combining religious beliefs of two or more faiths
Tambor	Yoruba drumming ceremony
Terreiros	Public spaces in Brazil where ex-slaves performed religious rituals recalling Yoruba *Orisas*
Ulrick Jean-Pierre	Contemporary Haitian-born artist living in New Orleans
Vodou	Haitian syncretic religion combining Creole and Yoruba religious beliefs
Wole Soyinka	Contemporary Nigerian poet and playwright
Xango	*Orisa* of thunder and lightning; the fourth ruler of Oyo Empire
Yoruba Andabo	Contemporary Afro-Cuban jazz band known for injecting Yoruba chants and rhythms into their popular recorded music
Yorubaland	Region in southwestern Nigeria, Benin, and Togo
'Zulu Sọfọla	20th century Nigerian playwright; broke new grounds for female artists in Nigeria

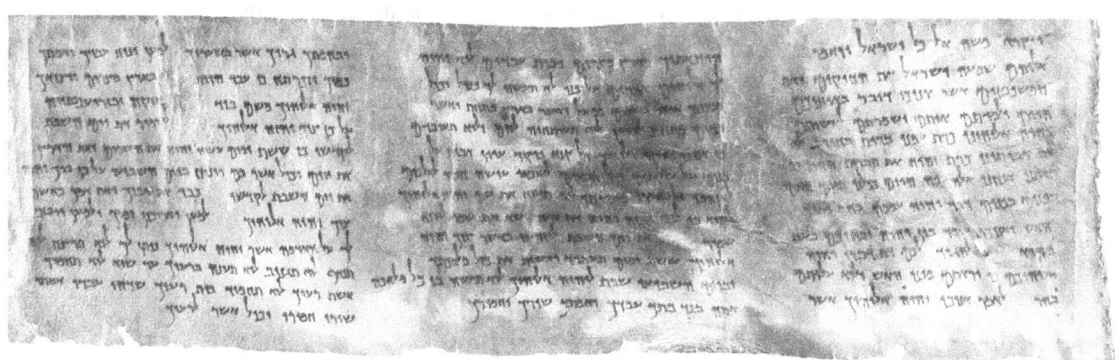

Part Two
TWO WORLDS

CHAPTER FIVE
Judaism: The Oneness of God

CHAPTER SIX
Christianity: Transcendence

CHAPTER SEVEN
Islam: Strangers Welcome

Chapter Five
Judaism
The Oneness of God

"Hear O Israel, the Lord is God. The Lord is One."

The *shema* prayer is one of the holiest prayers uttered in the Jewish religion. It is also one of the oldest known affirmations of **monotheism** in the world, emphasizing oneness and the interconnection of all living things.

The oral stories collected in the **Hebrew Bible** tell of a people who came to believe in one God that surpassed all others in wisdom, power, and goodness. It is a philosophy that not only shaped the Jewish religion, but also provided the foundations for Christianity and Islam, the two most popular religions in the world today.

The Jewish God enters into agreements with the Israelites that promise a merging of two worlds: the fleeting experiences that shape our daily lives and the more lasting wisdom we require to make sense of it all. In this high-stakes relationship between Jews and their God, success depends on one's ability to cultivate curiosity and humility, patience and persistence.

There is a story about a theological argument between two respected second-century Jewish rabbis. Rabbi Eliezer knows he is right and calls on God to back him up. When God intervenes on Rabbi Eliezer's behalf, his rival, Rabbi Yehoshua, essentially kicks God out. Rabbi Yehoshua argues that the one God put us here on earth and already gave us the guidelines for how to live. It's up to us, now, to use our limited, imperfect knowledge and try our best to figure things out on our own. Happily defeated, God leaves the debate to the rabbis, confident that creation is in good hands.

The Limits of Human Knowledge

In the opening chapters of the **Torah** we learn that the first human beings took tremendous risks to gain knowledge. **Adam and Eve** were sheltered in the **Garden of Eden** where their immediate needs were fully met. Still, they were intellectually restless. They knew God would penalize them harshly if they got caught eating from the forbidden Tree of Knowledge. But they took that risk anyway. Why?

The knowledge Adam and Eve acquire in the story was not the scientific kind of knowledge gained by observing and discovering the hidden laws of nature. Instead, their newfound wisdom was ethical, knowing good and evil, right from wrong. At the root of the human condition, the Torah tells us, is our desire to be better people. Not only do we want to know right from wrong, we want to use that wisdom to do the right thing. It's the kind of wisdom only God and the angels were privy to.

The story of the Garden of Eden presents a tension that is developed throughout the Hebrew Bible. What Adam and Eve want most is an ethical certainty that will help them live their lives meaningfully and purposefully. But it is precisely this certainty that is constantly denied us. Whenever humans try to learn what God knows, we get thwarted. In the story of Babel, for example, the Hebrews built a tower so they could learn God's secrets. But because of such ambitions, they were deceived, broken, and in the end, scattered.[160] The Hebrew Bible teaches us that humans can never know what the one God knows. And yet, Jews are continuously called on to act with such incomplete knowledge.

> ## The Book of Genesis
>
> 3:1 Now the serpent was cunning, more than all the beasts of the field that the Lord God had made, and it said to the woman, "Did God indeed say, 'You shall not eat of any of the trees of the garden?'"
>
> 3:2 And the woman said to the serpent, "Of the fruit of the trees of the garden we may eat.
>
> 3:3 But of the fruit of the tree that is in the midst of the garden, God said, 'You shall not eat of it, and you shall not touch it, lest you die.'"
>
> 3:4 And the serpent said to the woman, "You will surely not die.
>
> 3:5 For God knows that on the day that you eat thereof, your eyes will be opened, and you will be like angels, knowing good and evil."

In the Book of Genesis, God speaks to **Abraham**, imploring the simple shepherd to leave his home and everyone he knows on a promise that his new life will be richer. If he agrees to God's **covenant**, Abraham's monotonous days of working for a living will be blessed with purpose. His ordinary life will become extraordinary.

Is such faith justified? Abraham must ask himself this question when God commands him to hike into the mountains of Moriah and sacrifice his beloved son **Isaac**.[161] Abraham is tested to choose between the love of his son and his faith in God. He attempts to strike down his son. In the end, there is joy and forgiveness as a messenger from God stays Abraham's hand. But why would Abraham agree to do it in the first place? What kind of faith does this God require of the Jewish people?

This story from the Torah has understandably troubled Jews, Christians, and Muslims for thousands of years. Danish philosopher Søren Kierkegaard spent sleepless nights trying to grasp Abraham's faith.[162] Hiking up Mount Moriah would have taken Abraham and Isaac three days. How Kierkegaard would have loved to hear what they talked about on that fateful hike, for in that conversation would lie the essence of faith and the sometimes painful struggle to realize it in this world.

The spiritual affliction of Abraham binding Isaac is told every fall on **Rosh Hashanah**, the Jewish New Year celebration that marks the beginning of the Ten Days of Awe, ending with **Yom Kippur**. Yom Kippur marks the final chance for repentance before God seals shut the book of life, finalizing who will survive and prosper in the upcoming year. In the opening prayers of the

Yom Kippur service, Jews pray for forgiveness for themselves and for "everyone who acted unwittingly." Built into the prayers of the High Holy Days is the implication that we need help, that we don't always know the right thing to do—and that even when we *do* know, we don't always have the courage or energy to do what's right.

Searching for God

Searching for the one God is a recurring theme in the Hebrew Bible and in the history of Jewish wandering. The second book of the Torah, the Book of **Exodus**, tells the story of **Moses** leading the Israelites on a forty-year journey through the Sinai desert, in search of God's Promised Land.

The faith of the Israelites is continuously tested. Not only are the freed but weary slaves denied God's knowledge, they don't even know *what* exactly God is. When Moses asks who God is, God responds cryptically, saying only, "I am what I am."[163] Later, when Moses begs to finally see God's glory, he is shown only God's back. God tells Moses, "Thou canst not see my face: for there shall no man see me, and live."[164] This idea of a partially hidden God moving away from us proves crucial to understanding Jewish monotheism.

In the year 70 CE, the Romans destroyed most of the Jewish Temple in Jerusalem, and banished Jews from Canaan, their "Holy Land." For two thousand years Jews scattered across Europe, the Middle East, and later the Americas, in what is known as the Jewish **diaspora**.

Bereft of a spiritual center or political homeland, Jewish rabbis codified prayers, rituals, and Biblical exegesis in books known as the **Talmud**. Sprinkled into many different cultures and lands, these Jewish discussions and debates acquired special significance. The words and the books themselves were treated as sacred. The Torah was literally crowned and dressed in kingly robes, a practice still adhered to today in synagogues around the world.

Reading and praying at home or in small group settings became the norm. We see this most notably in the philosophy behind the Jewish **Sabbath**, the seventh day of the week. Keeping the Sabbath is one of the **Ten Commandments** that God gives Moses on Mount Sinai, and it is especially relevant to a people without a true homeland. Jewish tradition marks Friday sundown to Saturday sundown as the time to celebrate the Sabbath. Through candle lighting, prayers, and ritual meals, Jews are taught to disconnect, literally unplug from worldly things, and focus on family, community, and other spiritual matters. On the Sabbath, God is not found in a particular place, but rather in time. It is not at any agreed-upon sacred location but rather on the seventh day when Jews are closest to God.[165]

> ### Yehuda Amichai
> *My Parents' Motel*
>
> My father was God and didn't know it. He gave me the Ten Commandments not in thunder and rage, not in fire or cloud, but with softness and love.

Maimonides and the Mystics

In the 12th century, Jews, Christians, and Muslims formed vibrant intersecting communities in Europe and Northern Africa. After studying at the University of al-Qarawiyyin in Fez, Morocco (the world's oldest university), philosopher **Moses Maimonides** struggled with the question of how to find the elusive Jewish God. Indebted to Islamic philosophers of his time, Maimonides' forays into **negative theology** had a lasting influence on inquiries into the mystery of the Judeo-Christian-Muslim God.

As Maimonides pointed out, there are a number of problems with saying anything positive or certain about a God that is bigger than anything humans can conceive. Oft-repeated phrases like, "God is merciful" or "God is all-knowing," can only be partial truths since the Jewish God is much more than merciful and all-knowing. And saying insufficient things about God is problematic. Such statements also have the unintended consequence of breaking God down into composite parts that serve to break up God's perfect unity.

> ### Moses Maimonides
> *Guide for the Perplexed*
>
> Since it is a well-known fact that even that knowledge of God which is accessible to man cannot be attained except by negations, and that negations do not convey a true idea of the being to which they refer, all people, both of past and present generations, declared that God cannot be the object of human comprehension, that none but Himself comprehends what He is, and that our knowledge consists in knowing that we are unable truly to comprehend Him…. The idea is best expressed in the book of Psalms, "Silence is praise to Thee" (lxv. 2). It is a very expressive remark on this subject; for whatever we utter with the intention of extolling and of praising Him, contains something that cannot be applied to God, and includes derogatory expressions; it is therefore more becoming to be silent, and to be content with intellectual reflection, as has been recommended by men of the highest culture, in the words "Commune with your own heart upon your bed, and be still" (Ps. iv. 4).

A trained physician, Maimonides was ever wary of such futile efforts. He saw too many people who "fatigue minds with what they cannot apprehend," a common disease of religious zealots with "some sort of mad obsession."[166] If saying anything positive about God is misguided at best and madness at worst, how then are Jews supposed to talk about or even think about God?

Maimonides believed that it was more accurate to say what God is *not*. God is not good, bad, smart, or silly. There is a nearly infinite list to choose from since God is not anything that imperfect mortals can conceive. With each negation, Maimonides argued, one chips away the superfluous distractions and gets closer to the essence of God.

Maimonides was certain that there was a God that spoke to Abraham and gave Moses the Ten Commandments on Mount Sinai. But he believed that any rational investigation into who or what exactly God was could only deepen the cracks between the two interconnected worlds. Can we still get closer to God, without ever rationally understanding just what this one God is? That has been a central question for Jews following in the footsteps of Maimonides.

After Jews were expelled from Spain in 1492, the city of **Safed** (in modern-day Israel) became one of the most important intellectual centers of Jewish life. In Safed, Jewish leaders sought new ways for establishing a closer relationship with a distant God. They wrote new prayers pleading for God to reveal an ancient light to the world. On the Sabbath, they sought to connect more directly with God.

In one central prayer, *Lecha Dodi*, Jews chant in unison for the Sabbath "bride." At such a sacred moment, the love for God transcends the more ordinary thoughts and emotions typically experienced throughout the work week. The hope is that even without a clear understanding, one can still experience God in the way that lovers feel love without being able to fully grasp what it is they are experiencing.

In Safed, **Isaac Luria** made the startling proclamation that God's light was fading because God was withdrawing. Creation was broken. Because of this disintegration, God suffered alongside all living creatures. For Luria, it was up to humans to find the broken pieces, the "fallen sparks of light" in everyday places. Every good act lifted one more spark to heaven, fortifying one more gap that separated God from the world.

Direct experience with the one God was encouraged above all else. "Taste and see that the Lord is good,"[167] wrote the Psalmist of the Hebrew Bible. By the 18th century, Jewish leaders in the tradition of Maimonides and Luria were convinced that scientific thinking was an inadequate tool to reach God. Instead, they sought out new avenues of prayer that bypassed rationalism altogether.

In the early 1700s, one poor orphan took a job picking up village kids to attend the Jewish House of Prayer. According to legend, this orphan led the children down a scenic path through the forest, encouraging them to sing out to God at the top of their lungs. The orphan became known as the **Baal Shem Tov** (the Master of the Good Name), and his insistence on ecstatically crying out to God earned him instant notoriety. For the Baal Shem Tov, even drunken singing outside the taverns could be examples of religious confessions.

The Baal Shem Tov's inner circle began a new movement in Judaism known as **Hasidism**. Hasidism offered more passionate and poetic relationships with God. The Hasids of Eastern Europe fervently prepared for the coming of a **Messiah** who would help heal the world for God's return. They sang and danced, and told fantastical and mysterious stories.

The Baal Shem Tov's great-grandson, Rabbi **Nachman of Bratslav**, was the greatest storyteller of them all. In his stories of daring feats of discipline, anonymous princes, kings and paupers find their faith rewarded in a troubled and violent world. The stories appeal to our non-rational sides, showing us "that a person is more than he appears to be and that he is capable of giving more than he appears to possess."[168]

Rabbi Nachman was known for defying convention. He encouraged religious Jews to go out into the forests late at night to pray and pour out their souls to God like children crying out to their parents. He believed that putting ourselves in vulnerable positions would make us react in emotional and spontaneous ways that could bring us closer to the one God. When Rabbi Nachman met "enlightened" Jews who were too enthralled with science and logic, he played chess with them, never once speaking of God. Everybody had their own path to God, according to Rabbi Nachman, and no path made any more sense than the other.

God's Gender

Despite Maimonides' cautions, it's worth noting that the Hebrew Bible does give its Creator of the world a number of descriptive metaphors (like Creator). God is also described as a jealous, powerful, and sometimes vengeful king. There are some apparent advantages to describing God

> ### *Lecha Dodi* Prayer
>
> Arouse thyself, arouse thyself, for thy light is come: arise, shine; awake, awake; give forth a song; the glory of the Lord is revealed upon thee.
>
> Come, my Beloved, to meet the bride; let us welcome the presence of the Sabbath.
>
> Come in peace, thou crown of thy husband, with rejoicing and with cheerfulness, in the midst of the faithful of the chosen people: come, O bride; come, O bride.

with human or heroic attributes. It helps us relate to an all-powerful being who still acts and appears as we do. Conceiving God as a stern but loving father is more intimate and inviting than characterizing God as distant and incomprehensible. Such metaphors are meant to help us relate to the world in ways we wouldn't ordinarily. Metaphors can deepen, concretize, even enhance ordinary relationships.

Most of the metaphors of God that are used, however, are also gendered. In the many editions of the Hebrew Bible on the market today, God is most commonly translated as a "he." In cultures where many gods are worshipped, there can be more leeway for varied depictions of the gods. But after the Jewish God "had successfully vanquished the other gods and goddesses of Canaan and the Middle East and become the *only* God, his religion would be managed almost entirely by men."[169] Since humans can only speak of God in human languages, assigning God a pronoun simplifies the ways we can fathom such a complex being. The use of the masculine pronoun, some argue, can be understood as neutral.

But Jewish feminist authors in the late 20th century challenged such views of religious neutrality. If we started calling the Jewish God a "she," would it carry the same **gender-neutral** significance, and if so, why haven't we done it? If a perfect being is described as male, what does that mean for all the people who don't identify as male? As philosophers of language long ago pointed out, the words we use to describe things say more about us than the things the words refer to.

In more recent times, some Jewish prayer books have been re-written to include more gender-neutral translations. Some Jewish scholars believe we should create new metaphors of God that draw from the same original Biblical sources, but emphasize attributes of God that aren't defined as traditionally male. Such metaphors can include the one God as an artist who creates worlds out of nothing, as a mother who gives birth to new beings, as a garden that nourishes all life, as a lonely, suffering partner reaching out for human compassion, as an unfolding verb (rather than a static noun).

Today's Jewish feminists emerge from an ancient tradition of Jewish philosophers and theologians who don't have all the religious answers, and therefore fully engage themselves in the questions.

> ### Judith Plaskow
>
> *Standing Again at Sinai*
>
> Obvious and innocuous as male God-language has come to seem, metaphors matter—on both an individual and social level. Though long usage may inure us to the implications of our imagery, religious symbols are neither arbitrary nor inert. They are significant and powerful communications through which a religious community expresses a sense of itself and its universe.... The male images Jews use in speaking to and about God emerge out of and maintain a religious system in which men are normative Jews and women are perceived as Other....

Buber's Dialogue with God

Martin Buber grew up in a pious Jewish home in Vienna, Austria at the end of the 19th century. But he struggled with his faith in God and sought out **existentialist philosophers** who challenged traditional conceptions of an all-merciful, caring God. Nominated for the Nobel Prize in Literature ten times and the Nobel Peace Prize seven times, Buber wrote numerous books and essays that show how contemporary, secular Jews can rediscover pathways to communing with God.

Buber accepted a Jewish view of God as an "eternal mystery." Like Jewish theologians before him, Buber argued that we may never be able to fully understand the one God. However, that ignorance doesn't have to rule out a lasting, intimate relationship. "It is not necessary to know something about God in order to believe in Him," Buber writes. "Many true believers know how to talk to God but not about Him."[170]

Buber focuses much of his attention on how to talk to God in the absence of significant knowledge. Instead of conceiving God as an "It," he argues that it's better to think of God as another "You" (sometimes translated as "Thou"). If God is conceived as a remote "It," then we only think of ourselves and how we can benefit from an isolating relationship with an inaccessible higher being. But if we think of God as another being worthy of our respect, then we enter into a richer dialogue, one that is eternally ongoing and unfinished. In place of dogmatic rules and routinized prayers, Buber encouraged spontaneity and depth of passion.

Related to our relationship with God is our relationship to other people, strangers from other cultures, faithful believers of other gods. "That we can no longer carry on a genuine conversation from one camp to the other is the severest symptom of the sickness of present-day man," Buber wrote.[171] Genuine dialogue with other people means looking beyond oneself to see things from each other's point of view. It doesn't mean we need to agree with or like everyone we meet. But for Buber, it's important to build community with others by recognizing and affirming the dynamic ways we think differently, while still all sharing a common humanity.

Though we may not always understand or agree with each other, Buber believed that we should fully open ourselves to communication and sharing with all living beings, be they strangers or lovers, animals or trees. Buber's God prefers we cultivate relationships with each other instead of always confining ourselves in silent prayer. Separating God from our everyday world causes fissures in the ways we approach each other and ourselves.

Buber challenges us to think of ways we can more fully engage in our everyday activities. Holiness doesn't come from ducking mundane responsibilities. For Buber, holiness means approaching every day with humility, compassion, and intensity. "The world in which you live, just as it is and not otherwise, affords you that association with God which will redeem you and whatever divine aspect of the world you have been entrusted with."[172]

God's Silence

The search to find and know God is more than a philosophical puzzle for many Jews. When Jews pray to God they do so with the hope, and sometimes trust, that there is an unseen being who is out there listening and caring. This is especially true in bad times when real people suffer and need reasons to believe that help is on the way. These are often the times that religion matters most poignantly in our lives.

The Jewish God is defined as all-powerful and all-good. That means God can stop bad things from happening to anyone. And yet, as we know, horrible things happen to undeserving families somewhere in the world every minute of the day. How can this be justified, or even understood? Regardless of whether or not we can know anything about God, Jewish theologians question whether we can count on God's support when we need it most. In the philosophy of religion, the attempt to explain God's goodness in bad times is known as **theodicy.**

As Rabbi Harold Kushner writes, "The misfortunes of good people are not only a problem to the people who suffer and to their families. They are a problem to everyone who wants to believe in a just and fair and livable world. They inevitably raise questions about the goodness, the kindness, even the existence of God."[173] For thousands of years Jews have struggled with the question of why a perfectly good God allows terrible things happen to innocent children, good people, even unsuspecting animals.

In the Hebrew Bible, the Book of **Job** directly engages with theodicy. Job is described as a God-fearing, good man who tries to do all the right things. Instead of getting rewarded for his efforts, he is made to bear witness to death of his children and the destruction of his fortunes. His own body is beset with painful boils. In his deepest despair, Job calls out to God, but is met with silence. "Though I cry, 'Violence!' I get no response; though I call for help, there is no justice."[174]

In the Book of Job, a new relationship between Jewish people and their God is explored: that of a frustrated victim accusing his Creator of staying silent instead of more actively caring for the people God once lovingly created.

In the end of the story, God does finally respond to Job, but not to the question about why Job's loved ones needed to suffer such pain. Instead, God reminds Job of his small place in the universe and the vast space between his world and God's.

In more recent times, Jews have again been forced to confront the seemingly infinite and empty spaces between them and their God. During the **Holocaust**, German Nazis killed over six million Jews. Many survivors and descendants of survivors of the German concentration camps still struggle to reconcile comforting depictions of the Jewish God with the horrors of their lived history.

> ### Elie Wiesel
>
> *Night*
>
> Never shall I forget those flames that consumed my faith forever.
>   Never shall I forget the nocturnal silence that deprived me for all eternity of the desire to live.
>   Never shall I forget those moments that murdered my God and my soul and turned my dreams to ashes.
>   Never shall I forget those things, even were I condemned to live as long as God Himself.
>   Never.

Elie Wiesel, a survivor of German concentration camps, struggled throughout his life with the questions of Job in light of modern day tragedies. Like Job, Wiesel longs to know God's plan. Without this knowledge, Wiesel argues for the need to protest. In one of his plays, a Jewish peasant puts God on trial for allowing such pain to endure. As the fictional peasant Berish argues, "it is as a Jew that, with my last breath, I shall shout my protest to God."

Even if we learn to make peace with God's actions, can we ever forgive God's non-actions? No matter how long we've studied God's words, can we ever fully comprehend God's silences? Poet **Rivka Miriam** often expresses anger and disappointment in God's silence. In her poem, "Who Will Take Us," she writes:

> Who will take us to his chest in
>   the evening—
> The great God is so tired,
> He has no strength to bear us anymore.
> We're too much for Him.[175]

Born in 1928, Elie Wiesel survived imprisonment in the Auschwitz and Buchenwald concentration camps, and was among the prisoners freed by Allied troops in 1945. After the war he became a journalist. Wiesel lived in France until 1955, when he moved to the United States. He joined the faculty of Boston University in 1976. Wiesel received the Nobel peace prize in 1986, and died in 2016.

The Holy Land

Throughout the Hebrew Bible, the places where the ancient Hebrews interact with their God are made sacred. Such historical markers help bind us to a distant past, building tradition and creating a shared culture. The marked places also serve as reminders to think deeper about the ways we treat each other when we're near such holy sites.

In the Book of Genesis, God sends Abraham to the land of Canaan. "Go forth from your land and from your birthplace and from your father's house, to the land that I will show you."[176] Years later, God again promises his prophet Jeremiah, "I will return your captivity and gather you from all the nations and from all the places where I have driven you ... and I will return you to the place whence I exiled you."[177] Because of these agreements the land is made holy and marked by Jews as the Promised Land.

King David authorized the building of the holy temple in Jerusalem to house the ark of the covenant. The construction of the temple was completed by King Solomon in the tenth century and was destroyed four hundred years later. A second temple was subsequently built and destroyed by the Romans in 40 CE. At that point Jews were forced out of their homeland and primarily scattered across the Middle East, Russia, and Eastern Europe.

By the end of 19th century, **anti-semitism** was sweeping over Europe and the Russian Empire. In 1897, approximately 200 Jews from 17 different countries gathered in Basel, Switzerland to discuss returning Jews to the Holy Land. Led by the writer, **Theodor Herzl**, the movement known as **Zionism** (for Mount Zion) began to take shape. For Herzl the land was more than a place of refuge from hatred and violence. Like Abraham moving from one place to another, Zionism promised Jews the chance to rediscover and re-forge their relationship to the one God. They could return to Jerusalem to pray at the **Wailing Wall,** the last standing wall of the Second Temple. In his opening statement at the **First Zionist Congress**, Herzl said, "Zionism is a homecoming to the Jewish fold even before it becomes a homecoming to the Jewish land."

Following the end of World War II and the devastation of the Holocaust, the United Nations set aside a section of Palestine for Jewish statehood. This new country was called Israel, which in Hebrew means "the place where one wrestles with God."

Israel's first Prime Minister, **David Ben-Gurion**, frequently made connections between the Biblical stories and the Israeli state. He noted the religious and moral struggle of the Jewish people that "began in the earliest period of our history, as far back as authentic, recorded history will take us." Ben-Gurion believed all Jews "will face this struggle until the end of time; until the coming of the messianic age."[178]

After the founding of Israel, millions of Jews emigrated there to improve their lives, both socially and economically. But Palestinians who live on the same land have similar dreams. Religious,

Theodor Herzl

Old New Land

"Jerusalem!" cried Friedrich in a half-whisper, his voice trembling. He did not understand why the sight of this strange city affected him so powerfully…. Suddenly he saw himself a little boy going to synagogue with his father. Ah, but faith was dead now, youth was dead, his father was dead. And here before him the walls of Jerusalem towered in the fairy moonlight. His eyes overflowed. He stopped short, and the hot tears coursed slowly down his cheeks.

Above photo: Jewish women pray at the women's side of the Western Wall in Jerusalem in 2007.

political, and economic differences between Jewish Israelis and Muslim Palestinians continue to be a divisive sticking point in the Middle East.

In 1983, American Rabbi Hanan Schlesinger became a settler, moving to the West Bank in disputed territory between Palestine and Israel. There he built walls shutting out all opposing viewpoints. "For us the Palestinians are the consummate other. The other that you ignore, that you never see.… The other from whom you are completely distant, the other of whom you are thoroughly suspicious."[179] After meeting Palestinian families who lived on the other side of the fence, however, Schlesinger began to recognize that his narrative was only a partial truth. Confronting his narrow-minded thinking was "unmooring," he observed, but it helped lead him to create a number of programs and peace initiatives that educate people on the need to foster peace and understanding between Palestinians and Israelis.

Isaac Kook, the chief rabbi of Jerusalem, understood that Israeli Jews wouldn't always agree on religion, nationality, or the need to modernize along more liberal principles. In Judaism, he argued, it's not enough to believe one is right. One must respect arguments for the opposing point of view or risk following one's passionate ideas to "the perilous detriment of excess."[180]

Jewish Humour and the Cosmic Joke

Throughout the 20th century, Jews came to North America in unprecedented numbers. New York City became the melting pot for the great majority of Jewish immigrants seeking a better life in the New World. The question for many believers was whether the Jewish God would come too. Would God "stand beside her and guide her / through the night with the light from above," as **Irving Berlin** pleaded in his famous anthem, "God Bless America"?

Berlin was by far the most successful composer in New York's **vaudeville** scene. His variety shows irreverently poked fun at racial and cultural differences springing up all over New York's makeshift ghettos. Many Eastern European Jews joined in the merriment of the bawdy, anti-authoritarian nightly shows. The actors, comedians, and musicians gleefully questioned their status in America and, more controversially, their place in God's universe.

Jewish psychologist **Sigmund Freud** wrote a book on the importance of such kinds of humour, noting how good jokes can recall and relieve the pressure of traumatic experiences. "I do not know whether there are many other instances of a people making fun to such a degree of its own character,"[181] he wrote about the Jewish people. Jewish comedians were important figures in the **Theatre of the Absurd**, finding humor in the seemingly futile attempt to take solace in God's incomprehensible universe.

In the 1930s, nobody made fun of their small place in the world more hilariously than the **Marx Brothers**. In theatre, on film and later on television, Groucho's fake moustache and oversized cigar become an iconic symbol of the blasphemous immigrant poorly negotiating the newly established secular authority. Groucho's Jewish humor "made the outsider a permanent fixture of mainstream American public life."[182] After the Holocaust, Jewish humour not only challenged American authority at home, but also God's authority in the cosmos.

Groucho once called American comedian **Woody Allen** "the sixth Marx brother" because of Allen's pithy depictions of God's creations. "If it turns out that there is a God, I don't think that

Original movie theatre poster for the Marx Brothers comedy *A Night at the Opera*, released by MGM in 1935. Groucho Marx later hosted the popular radio and TV quiz program *You Bet Your Life* for 14 seasons, from 1947 through 1961.

he's evil," Allen's character says in his 1975 film *Love and Death*. "I think that the worst you say about him is that basically he's an underachiever." In his films and his stories, Allen never quite reconciles with the God of Job who can appear to make things more difficult for people on earth. Although Allen maintains that "the best thing that gives you a chance to triumph in life is religious faith,"[183] such faith is often problematic for the theologians and comedians whose families suffered under a seemingly absent God.

In the late 1980s, Jewish comedians **Larry David** and **Jerry Seinfeld** combined to create the television comedy *Seinfeld*, which ran nine seasons and became the most popular sitcom of the 1990s. The stubbornly anti-authoritarian Seinfeld sees a religious debt he owes his ancient and not so ancient ancestors. "How to be a comedian, and how to think funny, or talk funny," he explained at the National Museum of American Jewish History, "some of that was put in me from other Jews."[184]

Today, Jewish comedians continue to challenge an all-loving, merciful God. "To be honest, I would like to go about my life exploiting the subject of Jewishness for comedy," comedian **Sarah Silverman** writes in her autobiography.[185] For Silverman the Jewish God represents many of the characteristics of the petty American men she encounters in her everyday life. In one controversial episode of *The Sarah Silverman Program*,[186] God is angrily put out when no one will validate his $2 parking fee at Silverman's high school reunion.

Amy Schumer is another comic who exposes the tensions inherent in the quest for developing more meaningful relationships in our fast-paced, pleasure-seeking world. In one skit on her television show, *Inside Amy Schumer*,[187] God is visibly frustrated at Schumer. Embittered, God points out that the last time Amy thought to pray was while rooting for the Green Knights in a Medieval Times show.

Many television viewers find such depictions of God blasphemous. But beneath the surface of such ribald humor, some critics see a therapeutic airing of grievances with a seemingly indifferent Creator of the universe. Such humour has deep roots in the Jewish tradition. "In this sense, jokes about God afforded Jews the opportunity to soften blasphemy with wit, to raise serious questions about the nature of belief, and laugh through the pain."[188]

What all these comedic scenes have in common are the ways they expose the challenges of balancing our petty day-to-day concerns with a transcendent yearning for God's wisdom and goodness. Such tensions have long been embedded in the Jewish experience since the earliest Biblical stories first recorded thousands of years ago.

Discovery Questions

1. Read the Biblical story about Abraham and Isaac (Genesis 22). Write a short dialogue between father and son as they walk up Mount Moriah. What questions might Isaac pose? How might Abraham answer his son?

2. This Friday night, light candles and eat dinner in your dorm room or home. Invite friends and encourage them to turn off their devices. How did it go? What did you talk about? How did it differ from what you would ordinarily do at the same time?

3. Listen to a podcast episode of the 2018 Chutzpah Project by the Jewish Orthodox Feminist Alliance (JOFA). How are Orthodox Jewish women reinterpreting ancient Jewish practices? What challenges do they face? What can you do to help?

4. Go to the Jewish Virtual Library and read Martin Buber's letter to Mahatma Gandhi about the importance of establishing a Jewish state in Israel. Do you agree that "dispersion becomes dismemberment"? Write an email in response that addresses fundamental Jewish themes.

5. Go to the United States Holocaust Memorial Museum website and click on the nine-minute video link, "Why We Remember the Holocaust." Explain the "moral challenge" to "not become indifferent." What can you do to help?

6. Attend an open-mic comedy performance on or near campus. Describe a joke that might be considered blasphemous to the Jewish God. Explain why. When does humour cross a relevant ethical line?

7. Describe one thing you know with absolute certainty to be true. How do you know it is true? What would it take for you to question your belief?

Glossary

Terms	Definitions
Abraham	Husband of Sarah, father of Isaac and Ishmael
Adam and Eve	The first man and woman; created by God in the Garden of Eden
Anti-Semitism	Discrimination and bigotry against Jews and their religious beliefs
Baal Shem Tov	18th-century mystical Rabbi considered to be the founder of Hasidism
Covenant	A binding agreement between God and the Jews
David Ben-Gurion	First prime minister of Israel
Diaspora	A population that is scattered beyond its own homeland
Existentialist philosophers	Individuals of a school of philosophy (existentialism) who emphasize individualism and agency
Exodus	Second book of the Torah in the Hebrew Bible
First Zionist Congress	An 1897 convention marking the beginning of Zionism as an organized political movement
Garden of Eden	Earthly paradise where Adam and Eve were created
Gender-neutral	Using or understanding concepts in non-gendered ways
Genesis	First book of the Torah in the Hebrew Bible
Hasidism	Jewish mystical tradition founded in the 18th century
Hebrew Bible	Collection of sacred Jewish texts; also referred to as the Old Testament
Holocaust	Planned genocide of six million Jews from 1941 to 1945
Irving Berlin	Early 20th century American songwriter
Isaac	Son of Abraham and Sarah
Isaac Kook	Renowned 20th century Jewish scholar and chief rabbi of Jerusalem
Isaac Luria	16th-century Jewish mystic and central contributor to the Kabbalah
Jerry Seinfeld	20th-century Jewish-American comedian, featured in popular television sitcom, *Seinfeld*
Job	Prophet of God in the Book of Job
King David	Second king of Israel and Judah; author of Biblical Psalms

Larry David	20th-century Jewish-American comedian, helped create popular television sitcom, *Seinfeld*
Martin Buber	20th-century existentialist philosopher
Marx Brothers	Early 20th-century comedy family
Messiah	An anointed being prophesized to deliver creation from the sufferings of sin
Monotheism	Belief in the singular nature of God
Moses Maimonides	12th-century philosopher and physician of the Middle Ages
Nachman of Bratslav	19th-century mystical rabbi and great-grandson of Ball Shem Tov
Negative theology	Approaching God by negating all that is known regarding God
Rivka Miriam	Contemporary Israeli poet and artist
Rosh Hashana	Jewish New Year, celebrated in the fall
Sabbath	A time of worship and rest from Friday sundown to Saturday evening
Safed	One of four holy cities for Jewish mysticism
Sarah Silverman	Jewish-American comedian; television star of "The Sarah Silverman Project"
Shema	An ancient Jewish prayer that emphasizes the unity and interconnectivity of all beings
Sigmund Freud	Father of psychoanalytic therapy
Talmud	Compilation of Jewish law and philosophy providing interpretations of the Hebrew Bible
Ten Commandments	A set of laws given to Moses by God on Mount Sinai
Theatre of the Absurd	Theatrical presentations emphasizing the purposelessness of human existence
Theodicy	A defense of God's benevolence in the wake of inexplicable suffering
Theodor Herzl	Founder of political Zionism
Torah	The first five books of the Hebrew Bible
Vaudeville	Popular 19th- and 20th-century theatrical presentation including dance, comedy and song
Wailing Wall	Remnant of Jewish temple in Jerusalem; contemporary site for worship and lamentation
Woody Allen	Jewish-American comedian, director, and actor
Yom Kippur	A day of atonement, consisting of worship, introspection and fasting
Zionism	A religio-political movement that advocated for self-rule of the Jews in Israel

Chapter Six
Christianity
Transcendence

Few people have exhibited Christian virtue more profoundly than **St. Seraphim of Sarov**, Russia. In 1804 he was viciously attacked by thieves, forcing him to live as a hunchback for the rest of his life. But his oversized soul could not be contained by his contorted body. He pleaded with the law courts to forgive the thieves. When word of his forgiveness spread, Seraphim patiently received a steady stream of pilgrims, helping them find some joy in their otherwise meager lives.

In 1946 the USSR established a nuclear weapons research facility in the holy city of Sarov, and as the site of the Russian Federation Nuclear Centre, the city remains closed to non-residents today. The saint's remains were shut away in Moscow's Museum for Religion and Atheism. But like his faith in Christian transcendence, the holy man from Sarov could not be kept down. In 2016, his remains were carried up by a Russian astronaut to the International Space Station, where they orbited—and consecrated—the earth for six months. Science and religion had once again joined forces in the confidence that the human story isn't necessarily limited to what we see, hear, and touch in our everyday world.

Transcending one's earthly body is at the centre of the Christian religion. The word "transcendence" means to cross over, to go beyond ordinary limits and change into something better. The promise of transcendence is one of Christianity's greatest gifts to the world. It comes with the faith that we can be better than we are. We can do better than we're doing. And it isn't too late to get to work.

Mother Mary and the Incarnate God

At the core of the Christian **Gospels** is the story of how, over 2,000 years ago, the One God took the form of a human body to live among the Jewish people in the land of Israel.

For many Christian theologians, God became incarnate for at least three reasons: "to provide a measure of reconciliation with God for a broken relationship, to identify with our suffering, and to show and teach us how to live and encourage us to do so."[189] By living, suffering, and dying in the human world, God could help humans repair their damaged world by suffering alongside us and exhorting us to be better people. For this purpose, God chose a woman to carry the incarnated God in her womb and give birth to the human form of God.

In the Gospels, the Book of Luke tells the story of how the angel Gabriel approached a Jewish peasant woman named **Mary** (or Miriam) and proclaimed, "You will conceive and give birth to a son, and you are to call him **Jesus**. He will be great and will be called the Son of the Most High."[190] By giving her consent, Mary establishes herself as a central figure in the Christian story. Mary's pregnancy was caused by **immaculate conception** in the tradition of holy birth stories in the Old Testament.

During the holiday of **Christmas**, Christians recount Jesus' birth in **Bethlehem**. A star in the sky marked the fulfillment of an Old Testament prophecy:

> "But you, Bethlehem, in the land of Judah,
>   are by no means least among the rulers of Judah;
> for out of you will come a ruler
>   who will shepherd my people Israel."[191]

The baby Jesus slept in a manger since there was no room for his family in the inn. Tasked with caring for this holy child, Mary and her husband Joseph raised Jesus in the city of **Nazareth**. Years later, Mary's role in the birth of Jesus would be officially noted at the **Council of Ephesus**. In the year 431, **Cyril of Alexandria** definitively stated that God chose to be born in the world "in order that he might bless the beginning of our existence … seeing that it was a woman that had given birth to him, united to the flesh.…"[192] Through Mary, we see the joining of two worlds: spirit and flesh, heaven and earth, God and human.

Michelangelo sculpted the *Pietà* in 1498–99. The sculpture is located in St. Peter's Basilica.

Throughout the Middle Ages, the image of Mary grew into an international symbol of motherhood, with all its human hardship, unconditional love, and constant care. As St. John of Damascus stated in the eighth century, "The very name of the Mother of God contains the whole mystery of the economy of the Incarnation."[193] Blessed by God, Mary learned the joy of parenthood and the heartache of outliving her child.

In the 15th century, a 23-year old sculptor, **Michelangelo Buonarotti**, was commissioned to immortalize Mary's bittersweet understanding of the human condition in stone. His *Pietà* captures Mary's pain and patience as she holds her dead child in her arms. Housed in **St. Peter's Basilica** in the **Vatican**, Michelangelo's *Pietà* is visited by millions of tourists every year. As the sculptor's first biographer proclaimed in the 16th century, Michelangelo was able to express something eternal and transcendent in the mother-and-child love story. It is miraculous "that a stone, formless in the beginning, could ever have been brought to the state of perfection which Nature habitually struggles to create in the flesh."[194] Over 500 years later, the statue of Mary continues to draw tourists and pilgrims alike to witness the transcendent embodiment of the human spirit in stone.

The story of Mary's compassion took on new life in Mexico after the fall of the Aztec Empire. In 1531, Juan Diego, a recently converted Christian, heard the singing of birds on the way to his religious instruction. Astounded, he then saw a vision of Mary beckoning him to build a church. The church was to be on the top of a hill, where Mary could give the people all her love and compassion. To Juan Diego Mary offered flowers as a sign of her love, along with an imprint of her likeness on his cloak. In the imprint, Mary is brown-skinned and wearing the traditional dress of the Aztec goddesses. After initial skepticism, Juan Diego's Bishop verified the truth of the peasant's encounter and built a chapel in the city of Tepeyac, in honour of the **Virgin Mary of Guadalupe**. Miraculously, the imprint of Mary along with the original cloak of cactus fibres has remained intact in the church for almost 500 years.

Today, the 16th-century church is the most visited tourist site in all of Mexico. As in many other places around the world, apparitions of Mary help blend native folklore with the tenets of early Christianity. Mary's presence in a small village in Mexico comes with a unifying message: "because the vision occurred during the period of the Conquest, the seer was Indian, the Madonna was black, and the site was one originally dedicated to the indigenous goddess."[195]

For Christians around the world, Mary offers hope, love, and community with diverse people from sometimes violent histories. And, as many contemporary Christian feminists point out, the evolving story of Mother Mary helps us see how "female imagery rightly belongs in our discourse about the divine mystery."[196]

Repentance and Forgiveness in Jesus Christ

Before Jesus, it was **John the Baptist** who acted as "the voice of one calling in the wilderness,"[197] imploring the Jews of Judea to repent and strive to be better people. In his **baptism** rituals at the Jordan River, John the Baptist gave people hope that their past mistakes did not need to define them forever. As his own father had prophesied, John gave his people "the knowledge of salvation through the forgiveness of their sins."[198] The promise of baptism is that we can transcend not only our past, but also our bodies, race, gender, and social class not by defeating others, but through the more difficult act of repenting for our own mistakes.

Though he was already without sin, Jesus was baptized by John. When he emerged from the river, Jesus was more than merely the son of a carpenter. He was publicly revealed to be the Son of God, with whom the Lord was "well-pleased."[199]

After his baptism, Jesus embarked on a mission to convince others that they could transform themselves as well. He performed miracles like turning water into wine, restoring sight to

> **The Beatitudes (Matthew 5: 2–10)**
>
> 2 And he opened his mouth, and taught them, saying,
>
> 3 Blessed are the poor in spirit: for theirs is the kingdom of heaven.
>
> 4 Blessed are they that mourn: for they shall be comforted.
>
> 5 Blessed are the meek: for they shall inherit the earth.
>
> 6 Blessed are they which do hunger and thirst after righteousness: for they shall be filled.
>
> 7 Blessed are the merciful: for they shall obtain mercy.
>
> 8 Blessed are the pure in heart: for they shall see God.
>
> 9 Blessed are the peacemakers: for they shall be called the children of God.
>
> 10 Blessed are they which are persecuted for righteousness' sake: for theirs is the kingdom of heaven.

the blind, and raising the dead. Such remarkable feats helped convince the villagers that they were not limited to their worldly bodies. Jesus' miracles showed his followers that the smallest amount of faith in another world could help move even mountains. Everything now was changeable, Jesus promised. "Nothing will be impossible for you."[200]

While celebrating the story of the Jewish Exodus to freedom at a Passover Seder, Jesus sought to give strength to his twelve disciples before they embarked on their own rigorous spiritual journeys. Performing the first **eucharist**, Jesus gave his followers the bread of his body and the wine of his blood, "which is poured out for many for the forgiveness of sins."[201]

After the **Last Supper**, the company retreated to a forest in **Gethsemane** to pray. Jesus understood that forgiving humanity's sins would come with the most torturous suffering imaginable. "Take this cup from me," he implored God.[202] But his faith in God's forgiveness gave him strength, "[a]nd being in anguish, he prayed more earnestly, and his sweat was like drops of blood falling to the ground."[203]

As he prophesied, Jesus was arrested by the Roman authorities. When the Roman governor Pontius Pilate asked if he were some kind of king, Jesus responded, "My kingdom is not of this world."[204] Jesus was found guilty and sentenced to death by **crucifixion**.

On the appointed day, Jesus was whipped and forced to carry his **cross** through the streets of Jerusalem before arriving at Golgotha. There, Roman soldiers nailed his body to a cross between two other convicted criminals. In the moment of his most intense suffering, Jesus said a prayer for his oppressors. "Father, forgive them, for they know not what they do."[205] Just before dying, he called out to God, recalling the trials of King David in the Book of Psalms. "My God, my God, why have you forsaken me?"[206]

On the third day after Jesus' burial, his garments were discovered in his tomb, but his dead body was nowhere to be found. What was the meaning behind his missing body? While the disciples were grappling with this question, Jesus showed himself to them, saying, "Why are you troubled, and why do doubts rise in your minds? Look at my hands and my feet. It is I myself!"[207]

For the disciples and future Christians, the resurrection of Jesus definitively proved that humans are more than worldly flesh and blood. The holiday of **Easter** celebrates this hope of transcending ourselves into something greater than we are today. With the curse of the Garden of Eden lifted, our sins forgiven, even death itself might be overcome. As **Paul the Apostle** explained, such is the mystery of the Christ incarnate. "We will not all sleep, but we will all be changed—in a flash, in the twinkling of an eye, at the last trumpet. For the trumpet will sound, the dead will be raised imperishable, and we will be changed."[208]

Bodies and Souls of the Catholic Saints

In the Christian cosmology, human beings move between two worlds: what **St. Augustine** called the "City of Man," and the "City of God." The City of Man is the world of finite, material things, that shine forth but then decay, break apart, and die. Our bodies and our bodily desires bind us to this earthly realm, try as we might to seek out the eternal, immaterial City of God.

A young man in the fifth century, Augustine was a slave to his desires and lusts. With his like-minded, good-timing companions he chased temporary pleasures, and "rolled in its dung as if rolling in spices and precious ointments."[209] But even in his darkest moments, Augustine believed there was something eternal housed in our temporary bodies. And that something, called a **soul**, was our ticket out of the City of Man. "Through my soul I will ascend to him," Augustine wrote. "I will rise above the force by which I am bonded to the body and fill its frame with vitality."[210] Augustine's story is typical of many **saints** in the **Roman Catholic** tradition. He didn't live a perfect life. Rather, he is venerated because he desperately sought longer lasting ways of fixing his flaws by searching his soul and demanding more of his body.

In 13th-century Italy, troubadour poets were moving from town to town, singing of the beauties of nature and romantic love. **St. Francis of Assisi** was enchanted by the chivalrous poetry, but he saw something deeper than pleasure in nature's wonders. He slept in the caves and the fields of the Great Outdoors. The trees, the rivers, the wild animals all had their own dignity instilled by their Creator. Just as good music makes us curious about the composer, so did natural beauty bring St. Francis out of his everyday doldrums and move him closer to God. In his well-known **"Canticle of the Sun,"** St. Francis praised God through his natural creations: to Sir Brother Sun ("Of You Most High, he bears the likeness"), through precious Sister Moon and the stars, and Brother Fire who "is beautiful and playful and robust and strong."

According to St. Francis, all God's creatures are invested with the Holy Spirit and therefore worthy of our reverence and our care. One time, a frightened rabbit leapt into St. Francis' arms. Deeply moved, St. Francis hugged the animal, and "pressing it to him with tender affection, admonished it with motherly compassion not to let itself be taken again, and then set it free."[211]

Today, the patron saint of animals continues to inspire people from Pope Francis (who took the saint's name) to secular animal rights organizations like People for the Ethical Treatment of Animals (PETA). "For who can afford to ignore the example of one ... whose responsiveness to the beauty of the environment was so great, his joyful openness to it so boundless, that he experienced mystical ecstasy while contemplating a flower?"[212]

St. Teresa of Ávila wasn't expected to change the face of Christianity during the days of the **Inquisition** in 16th-century Spain. She couldn't read Latin, had trouble dissecting subtle theological debates, and more troubling, she wasn't a man. But these same disadvantages put her in the tradition of New Testament saints who were guided more by feeling than by intellectual arguments.

After reading St. Augustine's **Confessions**, St. Teresa was convinced that the soul could experience God directly without the aid of logic or rationality. "When the Lord suspends the understanding and makes it cease from its activity," she wrote, "He gives it something which both amazes it and keeps it busy, so that, without reasoning in any way, it can understand more in a short space of time than we, with all our human efforts, in many years."[213] St. Teresa experienced such **rapture** firsthand. In her writings, she guided other Christians whose souls had been hardened by bad habits and worldly bustle. For even "when a person is quite unprepared for such a thing, and is not even thinking of God, he is awakened by His Majesty, as though by a rushing comet or a thunderclap … it goes and comes again; it is, in short, never permanent, and for that reason it never completely enkindles the soul; for, just as the soul is about to become enkindled, the spark dies, and leaves the soul yearning once again to suffer that loving pain of which it is the cause."[214] Suffering this "loving pain" continues to be a hallmark for Christians around the world who live divided between two worlds.

Icons to Another World: Russian Orthodoxy

Icons are a genre of paintings of Jesus, Mary, or any of the Biblical prophets and the Christian saints who followed them. The images are usually painted on wooden panels with rich colors: often red, yellow, and gold. Holy people in the icons are frequently distinguished by halos, or unusually stretched out bodies to "show that the person portrayed belongs to another dimension."[215]

> ### Nicaea II (787)
> … these are the images of our Lord, God and saviour, Jesus Christ, and of our Lady without blemish, the holy God-bearer, and of the revered angels and of any of the saintly holy men. The more frequently they are seen in representational art, the more are those who see them drawn to remember and long for those who serve as models… Indeed, the honour paid to an image traverses it, reaching the model, and he who venerates the image, venerates the person represented in that image.

In Russia, it is not uncommon to see Christians parading icons at festivals, or walking long distances to kiss the artwork. In 787, at **Nicaea II**, it was decided that it was entirely proper to bestow icons with "a fervent and reverent adoration." After all, humans were made in God's image (in Greek, "*eikon*"). The Church decreed it was possible for the Holy Spirit to reach people through Christian images and relics.

Holy images are meant to radically transform us, helping us transcend our immediate environment. Icons serve as "gateways to another world."[216] Just as Christ incarnate was of two worlds, so might we be. The gentle facial expressions portrayed in icons, alongside the sharpness of the colors are meant to inspire us to live up to the divine inside us. "The icon bears witness to a mystical interaction between the creator and creation,"[217] a partnership with something bigger and bolder than what we ordinarily see.

In the **Great Schism** of 1054, the **Eastern Orthodox Church** centred in Constantinople parted ways with the Roman Catholics of the West. Deepening theological divides over the Trinity and the concept of original sin and longstanding political and ethnic issues over Papal authority proved to be too large a rift to bridge. In the Christian East, and in Russia in particular, holy icons became essential passageways for religious communities to tap into the relationship between a God on high and the humans below, created in God's likeness.

In the 15th century, **Andrei Rublev** attempted the impossible task of capturing the **Trinity** on canvas. In Rublev's *Trinity* we see the three angels who visit Abraham in the Book of Genesis. The way the painted faces often stare back at us places the viewer in an active relationship with the ancient mystery of Christ.

Russian director **Andrei Tarkovsky**'s 1966 film *Andrei Rublev* helped return once forgotten iconography to a new generation of modern viewers. The challenge Tarkovsky presents in the film was "how to raise the profane art of the cinema to the level of the icon."[218] His epic 3½-hour film on Rublev was an exploration into the question of whether the mystery of Christian transcendence could be expressed in contemporary cinema. For Tarkovsky, and a slew of modern directors he influenced, it was possible to brush up against another more spiritual world within our reach. As Tarkovsky once wrote, "Through the image is sustained an awareness of the infinite: the eternal within the finite, the spiritual within matter, the limitless given form."[219]

The Russian icons show us how an image can reflect the Christian God. And if that's true, then there's hope that other Christian art forms can succeed as well.

The Struggle to Forgive: Lev Tolstoy and Fyodor Dostoyevsky

In 1879, **Lev Tolstoy** (also and perhaps better known as Leo Tolstoy in English) should have been on top of the world. He had already written his masterpieces, *War and Peace* and *Anna Karenina*, two novels that forever changed the way fiction is written and read today. And yet what could fame and fortune offer the celebrity author confronting his own inevitable mortality?

Time and again Tolstoy would read the Gospels, but still he felt empty. Then he read Jesus' Sermon on the Mount[220] and was transformed. "My life and my desires were completely changed; good and evil interchanged meanings," he wrote. "Why so? Because I understood the doctrine of Jesus in a different way from that in which I had understood it before."[221]

> ### Lev Tolstoy
> *Resurrection*
> Now he saw clearly what all the terrors he had seen came from, and what ought to be done to put a stop to them. The answer he could not find was the same that Christ gave to Peter. It was that we should forgive always an infinite number of times because there are no men who have not sinned themselves, and therefore none can punish or correct others.

Tolstoy was particularly struck with Jesus' command to "resist not evil." Though he had read the words thousands of times before, he always took it as a worthy ideal that had no firm application in the real world. As a Christian he had fought in wars to defeat evil and the people who pursue it. Now, for the first time, he sensed hypocrisy in his actions. He also sensed a disconnect with other Christians who lived in Russia and around the world.

Photograph of Lev Tolstoy, taken in 1908 by Sergei Prokudin-Gorsky.

Instead of heroically combating evil, Jesus commands we meet anger with kindness, violence with love. In his final novel, *Resurrection*, Tolstoy opens with a quote from the Sermon on the Mount. "How often shall my brother sin against me and I forgive him? Not seven times but seventy times seven."

The message sounds so simple, and yet Tolstoy found it difficult to truly enact it in the world. Too often he looked to his own pleasures or personal glory. "The orgies and duels in which I took part as a student, the wars in which I have participated, the diseases that I have endured," he wrote, were "exacted by fidelity to the doctrine of the world."[222] Whenever Tolstoy could summon the strength to live a life of love and forgiveness, he found himself immeasurably happier.

Tolstoy interpreted Jesus' message to turn the other cheek as a radical break from the cycle of cruelty and violence the secular world encouraged—and not just the secular world. Religious organizations like the Russian Orthodox Church, Tolstoy argued, also divided people, instilling fear and intolerance for others who appeared different from the community. These behaviours and "rules of the Church weakened and sometimes destroyed the desire for Christian truth which alone gave meaning to my life," Tolstoy wrote.[223] Excommunicated by the Church, Tolstoy challenges us to decide who has the authority to enact Jesus' message: whether it be the town leaders and the Church, or simple human beings putting their community's interests above their own.

Tolstoy's contemporary, **Fyodor Dostoyevsky**, was raised by a strict orthodox father. In the late 19th-century, the old Russian Orthodoxy was confronted with the economic successes of Western Enlightenment and the pleasures of secularism. Why live a religious life, when it seemed so much more fun to strike it rich in this world?

Dostoyevsky, by his own account, lived a dissolute life of gambling and drinking, attended by troubling bouts of deep self-loathing. Many of his fictional characters are also imbued with such depravity. But in most of his stories, Dostoyevsky shows these same characters always reaching for a way out. Dostoyevsky admits that his own crisis "is the one by which, consciously or unconsciously, I have been tormented my whole life: the existence of God."[224]

In his groundbreaking novel, *Crime and Punishment*, Dostoyevsky portrays a morally depraved student, Raskolnikov (or "Rascal"), who sets out to see if he can get away with murder. Throughout the story, the police close in while his own conscience steadily eats away at him. Towards the end of the book, Raskolnikov dons a wooden cross around his neck, crosses himself "sincerely," and confesses his crime. In the final scene we see him in a Siberian prison camp, with a Bible by his side. It brings a fitting end to "the story of the gradual renewal of a man, the story of his gradual regeneration, of his passing from one world into another, of his initiation into a new unknown life."[225]

In his life and his fiction, Dostoyevsky never strayed far from his fascination with these dual themes of sin and forgiveness. Father Zossima, a character in his final book, *The Brothers Karamazov*, is partly based on the real-life Russian Bishop, **St. Tikhon**. St. Tikhon battled with his own depression and mood swings. But he never fell victim to despair, which he defined as "having no hope in the mercy of God."[226]

Like St. Tikhon, Dostoyevsky's portrayal of Father Zossima is one of internal suffering, struggle, and in the end, peace. On his deathbed, Father Zossima poetically proclaims, "It's the great mystery of human life that old grief passes gradually into quiet, tender joy ... gentle memories that come with them, the dear images from the whole of my long, happy life—and over all the Divine Truth, softening, reconciling, forgiving!"[227] In Father Zossima and his disciple Alyosha, Dostoyevsky offers a convincing answer to his own persistent religious doubts.

But perhaps the best-known chapter from *The Brothers Karamazov* is entitled "The Grand Inquisitor." In the fictional story retold by an atheist, Jesus has returned to earth during the time of the Spanish Inquisition. The Inquisitor recognizes Jesus and arrests him. The people don't want the promise of another world, he says to Jesus. Given the choice of two worlds they'll always choose the earthy realm over heaven. "For the sake of that earthly bread the spirit of the earth will rise up against Thee," he asserts.[228]

Throughout the Inquisitor's rant, Jesus never says a word. Finally, the Inquisitor longs for the God incarnate to respond. Jesus' answer, as Dostoyevsky knew all too well, could only be one of infinite love and forgiveness. Instead of picking apart the Inquisitor's arguments, Jesus leans over and "kissed him on his bloodless aged lips."[229] The kiss proves more powerful than the hatred sowed between people struggling for worldly power.

For both Tolstoy and Dostoyevsky the Christian promise of spiritual transcendence was both a struggle and an aspiration. Though it's unclear whether either author achieved it in their own lives, their struggle to be something more is what gave their troubled lives meaning and their fiction such enduring popularity.

Reformation and the Puritan Revolution

Like Russians, European Christians were also concerned with the worldly power of the Roman Church. To rebuild St. Peter's Basilica in Rome, some 16th-century bishops were promising poor Christians salvation if they helped foot the bill. In Germany, **Martin Luther** had enough of such money grabs. The Pope, he argued was tyrannical and abusive, straying far from Jesus' clear message against authoritarianism. Luther detailed the Roman Catholic Church's abuses in **Ninety-five Theses**, calling out the corrupt priests who "are let go free, without having made good the damage they cause."[230]

Luther also questioned **Papal infallibility**. All human beings, Luther argued, were capable of grasping the full import of the Gospels on their own. What mattered most was the devotion of their faith and their acts of charity in the world. This renewed emphasis on worldly acts of kindness and personal responsibility was a hallmark of the **Protestant Reformation** that Luther spearheaded.

As many religious scholars have pointed out, the anti-authoritarian underpinnings of the Protestant Reformation dovetailed easily with the rise of capitalism, Western democracies, and the individual's pursuit of happiness. The German sociologist Max Weber famously argued that the Protestant spirit championed "the fulfilment of duty in worldly affairs as the highest form which the moral activity of the individual could assume. This it was which inevitably gave everyday worldly activity a religious significance."[231] The clear distinction between St. Augustine's two worlds was beginning to blur.

In the 17th century, a sect of Protestants known as the **Puritans** grew tired of English tyrannical excess and the King's close ties with the Roman Catholic Church. Ten years after the departure of the *Mayflower*, **John Winthrop** left England to start a new religious community in America. The stakes were high. Could a new society be built with a Christ-like love, "divine, spiritual, nature; free, active, strong, courageous, permanent"? This New World, as Winthrop well knew, was an untried experiment. "For we must consider that we shall be as a city upon a hill. The eyes of all people are upon us."[232]

Winthrop Heading to America

We must delight in each other; make others' conditions our own; rejoice together, mourn together, labor and suffer together... The Lord will be our God, and delight to dwell among us, as His own people, and will command a blessing upon us in all our ways, so that we shall see much more of His wisdom, power, goodness and truth, than formerly we have been acquainted with....

In England, Oliver Cromwell, known as the "Puritan Moses," had already led a revolt against the **divine right of kings** in the hopes that a more reasoned parliamentary debate would someday rule the country. In America, this revolutionary spirit was taken up by Puritans like **Benjamin Franklin** and **Samuel Adams**. A deacon at the Old South Church in Boston, Adams's father was also a political activist. His generation's interest in combining worldly commerce and politics with other-worldly religion was passed down to his son. It was from the Old South Church that the younger Adams led the Boston Tea Party, commencing the symbolic onset of the American Revolution.

Four years after the signing of Declaration of Independence, Adams continually cautioned Americans about the need to preserve community values over the ambitions of dictators. "If ever the time should come, when vain and aspiring men shall possess the highest seats in government," Adams wrote, "our country will stand in need of its experienced patriots to prevent its ruin."[233]

Christianity: Transcendence • 103

Shouting the Gospel

In the 19th century, many Black **Baptist** churches of the American South developed the practice of shout-outs in which the preacher would call out to the congregation and the congregation would respond with an "Amen," "Hallelujah," or other words of praise. Sunday mornings at these African-American churches were often rollicking, emotional, and actively participatory experiences.

In the 1920s and 1930s record producers eager to take advantage of the popularity of phonograph sales, began recording musical acts that featured shouting preachers introducing and singing along to music. The growing popularity of the Southern Baptist church services soon gave rise to a new high-energy musical style known as **gospel**.

Gospel music began as an amalgamation of local blues music that captured the despair of post-slavery poverty and set it to hopeful themes of Christian transcendence. In 1932, **Thomas Dorsey** lost his wife and baby in childbirth. That soul-crushing experience led him to write the words to **"Precious Lord, Take My Hand,"** one of the most widely recorded gospel songs of all time. Dorsey's lyrics capture the heartache of a person seeking transcendence and salvation from their earthly plight: "Through the storm, through the night, / Lead me on to the light."

In the 1940s Dorsey teamed up with singer **Mahalia Jackson,** barnstorming black churches across the country. "All by herself, Mahalia was the vocal, physical, spiritual symbol of gospel music."[234] Born in New Orleans, Jackson used to sing **hymns** in the all-night wakes that followed the deaths of Christians in her community.

Jackson took Dorsey's music and added physicality, sex appeal, and a booming voice. "At her best, Mahalia builds these songs to a frenzy of intensity almost demanding a release in holler and shout. When singing them she may descend to her knees, her combs scattering like so many cast-out demons."[235] Jackson often closed her show with the classic, "When the Saints Go Marching In," a song frequently played at Christian funeral processions in New Orleans.

An enthusiastic promoter of Civil Rights, Jackson befriended **Martin Luther King, Jr**. and often sang gospel songs before or after his speeches. Her rendition of **"We Shall Overcome"** became the soundtrack to sit-ins and protests of the 1960s. Before King's famous "I Have a Dream" speech at the March on Washington in 1963, Jackson sang the gospel tune, **"How I Got Over."** She sang at President Kennedy's inauguration in 1961, and at King's funeral in 1968.

While gospel music continues to fill the airwaves on radios across North America, its biggest link to popular culture is its legacy of influence on old-school rhythm-and-blues shouters like Little Richard and Ray Charles. Gospel music is also credited as being the inspiration for white rock-and-roll shouters like Elvis Presley, the Beatles, and the Rolling Stones. Today, contemporary hip-hop stars like Beyoncé and Drake frequently sample gospel beats to animate their music. The popularity of hip-hop, rock-and-roll, and R&B are all built on the transcendent shouting of gospel preachers and the ancient Christian religion that gave them hope.

Discovery Questions

1. Read Petrarch's 14th-century letter, "Ascent of Mont Ventoux," about his physical and spiritual struggles to hike up a mountain. What Christian themes are discussed? Have you encountered any similar challenges?

2. Ask a friend or family member forgiveness for something you did or said in the not-too-distant past. Was it hard? How do you feel about it now? What's changed?

3. Read the "Rebellion" and "Grand Inquisitor" chapters in Dostoyevksy's *The Brothers Karamazov* (Book 5, Chapters 4 and 5). What arguments does the philosopher Ivan make against Christ? How would you respond?

4. Do an image search for Rembrandt's "The Holy Family by Night," a painting that had a profound impact on Vincent Van Gogh. What Christian themes do you see in the painting? Are any of these themes also present in Van Gogh's famous "Starry Night"?

5. Listen to Beethoven's Ninth Symphony, the fourth movement of which includes the "Ode to Joy." The music has often been the backdrop for political protests around the world. Describe how it makes you feel. Which sections of the symphony best represent suffering, and which sections best represent freedom?

6. Volunteer at an off-campus food bank or housing shelter for one day or night. How did you help others? How did others help you?

7. Watch parts of the 2003 documentary, *20 Feet from Stardom*. How have the gospel singers helped shape modern day rock-and-roll music?

Glossary

Terms	Definitions
Andrei Rublev	15th-century Russian icon painter
Andrei Tarkovsky	20th-century Russian film director
Baptism	Water ritual of purification and religious initiation
Baptists	A branch of Protestantism
Benjamin Franklin	18th-century American scientist and political philosopher
Bethlehem	A town near Jerusalem; birthplace of Jesus
"Canticle of the Sun"	13th-century song composed by St. Francis of Assisi
Christmas	Winter festival celebrating the birth of Jesus
Confessions	Fifth-century autobiographical account of St. Augustine's life

Council of Ephesus	Fifth-century convention held to resolve theological issues of the Church
Cross	Symbol of Christianity representing the transcendence of suffering
Crucifixion	Punitive measure in which an individual is condemned to death by means of being nailed to a wooden construct
Cyril of Alexandria	Fifth-century philosopher and bishop
Divine right of kings	Doctrine which states that a King's rule is a result of divine will
Easter	Spring festival celebrating the resurrection of Jesus
Eastern Orthodox Church	The second-largest church in Christianity, popular in Russia and Eastern Europe
Fyodor Dostoyevsky	19th-century Russian novelist
Gethsemane	Garden in Jerusalem where Jesus was arrested
Gospel	A high-energy musical genre that emerged from the American Southern Baptist Church
Gospels	Accounts of the life of Jesus found in the New Testament
Great Schism	The separation of Eastern Orthodox Church from the Roman Catholic Church in 1054
"How I Got Over"	A gospel hymn made famous by Mahalia Jackson
Hymns	Songs praising Jesus and the Christian life
Immaculate conception	Pregnancy of the Virgin Mary, caused by God's will
Inquisition	A collection of Roman Catholic institutions dedicated to punishing heretics
Jesus Christ	God incarnate; foundational teacher of Christian ethics
John the Baptist	Preacher who baptised Jesus in the Jordan River
John Winthrop	17th-century English Puritan and American colonist
Last Supper	Final meal Jesus ate with his disciples before his arrest
Lev Tolstoy	19th-century Russian novelist
Mahalia Jackson	20th-century American gospel singer and civil rights activist
Martin Luther	16th-century religious reformer; leader of the Protestant Reformation
Martin Luther King, Jr.	20th-century Baptist minister who spearheaded the American civil rights movement
Mary	Mother of Jesus
Michelangelo Buonarotti	16th-century Italian Renaissance sculptor and painter
Nazareth	City in Israel where Jesus spent his childhood years
Nicaea II	Eighth-century Church council, encouraging adoration for Christian symbols and icons

Ninety-Five Theses	16th-century text authored by Martin Luther that challenged excesses of the Roman Catholic Church
Papal infallibility	A doctrine that exempts the Pope from any error in defining Christian ethics
Paul the Apostle	Apostle of Jesus who helped spread the teachings of Christianity
"Precious Lord, Take My Hand"	20th-century gospel hymn composed by Thomas Dorsey
Protestant Reformation	16th-century reform movement that encouraged greater emphasis on worldly acts and personal responsibility
Puritans	English Protestant sect that brought Christianity to the New World
Rapture	Mystical state in which an individual soul experiences divine revelation
Roman Catholic Church	The largest Christian Church, led by the Pope
Saints	Holy persons who have especially close relationships with God
Samuel Adams	18th-century American revolutionary
Soul	Intangible, immaterial, and Godlike aspect of the self
St. Augustine	Fourth and fifth-century theologian and philosopher
St. Francis of Assisi	13th-century friar and founder of the Franciscan order
St. Peter's Basilica	The Pope's residence in the Vatican; houses the tomb of Saint Peter
St. Seraphim of Sarov	18th- and 19th-century Russian saint
St. Teresa of Ávila	16th-century Spanish mystic and nun
Thomas Dorsey	20th-century gospel musician
Trinity	Unity of God in three distinct aspects: the Father, the Son and the Holy Spirit
Vatican	City-state in Rome, Italy; centre of Roman Catholicism
Virgin Mary of Guadalupe	Official Catholic title commemorating Mother Mary's mystical appearance in Tepeyac, Mexico
"We Shall Overcome"	20th-century gospel song that became the anthem of resistance in the American civil rights movement
"When the Saints Go Marching In"	A 20th-century gospel song and popular New Orleans jazz standard

Chapter Seven

Islam
Strangers Welcome

It's only a five-minute walk from the **Omayad Mosque** in Damascus, Syria to the most famous ice cream store in the Middle East, if not the world. But if you've been fasting for **Ramadan**, that night-time walk through the al-Hamidya market can feel like forever.

At Bakdash, they make their ice cream with ground orchid flour and sticky mastic to give it a gummy texture. They also pound it with giant wooden mallets to stretch the sweet, gooey cream before rolling it in pistachios. The ice cream, or *booza*, has been made the same way for over one hundred years. Before electricity, they used donkeys to carry in snow to keep the ice cream cold and stored it in caves.

Bakdash continues to thrive in the midst of civil war, COVID-19, and social unrest. Jews, Christians, Muslims, and people from all religions are welcome there. The founder of Bakdash was named after **Muhammad**, the last and most important prophet of Islam. The story of Bakdash, like the story of Islam, is built on welcoming people from all walks of life and giving them a little sweetness to take back home.

Strangers in a Strange Land: The Children of Abraham

"La ilaha illa Allah, Muhammadu rasool Allah" is the poetic opening of the Muslim testament of faith. "There is no God but God," it means, "and Muhammad is His prophet." Reciting it and taking it to heart is one of the **five pillars** of Islam, along with praying five times a day, helping the needy, fasting during Ramadan, and taking a pilgrimage to **Mecca** once in one's life.

The word "Islam" means "to submit" to the one God. As a persecuted people ever on the run, the earliest Muslims took hope in their relationship with a God who would shelter them and make them feel welcome. "He is with you wherever you are," it is written in the **Qur'an**, the holiest book of Islam.[236]

In the Prophet Muhammad, Muslims found a kindred spirit who never stopped finding God's handiwork in everyone he met. In flower beds or sick beds, the religious tradition of caring for strangers serves "as a moral challenge to humanity to rise above its personal grudges and pettiness and to respond to God by affirming belief in God's plan for the whole of humanity and working for its ultimate realization."[237]

In the Qur'an, Muhammad is instructed to "Follow the creed of Abraham, a man of pure faith."[238] Abraham trusted his God so completely he was willing to leave his home to become "a stranger and a sojourner" in a foreign land. In so doing, he became a *khalilullah*, a friend of God.

Perhaps because of his own nomadic history, Abraham shows compassion to other foreigners. When strangers come to his modest home, he overcomes his fears and invites them to stay for a meal. Because of this hospitality, Abraham and Sarah are blessed with their son Isaac, though Sarah is well beyond her child-bearing years. The story is told three different times in the Qur'an. From the earliest times, it was understood that we would need constant reminders to care for the foreigners in our communities.

After Isaac's birth, Sarah's handmaid **Hagar** was forced make her own way with her son **Ishmael** (whom she conceived with Abraham). In the Islamic tradition, special attention is given to the trials of Hagar and Ishmael. Alone in a seemingly inhospitable country, mother and child could not survive on their own. When their water ran out, Ishmael cried from thirst. Desperate to save her family, Hagar courageously raced from hill to hill, crying out for water. An angel of God heard her plea and mercifully looked after them, miraculously creating a well of water in the desert to nourish the needy foreigners. Such divine acts of kindness are models for us to provide for the most vulnerable strangers in our communities.[239]

The Qur'an describes how Ishmael's descendants remained foreigners for hundreds of years. It's why the **Hadith** reminds us: "Be in this world as though you were a stranger or a traveler."[240] Muslim commentators note how this journey of life we all undertake is short, unfamiliar, and filled with peril. All of us will someday come to rely on the kindness of strangers.

Every year, millions of Muslims travel to Mecca on the ***Hajj*** to circumambulate the ***Kabaa*** that Abraham and Isaac restored as proof of God's never-ending love for all people. Muslims from around the world also walk in Hagar's footsteps, between the Al-Safa and Al-Marwah hills in honor of the compassion shown to a frightened mother and child.

For many Muslims today, "true religiosity lies in renewing our hospitality to strangers, the marginalized and those who, for a variety of reasons, are vulnerable or even suspect in society."[241]

Muhammad: The Lonely Prophet

Muhammad was born in Mecca on the Arabian peninsula in the year 570. The land was full of businesspeople from a variety of religions, including Christianity and Judaism, running caravans

The Qur'an

42:13   In matters of faith, He has laid down for you [people] the same commandment that He gave Noah, which We have revealed to you [Muhammad] and which We enjoined on Abraham and Moses and Jesus: "Uphold the faith and do not divide into factions within it"—what you [Prophet] call upon the idolaters to do is hard for them....

along the desert trade routes. By age 25, Muhammad had already made a name for himself as a trusted, diplomatic trader who cared for those less fortunate. After impressing the successful businesswoman **Khadija**, 15 years his senior, they married.

At the age of 40, during a spiritual retreat in the mountains, Muhammad was visited by the angel **Gabriel** who told him the words of God that now make up the holy Qur'an. Shaken by the experience, and unsure of its meaning, Muhammad returned home and fell into his wife's arms, seeking comfort and guidance. After some questioning and consultations, Khadija understood that her husband's virtues had made him special in the eyes of Allah, the one God. She convinced Muhammad to take the recurring visitations seriously. Khadija then became the first Muslim, submitting herself to the one God and his prophet Muhammad.

Like many prophets of the Hebrew Bible and the New Testament, Muhammad was chastised by people in his community and made an outcast for his relationship with God. When the pain of isolation became too great, God would remind Muhammad to care for others who also felt alone and without a home. "Did He not find you an orphan and shelter you? Did He not find you lost and guide you?"[242]

On one mystical **Night Journey**, while Muhammad was sleeping near the holy *Kabaa*, the Prophet was transported to the "farthest mosque," understood to be the place where the *Al-Aqsa* **Mosque** stands today in Jerusalem. From there Muhammad ascended to heaven where he met other prophets like Jesus, John the Baptist, Moses, and Abraham. Finally, he was given direct access to God's glory as a sign that God's love for human beings has been fully restored through the line of the prophets, culminating in Muhammad.

Back home in Mecca, Muhammad's protection was fracturing. After the deaths of his beloved wife Khadija and his uncle **Abu Talib**, Muhammad barely survived assassination. He fled his home for the foreign city of Yathrib, later renamed **Medina**. This *hijra*, or journey, is the beginning of the Islamic calendar since it marks the starting point of the efforts to politically organize and socially structure the Muslim people.

Whether it was facing Mecca in their prayers, dreaming of Jerusalem, or praying to a sometimes distant God, "this traumatic dislocation was central to their new identity."[243] How the dislocated and disaffected Muslims of Medina sought to reach understanding with other strangers is one of the enduring messages of Islam today.

Grief and Resistance in Karbala

Not long after Muhammad's death in 632, the Muslim community was torn between following the Prophet's oldest and most faithful friend, **Abu Bakr**, and his nephew **Ali**. To this day, **Sunni** Muslims follow the line of Abu Bakr and **Shi'ite** Muslims follow the line of Ali.

In 680, Ali's son, **Hussein ibn Ali**, and approximately 70 of his followers were ambushed and killed in the city of **Karbala**, because they would not recognize the rule of the Islamophobic Yazid ruler. Hussein's sister **Zaynab**, the granddaughter of the prophet Muhammad, stood by Hussein's side, caring for the wounded and preserving the faith. Captured and paraded in a convoy to the Yazid stronghold of Damascus, Zaynab remained stubbornly defiant.

> ### Imam Musa al-Sadr
> The revolution did not die in the sands of Karbala; it flowed into the life stream of the Islamic world, and passed from generation to generation, even to our day. It is a deposit placed in our hands so that we may profit from it, that we draw out of it a new source of reform, a new position, a new movement, a new revolution, to repel the darkness, to stop tyranny, and to pulverize evil.

What was to be a celebration of the Yazid victory was marred when Zaynab stood up and publicly scolded the bloodthirsty warlord. Defending the martyrs who died for their faith in God, she said, "If you have gained something today by shedding blood, you will certainly be a loser on the Day of Judgment. On that day nothing but your deeds will count."

During the Muslim holiday of **Ashura**, Zaynab's words are recited in grief, while women and men take on the suffering of Muslim families everywhere, torn apart by war and hatred. Whether it is resisting the tyranny of Saddam Hussein in Iraq, the Israeli incursion into Lebanon, or American influence in the Middle East, the **martyrs** of Ashura and Zaynab's courage to resist oppression in the face of unimaginable sorrow continue to be a source of inspiration for Shi'ite Muslims around the world.

In Iran, National Nurses Day is fittingly celebrated on Zaynab's birthday to honor her legacy of fearlessly aiding the weak and downtrodden. In Lebanon, volunteers in orphanages, women's shelters, and charity centers are "seen to embody the very qualities in Zaynab that are desired—emotional strength, outspokenness, and dedication to others."[244]

In Karbala, sacrifice and sadness bleed into a flawed world where not everyone cares to submit to the ethical code set forth by the one God. In such complicated times, the Islamic virtues of caring and giving re-emerge stronger than ever.

Islam's Golden Age

From the ninth to the 14th centuries, a number of military victories transformed the Prophet's Muslim communities into one of the most advanced empires in the world. Middle Eastern cities like Baghdad, Damascus, and Cairo grew into cosmopolitan centers where people from many religions and cultures congregated to advance our understanding of science, theology, and the arts.

At the heart of the cultural explosion was the **Translation Movement**, a massive undertaking to translate the classics of Greek philosophy, Babylonian science, and Hindu mathematics into the Arabic language for Muslim scholars to freely access. At its peak, the most sought-after translators were earning the modern equivalent of over $20,000 per month for their efforts. The result was a revival of the classics that would eventually influence the foundational Renaissance and Enlightenment movements of Western Europe. For hundreds of years, translations of and debates on Western and Eastern philosophies were centralized in the **House of Wisdom** in Baghdad, while interest in the sciences was kindled across the Islamic Empire.

In modern day Uzbekistan, for example, **Ibn Sina** (Avicenna) was inspired to study medicine after memorizing the Qu'ran at age 10. He understood that compassion for the sick and healing

Ibn Sina (Avicenna)

illnesses are core Muslim beliefs. "For every illness," the Prophet Muhammad once said, "God gives us the cure." It's our job, then, to make sure we seek out cures for as many illnesses as possible. For that, it behooves us to learn from as many cultures as possible. In his seminal five-volume work, **The Canon of Medicine**, Ibn Sina drew on translated works to write his encyclopedic work on the health benefits of Chinese herbs and Indian spices, alongside technical anatomical studies of the human body. His *Canon* was later translated into Latin and served as the most important medical text in Europe and the Middle East for over five hundred years.

With the renewed interest in the medical sciences, wealthy Muslims helped fund ***bimaristans*** in the most teeming cities of the Islamic world. Prototypes for today's general hospitals and pharmacies, these *bimaristans* were places to treat the sick, provide appropriate herbs for healing, and educate the next generation of medical students. Patients from all religions were treated equally in these *bimaristans*. Jews and Christians were also welcomed to serve as doctors alongside their Muslim counterparts.

From the earliest days of the Islamic empire, Jews and Christians enjoyed protected status throughout the Middle East. They were known as **People of the Book**, the ones who were favored with knowledge of the one God. Muslims believed that "the Jews, the Christians ... all those who believe in God and the Last Day and do good—will have their rewards with the Lord."[245]

When the renowned Sultan **Salāh al-Dīn** (Saladin) captured Jerusalem in 1187, he spared the lives of many poor Christians who couldn't pay for their freedom. He also allowed Jews to return to Israel after Christian Crusaders had previously banished them. The most famous Jewish theologian, Maimonides, was a doctor for the sultan's son, and served in the royal court in Cairo.

In one famous proclamation protecting other religious believers, the Sultan cautioned Muslims "to abstain from harming and harassing them ... do not attack them in acts or words. Let them therefore not be subjected to hearing disagreeable, prejudicial, or unjust words."[246] In Arabic, Salāh al-Dīn means "righteousness of religion."

Even among his conquered people the Sultan was praised for "his attachment to Islam, his respect for Arab values: hospitality, generosity, forbearance, honor, courage."[247] In the 14th century, Saladin was the only Muslim to appear in Limbo (neither heaven nor hell) in Italian poet Dante Alighieri's *Divine Comedy*. Dante classified the sultan as one of the virtuous non-Christians, alongside Greek philosophers Plato and Socrates.

> ## Medieval Waqfa Document
>
> The hospital shall keep all patients, men and women, until they are completely recovered. All costs are to be borne by the hospital whether the people come from afar or near whether they are residents or foreigners, strong or weak, rich or poor, employed or unemployed, blind or sighted, physically or mentally ill, learned or illiterate. There are no conditions of consideration and payment, none is objected to or even indirectly hinted at for non-payment. The entire service is through the magnificence of Allah, the generous one.

Salāh al-Dīn followed a policy firmly set in place since the days of the Prophet. It was Muhammad who first diplomatically said to believers of other gods, "I do not worship what you worship, you do not worship what I worship ... you have your religion and I have mine."[248] The gains made in medicine and science during Islam's Golden Age could only emerge in a culture that not only tolerated different opinions, but actively sought them out.

In 1258, Islam's Golden Age came to an end when Genghis Khan's grandson led a Mongol invasion into Baghdad, killing many scholars and destroying the House of Wisdom. It's been said the **Tigris River** turned black with ink because of all the books that were thrown in the river. If the Mongols hoped to erase the legacy of Islamic scholarship, however, they were bound to be disappointed. Nearly a thousand years later, Muslims and non-Muslims continue to draw on those years as inspiration for a time when Islamic rulers encouraged the People of the Book to brainstorm together and strengthen their powers.

In 2006, Kuwaiti psychologist Naif Al-Mutawa created ***The 99***, a comic book series based on compassionate Muslim virtues that blossomed in the Golden Age. The story arc begins with 99 gemstones that were dropped into the Tigris River to soak up the wisdom from the books that were destroyed in the war. These gemstones give their bearers superpowers to work together and combat modern evils. The gemstones also update to modern times, reflecting Al-Mutawa's belief that the Qur'an is "a living, breathing document," that needs to be continuously refreshed and reinterpreted to keep the core medieval values relevant today.

In 2010, *The 99* joined forces with the Justice League of America, bringing together Muslim superheroes with Western comic icons like Superman and Batman, characters created by Jewish artists at a time of rampant anti-Semitism in Europe and the Middle East. Working together to fight hatred and intolerance was a common theme of Islam's Golden age. If the millions of *99* comics sold every year are any indication, it's a theme that still carries traction with Muslim children around the world.

Sufi Love and Longing

Not everyone was satisfied with Islam's popularity and material success of the Golden Age. As more and more cities contributed to the riches of the growing Islamic empire, many Muslims were concerned that people were becoming too enamoured of the things of the world, forgetting the Qur'anic message of fraternity and friendship. Religious ascetics began to leave behind their riches to live in closer proximity to God. They were called "Sufis," after the word for the coarse wool favored by ascetics of the time.

Sufis frequently eschewed public rituals and grandiose displays of piety, in favor of joining themselves more personally and directly with God. Because such avenues tended to bypass the hierarchical power structures of the Muslim capitals, impoverished women could earn respect and followers alongside wealthier men.

In the eighth century, **Rābi'a** of Basra (Iraq), "a stranger ... an orphan, a slave," was favoured by God because, as one medieval biographer notes, she was "on fire with love and longing."[249] More than performing the rites and practices, Sufis emphasized the dignity of eternal longing.

"The groaning and the yearning of the lover of God will not be satisfied until it is satisfied in the Beloved," Rābi'a once said.[250]

In 1095, the most famous theology professor of the Middle Ages quit his job in Basra because he lost his confidence that one could live a meaningful life by focusing merely on reading, writing, and teaching. While he compiled and parroted the wisdom of the ancients, **al-Ghazali** accepted the accolades, all the while feeling like he was standing "on the brink of a crumbling bank of sand."

Restless for something he couldn't quite place. al-Ghazali wrote, "Worldly desires were striving to keep me by their chains just where I was while the voice of faith was calling, 'To the road! to the road!'"[251]

Once al-Ghazali left his familiar and easy life, he became a stranger to himself and others. But being out of his comfort zone allowed the ex-professor to open himself to new ways of learning. As the famous Sufi **al-Arabi** argued, "we should be completely and utterly receptive to all doctrinal forms, for God, Most High, is too All-embracing and Great to be confined within one creed rather than another."[252]

On the road, Al-Ghazali soon learned that many Sufi Muslims drew on their feelings of isolation and spiritual

al-Arabi

Those who define love have not known it, those who have not tasted it by drinking it down have not known it, and those who say they have been quenched by it have not known it, for love is drinking without quenching.

restlessness to experience God's love more directly. Through desperate prayers, spontaneous singing, and physical activity, Sufis experienced first-hand the unity between God and humans.

For Sufi poets like **Rūmī,** it is the longing for love that is evidence of our connection to God. In one famous poem he compares a love for God with the longing of a reed flute cut from its roots and crying out through its music.

> Now listen to this reed-flute's deep lament
> About the heartache being apart has meant:
> "Since from the reed-bed they uprooted me
> My song's expressed each human's agony."[253]

In another poem Rūmī describes a man who has lost his fortune. "This man was empty, and the tears came." He leaves his home in Baghdad to become a stranger in Cairo, in search of something more than gold. Eventually he learns that God's love was with him always. "What I'm longing for lived in my house in Baghdad!" he realized. "But I had to come this long way to know it!"[254]

Today, people read Rūmī in hundreds of languages throughout the world. He continues to be the most popular poet translated in the English language, though he lived nearly 1,000 years ago. Through Rūmī, the Muslim longing of love speaks to us across the centuries. Calling out together is a way bringing us together. It's why many Muslim scholars believe "the unitive nature of Sufism is a powerful remedy for the disintegrated life from which so many people in the modern world suffer."[255]

Naguib Mahfouz's *Cairo Trilogy*

When **Naguib Mahfouz** accepted his Nobel Prize for literature in 1988, he boasted of Egypt's roots in Islam's Golden Age, and "the fraternity between religions and races that has been achieved in its embrace in a spirit of tolerance unknown to Mankind neither before nor since." More broadly, Mahfouz spoke of the artist's role in saving us from defeatism and powerlessness. "In this decisive moment in the history of civilization," he explained, "it is inconceivable and unacceptable that the moans of Mankind should die out in the void.... And just as scientists exert themselves to cleanse the environment of industrial pollution, intellectuals ought to exert themselves to cleanse humanity of moral pollution."[256] If such intellectuals were once again emerging from the Islamic world, so much the better.

In his seminal novel of the 1950s, **The Cairo Trilogy**, Mahfouz develops his favorite longstanding theme: everyday Muslims negotiating their daily tasks in the bustling streets and cramped quarters of old Cairo. There are criminals, hypocrites, lovers and revolutionaries, religious zealots, and bawdy singers. Especially singers. In the seedy lounges of old Cairo, the living pulse of Islam was coarsely expressed in tambourine time and transcendent shouting by holy, larger-than-life women. It's no coincidence that the names of Mahfouz's two real-life daughters recall two worlds: "Fatima," the sacred name of the Prophet's Muhammad's daughter, and "Um Kulthum," a nod to Egypt's most popular entertainer.

The three books of *The Cairo Trilogy*, *Palace Walk*, *Palace of Desire*, and *Sugar Street*, follow three generations of Egyptian Muslims who juggle their relationships, their faith, their ideas, their families and their country, while forces of destruction press ever closer. As one Israeli journalist writes, Mahfouz "speaks to all his readers because his stories are the stories of a struggle for things that are worthy in themselves in a ruthless and debilitating existential situation.... He hopes that he will arouse them to think, to be courageous, to struggle for justice and for beauty."[257]

Palace Walk

Mahfouz's first book in *The Cairo Trilogy* focuses on the Ahmad family: the moderately successful merchant al-Sayyid, his wife Amina, their two daughters, and three sons.

Amina is the caricature of the obedient Muslim housewife at the end of World War I. Worried only about her family, Amina is scarcely curious about the clashing world outside her home. "She did not feel in need of further education or suspect there was any new knowledge worth adding to the religious, historical, and medical information she already possessed."[258]

Amina never leaves her apartment, except for one fateful day when she dresses in disguise and sneaks off to pray at the **al-Hussein Mosque**. Before that she could only gaze on the mosque "with devotion, fascination, thanksgiving, and hope" from her rooftop garden.[259] At the mosque, Amina "sipped from the sweet spiritual waters of the shrine," but her journey ends abruptly when she breaks her collarbone in a car accident and is temporarily banished from the family for not knowing her place.

Her husband al-Sayyid is a controlling taskmaster at home, morphing into a lascivious tambourine player and carousing philanderer at night. Seducing a lounge singer, he carelessly jokes about Islam's stern ethical code, while privately apologizing to God. Such contradictions are not lost on the family, or his ex-lovers. As one intoxicated singer challenges him at his daughter's wedding party, "Why do you pretend to be pious around your family when you're a pool of depravity?"[260] Though the local **sheik** often cautions him against the sins he commits after hours, al-Sayyid can't tear himself away from the seductive pleasures of modern Egypt. Once the tambourines begin to shake, the unfaithful husband must confront the nightly defeat of the sternly religious family man he once aspired to become.

Palace of Desire

Of the five children, Kamal becomes the focus of the second book in the trilogy. His passion for religious studies vindicates his mother and bewilders his father. "Religion's one thing and men who make a career of it are something else," his father says disdainfully.[261] To the men of his father's generation, it's better to be an "esteemed bureaucrat" than a "wretched teacher."

Kamal, however, is not so easily deterred. "He could not understand how money entered into the question of learning.... He believed too deeply in its intrinsic value for his faith to be shaken."[262] Social status was one more trapping of the secular world. Instead, Kamal gravitated toward philosophy. "What is God? What is man? What is the spirit? What is matter?"[263] Those were the questions that interested him more than a life of commerce or law.

Throughout the second book, Kamal comes to realize that the youth of his generation also look down on the life of faith. On a picnic to the ancient pyramids outside of Cairo, Kamal notices differences between himself and his first true love, Aïda. A lover of French romance novels, Aïda is more familiar with newer European values than the older Muslim tradition. She drinks beer, eats ham sandwiches, and doesn't fast on Ramadan. She's long forgotten the Qur'anic sura "which speaks about God's unity and so forth," though it's only four verses long.[264]

In the end, Kamal rightly suspects Aïda looks down on him. His apartment is too small, his head is too big, his hair is too short, and perhaps implied in her rebuff, he's simply too Muslim.

Disillusioned with his religion and unfulfilled in his relationships, Kamal crosses the line when he publishes a paper in support of Charles Darwin's claim that humans come from animals instead of from God. Does Kamal's embrace of evolutionary science "announce the demise of his religious beliefs,"[265] or is it more complicated? Islam's Golden Age showed the world that the struggle between religion and science could be explored and confronted within a religious tradition. Though there are no easy answers, in science or religion, for Muslim intellectuals like Mahfouz, "that debate, no matter how painful, is better than resignation and slumber."[266]

Sugar Street

Mahfouz's final book in the trilogy follows Kamal's teenage nephews, Abd al-Muni'm and Ahmad. One brother joins the Muslim Brotherhood, a newly formed organization "with the goal of reviving Islam, intellectually and practically."²⁶⁷ The other brother stops performing his religious duties and finds work at *The New Man*, a socialist magazine that champions science.

At the end of the trilogy both brothers end up in prison for their beliefs. For Mahfouz, a fanatical insistence on religious precepts is as problematic as a righteous atheism that only serves to "destroy everything that makes man a human being."²⁶⁸

Rather than dictate one form of life over another, Mahfouz reminds us that the spirit of Islam welcomes all of its followers to find their own way. The journey should be encouraged, not coerced or shut down. "I see no problem in calling peoples to live in peace with each other on the basis of Islam," Mahfouz once said. "Such a calling fully accords with our faith."²⁶⁹

Malcolm X Walks the *Hajj*

In 1946 Malcolm Little began his sentence in Boston's Charlestown State Prison. In the fiercely segregated cities of America, it wasn't uncommon for a poor, orphaned black man to end up in jail for petty theft and larceny. Neither was it uncommon for the forgotten prisoners to seek belonging, guidance, and hope from religion, and specifically, Islam.

In prison Malcolm was introduced to the basic tenets of Islam. Soon after, the "petty criminal and trickster had transformed himself into Malcolm X, a serious political intellectual and Black Muslim."²⁷⁰ One of his first political acts of resistance was helping Muslim prisoners move into cells that faced Mecca. "I believe in religion," Malcolm would later say, "but a religion that includes political, economic, and social action."²⁷¹

Upon his parole from prison in 1952, Malcolm X quickly shot to prominence as one of the most important civil rights leaders of the 1950s and '60s. His eloquence, confidence, and spiritual discipline inspired a generation of American activists from poet laureate Maya Angelou to boxing champion Muhammad Ali.

In 1964, Malcolm sought to deepen his faith by embarking on the *hajj*. Participating in the ancient tradition that follows the footsteps of Abraham, Hagar, and the prophet Muhammad marked a decisive change in Malcolm's political views. Like so many Muslim pilgrims, Malcolm was most impressed with how the pilgrims saw each other as equals, regardless of social class or race. "All ate as One, and slept as One," Malcolm wrote. "Everything about the pilgrimage atmosphere accented the Oneness of Man under One God."[272]

> ### *The Autobiography of Malcolm X*
>
> The hardest test I ever faced in my life was praying.... Picking a lock to rob someone's house was the only way my knees had ever been bent before.
>
> I had to force myself to bend my knees. And waves of shame and embarrassment would force me back up.
>
> For evil to bend its knees, admitting its guilt, to implore the forgiveness of God, is the hardest thing in the world.... When finally I was able to make myself stay down—I didn't know what to say to Allah.

In Mecca, Malcolm met white people who didn't appear to harbor the deep stains of racism he faced back home. Struck by "*color-blindness* of the Muslim world's religious society and the *color-blindness* of the Muslim world's human society,"[273] Malcolm began to see a way out of insipid stereotyping and prejudices. "America needs to understand Islam," he wrote, "because this is the one religion that erases from its society the race problem."[274]

Islam taught Malcolm that the oneness of God also implied the oneness of humanity. Surrendering to the one God, he believed, could cause us to focus on our sameness rather than our differences. The *hajj* inspired Malcolm to imagine a future when we would "cease to measure, and hinder, and harm others in terms of their 'differences' in color."[275]

Benazir Bhutto and the Challenges of Democracy

In 1988 **Benazir Bhutto** was sworn in as the new prime minister of Pakistan. Just 35 years old, Bhutto became the youngest prime minister in the world. If the rest of the world was surprised that an Islamic country had its first-ever female leader, such gender concerns were lost on Bhutto. "Throughout the Holy Quran, there is example after example of respect for women as leaders and acknowledgment of women as equals," she wrote.[276]

The Prophet Muhammad's wife was a businesswoman, after all. If Khadija never gave up who she was after she married, why would Bhutto? After her arranged marriage, Bhutto did not take the name of her husband. "I'm not giving myself away. I belong to myself and I always shall," she said definitively.[277]

Pakistan has long posed difficult challenges for its Muslim leaders. Many of its leaders receive secular education in the very best universities of Europe and the United States. Bhutto herself was a Harvard graduate before moving to England to become student president of the Oxford Union. After the terrorist attacks of 9/11, Pakistan became a critical ally in America's war on terror, but it also provided safe haven to Osama bin Laden, the mastermind of the attacks. To this day the Waziristan region near the border with Afghanistan is a hotbed for the most violent offshoots of Islamic **fundamentalism**.

Benazir Bhutto on a visit to the United States in 1988.

118 • *Enchanted Wisdom*

Malala Yousafzai (centre) meets with U.S. President Barack Obama, First Lady Michelle Obama (second from left) and their daughter Malia at the White House in October 2013.

Can we reconcile so many seemingly contradictory paths of Islam under one banner? Bhutto thought it was possible and she used the story of Muhammad as inspiration. "Islam is committed not only to tolerance and equality but to the principles of democracy."[278] Bhutto believed we need to return to the Qur'anic roots of living and working together, while respecting one another's differences. She noted how "the vast majority of the billion Muslims in the world embrace a peaceful, tolerant, open, rational, and loving religion that codifies democratic values."[279]

Throughout her political life Bhutto was imprisoned numerous times for standing up for Islamic democracy in Pakistan. Time and again she survived violent challenges, until she was assassinated by a suicide bomber in 2008. Bhutto's life story details the tensions that many Pakistani women struggle with today. For example, in 2012, a 15-year-old education activist, **Malala Yousafzai**, was shot by a **Taliban** gunman on her way home from school in Pakistan. She survived the attack and just one year later, Malala delivered a speech to the United Nations wearing a pink shawl that once belonged to Bhutto. It was Bhutto's courage that first inspired millions of girls like Malala. In 2014, Malala was awarded the Nobel Peace Prize for her efforts to help all girls receive formal education. In her Nobel acceptance speech, Malala reminded us "that the very first word of the Holy Quran is the word '*Iqra*,' which means 'read.'"

In the new generation of Pakistani girls like Malala, Bhutto's unwavering belief that lasting democratic solutions are born from the ancient roots of Islam resound as loudly as ever. Bhutto reminds us that to this day, Islam "is an open, pluralistic, and tolerant religion—a positive force in the lives of more than one billion people across this planet, including millions in the growing populations of Europe and the United States."[280] If we're looking for well-trodden ways to get along with each other today, that's probably a good place to start.

Discovery Questions

1. Set your phone alarm every three hours one day. When it's time, stop what you're doing, go somewhere quiet, and reflect on your day. How did it feel? In what ways were you inconvenienced?

2. Go online and listen to some of the long, ecstatic songs of Egyptian singer Umm Kulthum. Do they strike you as love songs? Religious songs? How does the music make you feel?

3. Watch one of the animated episodes of Naif Al-Mutawa's *The 99* available online. How are some of the central themes of Islam exemplified in the episode you selected?

4. Describe a strong woman in your life. What similar character traits does this person have to Zaynab or Malala?

5. Watch Malcolm X's *Letters from Hajj*. How did his pilgrimage to Mecca inspire his struggle for social action?

6. Listen to NPR's 2005 "On Being" interview with Muslim scholar Leila Ahmed ("Muslim Women and Other Misunderstandings"). What misunderstandings does Ahmed describe? What issues does she raise about wearing the veil?

7. Play some music quietly in your room on repeat six or seven times. Dance in slow circles, the same speed each time. How did you feel by the end? Did you feel or think differently as the song repeated?

Glossary

Terms	Definitions
Abu Bakr	Companion and father-in-law of the Prophet Muhammed; Muhammad's rightful successor, according to Sunni tradition
Abu Talib	Uncle of the Prophet Muhammad
***Al-Aqsa* Mosque**	A holy site within Islam that marks the place from which the Prophet Muhammad began the Night Journey
Al-Arabi	12th-century Muslim mystic philosopher and scholar
Al-Ghazali	11th-century Islamic scholar and theologian
Al-Hussein Mosque	Burial place of Hussein ibn Ali in Cairo, Egypt
Ali	Son-in-law of the Prophet Muhammad; Muhammad's rightful successor, according to Shi'a tradition
Ashura	Day of mourning for Hussein's sacrifice
Benazir Bhutto	Pakistan's first female prime minister (1988–1990, 1993–1996)

Five Pillars	The Profession of Faith, Daily Observance, Charity, Fasting, and Pilgrimage
Fundamentalism	Unwavering dedication to a set of core religious beliefs or texts
Gabriel	Archangel who served as an intermediary between the Prophet Muhammed and God
Hagar	Handmaiden of Abraham's wife Sarah and mother of Abraham's son Ishmael
Hajj	Pilgrimage to Mecca
Hijra	Historic migration of the Prophet from Mecca to Medina
House of Wisdom	Grand Library of Baghdad, Iraq in Islam's Golden Age
Hussein ibn Ali	Grandson of the Prophet Muhammad; slain in Karbala in 680
Ibn Sina	Prominent Muslim physician and philosopher
Karbala	A city in modern-day Iraq that served as the battlefield between Hussein and Yazid
Khadija	Wife of the Prophet Muhammad; the first person to convert to Islam
Malala Yousafzai	Contemporary Pakistani activist and youngest Nobel Prize laureate
Malcolm X	American Muslim and civil rights activist
Martyrs	Those who are killed for their religious beliefs
Mecca	Birthplace of Islam and the Prophet Muhammad; located in today's Saudi Arabia
Medina	The second holiest city in Islam; located in today's Saudi Arabia
Muhammad	The main prophet and founder of Islam
Musa al-Sadr	A Lebanese spiritual leader in the Shi'a sect of Islam
Naguib Mahfouz	20th-century Egyptian writer and Nobel Prize laureate
Night Journey	Spiritual and physical ascent of the Prophet Muhammad
People of the Book	Jews, Christians and Muslims
Qur'an	Central revealed text of Islam
Rābi'a	Eighth-century Muslim Sufi mystic
Ramadan	Holy month of fasting in Islam
Rūmī	13th-century Sufi mystic and poet
Salāh al-Dīn	Unifier and first sultan of Egypt and Syria; founder of the Ayyubid dynasty
Sheik	An Arab leader or chief
Shi'ite	One who follows the Shi'a sect of Islam, popular in Iran and Lebanon
Sunni	One who follows the Sunni sect of Islam, the largest denomination of Islam
Taliban	Sunni Islamic fundamentalist movement based in Afghanistan

The 99	Animated series created by Naif Al-Mutawa
The Cairo Trilogy	Epic trilogy of colonial Egypt written by Nobel Prize laureate Naguib Mahfouz
The Canon of Medicine	Influential encyclopedia of medicine written by Ibn Sina
Tigris River	Iraqi river cutting through some of the most ancient known civilizations
Translation Movement	Massive Medieval effort to translate Greek philosophy, Babylonian science, and Hindu mathematics into the Arabic language
Waqfa	Document that highlights the charity of inheritance, approved by Islamic law
Zaynab	Outspoken critic of the Yazid ruler; the granddaughter of the Prophet Muhammad

ILLUSTRATION: ANNOTATED VERSION OF THE CONFUCIAN BOOK OF RITES, FROM BEFORE 907 CE

Part Three
LIVING TOGETHER

CHAPTER EIGHT
Confucianism: Family Harmony

CHAPTER NINE
Sikhism: Resisting Conformity

CHAPTER TEN
Navajo: Land of the People

CHAPTER ELEVEN
Shintoism: One with Nature

Chapter Eight
Confucianism
Family Harmony

In 2006, China's Central Television station broadcast a series of lectures by **Yu Dan**, a professor of media studies at Beijing Normal University. The subject was a modern understanding of Confucius' *Analects*. Yu Dan believed that the ancient past could teach us something vital about ourselves today. Specifically, she argued, "The wisdom of Confucius can help us to attain spiritual happiness in the modern world, to get used to the daily routine of our lives, and to find the personal bearings to tell us where we are."[281]

Confucianism is the religion that emerged from the Master's ancient teachings on ethics, comportment, and wisdom. Confucius (551–479 BCE) believed himself to be no more than a teacher or transmitter of ancient Chinese practices and behaviors. An avid reader of ancient Chinese texts that were steadily falling into obscurity, Confucius believed a growing apathy to ancestral history would leave people uprooted, spiritually empty, and ethically weakened. He therefore went against the tide of popular opinion and openly advocated for a more rigorous study of the ancient ways. Specifically he emphasized the value of dedicating time to studying the **Five Classics** of ancient China that included peasant songs, traditional codes of conduct, and theories on the origins of the cosmos.

Yu Dan's book, based on the televised lectures, was a runaway bestseller, reaching over 10 million people. While it's not uncommon to hear a Chinese scholar discuss the relevance of ancient wisdom today, nobody could predict just how well her teachings on Confucius would be received by so many different segments of the population, most of whom would not have considered themselves Confucianists.

"Be thoroughly versed in the old, and understand the new," Confucius said over 2,000 years ago.[282] What buried treasures did Confucius dig up from the ancient past, and why are millions of people in China and around the world so eager to discover the mystery for themselves?

From Thought to Action

The core of Confucius' teachings is detailed in the **Four Books**. Of these four books, the most popular is the ***Analects***, a collection of Confucius' aphorisms and snippets of revealing dialogue between the Master (as Confucius is often referred to) and his disciples.

Confucius constantly bemoaned that he was living in a dangerous time when people were easily ruled by fear and profit. Students only wanted to make their private fortunes. They therefore looked to copy and regurgitate answers, and that only when required. Few people had the motivation or the capability to think for themselves. In one famous remark, Confucius claimed that if he held up one side of a square, he expected his students to come back with the other three sides. But that happened rarely.

Confucius teaches us that we can take pleasure in learning rather than always seeing it as a chore. In the very first line of the *Analects*, "The Master said, Studying, and from time to time going over what you learned—that's enjoyable isn't it?" Studying the world means learning about ourselves and where we fit into this vast and constantly changing universe. The mystery of it should help supply us with a lifetime of questions that we can happily return to throughout our lives.

Kano Tan'yû (1602–1674), *Confucius and His Disciples Yanzi and Huizi at the Apricot Altar.*

Time and again Confucius reminds us that learning for learning's sake is insufficient. Memorizing formulas night and day was not the solution to complex social ailments. Instead, we also need experiential learning that applies our studies to real-life situations. "The Master said, A man may be able to recite all three hundred odes, but if you assign him as an envoy to some neighboring state and he can't give his answers unassisted, then no matter how many odes he might know, what good is he?"[283]

There's no point in blandly memorizing facts if you don't have the courage to put them into action. The 12th-century Confucianist **Zhu Xi** put it more succinctly. He wrote, "The student takes it and puts it into practice."[284] Spending too much time studying what others have said is fruitless at best and cowardly at worst. When told about a respected scholar and politician who always thought things over three times before doing anything, Confucius's answer was simple. "Twice is enough."[285]

Learning past history is only valuable if it helps us to do what's right in the present. The goal is not simply to print more books, but to develop **ren**, or humanity. *Ren* involves deepening empathy for others, recognizing their suffering and lifting them up through good words and deeds. Paying closer attention to how we comport ourselves in the world shows others what we respect and value, and the quality of our concerns. When we make it clear in our everyday interactions that small things matter, the bigger things tend to take care of themselves.

In Chinese the word *ren* (see next page) is written with two horizontal lines, which represent ourselves and our relationship with others. Attaining *ren* can never be accomplished in isolation. Confucianists maintain that "the virtue of humanity is meaningless unless it is involved in actual human relationships."[286] We need others to develop ourselves. Or put another way, we become our best selves in concert with others. Without this reciprocity, love is unfulfilled, societies fracture, and empires fall. In such times, simple acts of kindness are more important than ever.

ren

In the Confucian universe the human being is never powerless. Small changes in the way we act help to effect big changes in society. But self-cultivation, like studying the past, takes a lifetime to put into practice "Extend yourself," Zhu Xi wrote, "and bring it [empathy] to perfection so that even the selflessness of a sage does not surpass it. Wouldn't it make good sense to practice this for the whole of your life?"[287]

When people care so much to study others and make changes in themselves, humanity transforms into something more enchanted. Confucianists call it *he*, or harmony.

Living in Harmony

In Confucianism, the **sage** is someone who uses what they have learned to spread humanity. In Chinese, the word "sage" includes the root of the symbol "to listen." Humans have their own rhythms that constantly change and develop. Attuning oneself to such social cues is closely aligned with appreciating music. If we practice really hearing the music, we can better attune ourselves to the rhythms all around us.

Listening to music can also make our ordinary tasks more bearable, more meaningful, even more religious. Ancient Chinese farmers and townspeople frequently sang songs while they worked. These songs enchanted Confucius, hundreds of years later. Confucius is believed to have archived over three thousand songs, choosing only one-tenth of them for his classic *Book of Songs*.

Compiling the songs was more than a pleasant diversion for the Master, however. For Confucius, studying the *Book of Songs* could motivate us "to pursue self-cultivation, to exercise one's creative imagination, to ascend to levels of heightened awareness, and to develop a deepened sense of sociability."[288] Without such musical education, Confucius feared a humane and happy life was simply not possible.

All of us are consumed with conflicting emotions throughout our lives, some good and others less so. Listening to music is a tried and true way to calm our anxieties and order our emotions. "When one has mastered completely [the principles of] music, and regulates his heart and mind accordingly, the natural, correct, gentle and honest heart is easily developed."[289] When all of our natural, human emotions are given space to express themselves, "and all attain due measure and degree, it is called harmony."[290]

Music can also be used as a metaphor for how best to govern others. As anyone playing in a band knows all too well, terrific musicians can still perform poorly. So much depends on how well the

Xunzi

The Book of Music
Music is something which the sage kings found joy in, for it has the power to make good the hearts of the people, to influence men deeply, and to reform their ways... If the people have emotions of love and hatred, but no ways in which to express their joy or anger then they will become disordered. Because the former kings hated such disorder, they reformed the actions of the people and created proper music for them, and as a result the world became obedient.

bandmates listen to each other and make adjustments in real time. "The Master, speaking with the Grand Music Master of Lu, said, Music can be understood in this way. The players first in unison, then freely harmonizing, playing separately or carrying on from one another, and thus the piece is completed."[291]

Freely harmonizing means listening to each other and bringing out the best in other people, sometimes on the fly. Can we listen to people who don't share our politics? Can we still gel with people with whom we don't get along? If the answer to the above questions is yes, then we've learned some of music's most valuable lessons.

Beginning in the ninth century **neo-Confucianists** began organizing and interpreting Confucius' ideas into the coherent categories and ideals we still struggle to live up to today. Medieval Confucianists recognized that one bad apple can spoil the whole bunch. "When one man is greedy or avaricious, the whole country will be plunged into disorder."[292] Achieving harmony is always delicate. Rather than correcting or judging everyone's behavior, Confucianism teaches us how to listen and adjust our own personalities to live with others more harmoniously.

The Wisdom of our Ancestors

For Confucianists, learning the old songs is only the first step to attaining wisdom and harmony. The songs tell us something about our ancient ancestors, and our ancient ancestors tell us something about ourselves. Ignoring the past cuts us off from our roots and weakens our abilities to live a meaningful life, harmonizing with others and achieving *ren*.

Ancestor worship was popular in many Chinese folk traditions during Confucius' time. People prayed to or consulted with their dead relatives at important life junctures. Confucius never purported to understand what happens to the body or the soul when we die. Neither did he claim intimate knowledge of the gods or the spirits. But the Master passionately believed in observing the *li* (guides to rituals, etiquette, and comportment), passed down from long ago. "The veneration can serve important psychological functions as well as being an effective family glue. It contributes to our sense of who we are, and is of religious significance."[293]

More important than the rituals themselves is *how* we participate. What are our intentions? It's "more than jade or silk," just as making music is more than "bells or drums." If the musician is simply phoning it in, the passion and the art is sucked out of the performance. Similarly, if we half-heartedly pay respects to our ancestors, the world becomes a little colder, more robotic, less *humane*.

But are our ancestors actually listening to our pleas and our prayers? Intriguingly, Confucius had no idea. Instead of speaking knowingly of the heavens, Confucius preached the performance of ancient rituals "as if" the gods were present. That ignorance, he believed, was the core of all wisdom. "When you don't know, to know you don't know. That's what knowing is."[294]

Once we recognize that we don't really understand the ways of our ancestors, or what spiritual purpose their religious rituals provide, we approach history and religion with a renewed humility. Instead of confidently offering up our opinions on other people's practices, we might be better served by asking questions. "When the Master entered the Grand Temple, he asked questions about everything," because for Confucius, "asking is part of the ritual."[295] Asking questions is a critical component of showing interest in one's family history. It's the questions, more than the answers, that bind the present with the past.

Confucius' disciple, Hsiao Xing, wrote the **Book on Filial Piety**. He argued that the key to understanding *li*, and the importance of participating in ancient rituals, was to build deeper connections with the people of the past. "Given the Confucian emphasis on harmony," he wrote, "on the balance of opposing forces in the world, including the human world, it is to be expected that there is an emphasis on *li* in the family context."[296] Instead of solving our deepest questions, Confucianists implore us to show respect for the past by including its rituals in our everyday lives. In Confucianism, when people from different cultural and social backgrounds develop a humility for the questions and a passion for the ancient practices, a religious transformation takes place.

In China today, the Confucian ideal of venerating one's ancestors is as popular as ever. In 2008, in response to so many people invigorating the Confucian tradition, the Chinese government made April 5 a national holiday to honour one's ancestors. During the **Ching Ming Festival**, millions of people flock to cemeteries to weed, sweep, or otherwise beautify the gravestones of their loved ones. Relatives might also leave paper gifts resembling money, cars, or other signs of riches. Such modern enactments of ancient practices "point to a significant revival of a ritual practice that has long been claimed to be an essential part of the Confucian form of life, which takes filial piety as one of the most fundamental Confucian virtues."[297]

Filial Piety

Developing *ren* through personal relationships begins in the family. "Filial and brotherly conduct," Confucius said, "they are the root of humaneness, are they not?"[298]

Confucius believed showing reverence for one's parents involved much more than day-to-day care. It includes living in such a way that our parents' values can be readily apparent to everyone we meet. And not just during our lifetime, either. About a virtuous child, Confucius said, "While his father is alive, observe his intentions. After his father is dead, observe his actions."[299]

In one famous exchange, a government official bragged to Confucius about a boy so honest that he turned in his own father for stealing sheep. But Confucius wasn't impressed. Instead, the Master argued that family members should cover up for each other because "there's honesty in that, too."[300]

The point is that it does no good to talk about the state or the community when family relations are fractured. Lasting empires can only be built on the strength of pious children who respect their parents. **Mencius**, the "Second Sage," says it better: "Loving one's parents is benevolence; respecting one's elders is rightness. What is left to be done is simply the extension of these to the whole Empire."[301] When family

> ### Analects
> 2:6 Meng Wu Bo asked about filial devotion. The Master said, Your father and mother should have to worry only about your falling ill.
> 2:7 Ziyou asked about filial devotion. The Master said, Nowadays it's taken to mean just seeing that one's parents get enough to eat. But we do that much for dogs or horses as well. If there is no reverence, how is it any different?
> 2:8 Zixia asked about filial devotion. The Master said, The difficult part is the facial expression.

members know their place, they operate individually, but in harmony within their larger kinship groups.

In the aftermath of World War II, China embarked on a divisive **Cultural Revolution** that sought to permanently stamp out the Confucian tradition. But thousands of years of wisdom could not be made to simply disappear, and today Confucianism is in the midst of an unprecedented revival. The 17th-century "Rules for Students and Children" that reinforces proper behavior to parents, teachers, and elders is now ubiquitous in public schools, online, and sold in stores across China. In 2015, the Modern Filial Piety Culture Museum opened its doors to much publicity in China's Sichuan province. Combating modern feelings of loneliness and depression comes with a Confucian dose of family values.

But as many Chinese feminists have pointed out, such rigid family role-playing has been an all-too-easily available philosophy for people who want to justify unequal gender relations, providing ideological cover for keeping women in the home, subservient to their father in-laws, husbands, and sons. Traditionally, Confucian cultures across China and East Asia have made it easy to tune out the harmonic voices of half the population. "Only once in the Mencius, and never in the Analects, is there an expression of a woman's opinion—that of the wife of a man from Ch'i, who ironically is a fictional character."[302]

The question for many contemporary Confucianists is whether the tradition of filial piety still has something to contribute to more dynamic two-way relationships between men and women, children and parents, girls and boys. Can we "speak of the Confucian family in the modern context,"[303] and can we adapt its "robust, intricate, and well-articulated conceptions of family," to something "that is appropriate for the modern world"?[304]

Food for Thought

One thing often overlooked in the Confucian canon is the important role women have played in creating and enriching family harmony inside the home. Relegated to the kitchen and hidden from public view, mothers and daughters have long exemplified filial piety by passing on ancient values through the daily rituals of buying, preparing, and cooking food. Confucian rituals expressing filial piety are practiced every day, not only in male-dominated Confucian temples or elaborate prayer rooms, but also in simple, unadorned kitchens around the world.

The **wok** hanging in Confucian kitchens is, in many ways, a religious artifact. But it's not the kind of object to be preserved and protected in museums for tourists. The Confucian wok isn't meant to be worshipped from afar, but to be ritualistically warmed on a stove before joyous celebrations or ordinary family meals. The shape of the wok is designed for stir-frying different flavors, colors, and textures into one multi-sensory, delicious dish. As many Chinese-American chefs will tell you, the end goal is "the creation of harmony and balance among flavors."[305]

Cooking dumplings with a wok on an outdoor stove in Shenzhen, China.

In Confucian culture, food "is tradition, folklore, mythology, ritual, and religious observance as well as nutrition. Food is what commonly binds our families together," says one contemporary Chinese chef. Unlike the typical fast food available to most North American university students, Confucian meals recall "the enormous social, religious, and philosophical significance" of Chinese cooking.[306]

Such preparing, serving, and consuming of food has long been an important locus for Confucian ritual and wisdom. Mencius tells a story of Confucius walking out during a meal hosted by a local politician. The preparation was careless; no portions were reserved for the ancestors of old or the impoverished masses outside the gates. For Confucius, food preparation was always soaked through with ethical concerns. From the earliest days, "This rich world of food inspired an equally fascinating world of ideas."[307] Profound ideas can emerge from the disparate flavors that are joined together into one harmonious whole.

> ### Yuan Mei
> Sadly, today's people have forgotten the importance of considering the cultural roots of the host and cook when eating. Rather, they prefer to appease and humour each other at the expense of the cuisine. When a Han invites a Manchurian to eat Manchurian food, or a Manchurian invites a Han to eat Han food, what is served is a sad pastiche of the other culture's cuisine, prepared without the needed fundamental skills and technique; like a person trying to paint a majestic tiger but ending up with a mangy dog.... Such an individual will never achieve anything in life.

But *how* a meal is ritualistically cooked is equally important. "The dance of harmonizing the body through foods requires moderation and constant adjustment."[308] Adjusting temperature and taste takes an unusual focus that traditional chefs only develop through the cultivation of disciplined practice. Family cooks perform the time-consuming tasks because they care about what and how they serve others. "Into no department of life should indifference be allowed to creep: into none less than the domain of cookery."[309]

You can always tell if a person is faking virtue by the way they cook. Are they putting in the time? Are they using ingredients they chose for just this moment? Are they firing up the wok with love and compassion, and a desire to cultivate the diners they serve? Or are they thinking of themselves, cutting corners, saving money on cheaper ingredients? A person's character, says Mencius, "would be all over his face if he had to give away a basketful of rice and a bowlful of soup."[310]

Cooking for family meals can reveal how deeply the family members respect the Confucian value of filial piety. Modern Asian-American novelists like **Amy Tan** and **Kevin Kwan** write humorous cooking scenes that highlight the philosophy of sacrifice and tradition. Like the mother gently scolding her future daughter-in-law's dumpling-making technique in

> ### Amy Tan
> *The Joy Luck Club*
> I saw my mother on the other side of the room. Quiet and sad. She was cooking a soup, pouring herbs and medicines into the steaming pot. And then I saw her pull up her sleeve and pull out a sharp knife. She put this knife on the softest part of her arm. I tried to close my eyes, but could not.
> And then my mother cut a piece of meat from her arm. Tears poured from her face and blood spilled to the floor.
> My mother took her flesh and put it in the soup. She cooked magic in the ancient tradition to try to cure her mother this one last time....
> Even though I was young, I could see the pain of the flesh and the worth of the pain.
> This is how a daughter honors her mother.

Kwan's *Crazy Rich Asians*, initiation into age-old wisdom often happens in the kitchen.

A proper, ritualistically cooked meal harmonizes the Confucian values of *li* and *ren*. But only if the diner is equally prepared to chew on the philosophies stir-fried in the wok. It's no exaggeration to note that in the Confucian tradition, the "cutting of meat and cutting of words are one and the same thing."[311]

The Art of Calligraphy

The smallest details matter to Confucianists because they show the sincerity of our commitment to cultivating ourselves and doing right by others. For medieval Confucianists like **Chu Hsi**, everything, "even the meaning of one word or half a word," should be carefully examined.[312]

Because the Confucian sage is expected to use words seriously and cautiously, Chinese **calligraphy** has blossomed among scholars, philosophers and respected government officials. For over 2,000 years, calligraphy has been "widely celebrated as the soul of Chinese art."[313] Its long history of expressing core Confucian values in the most careful brush stroke is well documented in China and around the world.

Stories abound about how Confucius himself was a highly respected calligrapher. Modeling the brush strokes of previous sages is another example of showing respect for one's ancestors. "It also explains why it was a norm rather than an exception that Confucian literati throughout Chinese history have been accomplished calligraphy artists as well."[314]

It's not simply words themselves but the intentions and the philosophies behind them that are worthy of reverence. It might take years for a Chinese calligrapher to inscribe one worthy character. "Through calligraphy individuals are both taught discipline and given a sense of personal participation in a living culture of nearly incredible antiquity."[315]

In the Confucian universe, ordinary daily acts can and should be morally substantive. Writing brief notes is no exception. Do the brush strokes project something meaningful and original? Do we write in haste or with care? Does the ink "penetrate the wood," as **Sun Qianli** wrote in his landmark 13th-century treatise on calligraphy?[316]

Khoo Seow Hwa

Behind the Brushstrokes
In the hands of a master calligrapher, the brush opens up a fantastic array of artistic opportunities: the flow of black ink onto white paper, the twist of the brush, the delicate timing of a lift or a turn on a stroke are all fascinating. Chinese calligraphy can create the impression of music without sound, a melody for the eyes, as characters flow one after another in a rhythmic and pleasing pattern. One cannot resist falling for such beauty.

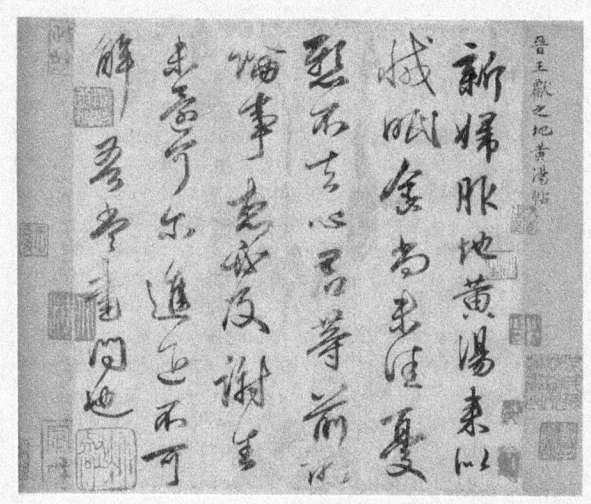

Wang Xizhi is the most famous example of a calligrapher whose brushstrokes could penetrate wood four inches deep. One story tells of a maid who scrubbed off Wang's inscription on a wooden table. However, because the inscription was written so powerfully, it magically reappeared on the table's surface.

Being substantive is not the same thing as being overly serious. It's worth keeping in mind that the most renowned work of calligraphy in the world was composed during a drinking game. Wang Xizhi completed his iconic "**Orchid Pavilion Preface**" in the year 353, after imbibing wine and challenging his lounging party guests to write poetry.

In modern times, Chinese calligraphers often use brushes made of animal hair, black ink ground down from fancy ink sticks (clockwise in a circular motion), a hollowed out ink stone for pouring in the ink, and fine paper (invented in China in the third century).

Though it may take years of discipline to master the particular brush strokes, the writing itself should be spontaneous and swift. If one goes back to correct a line, it will immediately appear sluggish and clumsy to the properly trained eye. The rhythm, balance, and delicacy of the calligrapher's brush stroke are often compared to the graceful movements of a dancer. The hand and the mind, the brush and the paper, even the symbols beside one another must work together in harmony or the art is lost.

Today, **Xu Bing**, China's most controversial contemporary calligrapher, is famous for composing symbols that challenge the religious significance of the written word. Created in 1991, his most famous installation, "A Book from the Sky," continues to tour museums and art galleries around the world. The installation consists of a number of open books underneath giant hanging sheets marked with 4,000 Chinese characters printed assiduously from his own woodcuts. But when you look a little closer you see they only look like Chinese characters. Xu Bing invented the entire language, divested of any apparent meaning at all.

Does the "book that refuses to be read"[317] show reverence for thousands of years of Confucian culture? Or is Xu Bing critiquing the sacred profundity of the art form? Or both? As one contemporary art critic writes, Xu Bing's artwork "calls attention to the ongoing crisis of modern China and at the same time calls into question any easy resolution of such a crisis which might be afforded by simple allegiance to culture and tradition."[318] The ancient Confucian tradition and the vicissitudes of modern life harmoniously intertwine in the modern art of calligraphy.

The Korean Wave

With its emphasis on education and filial piety, South Korea is considered one of the "four dragons" of Confucian culture that also includes Hong Kong, Taiwan, and Singapore. During the **Joseon Dynasty**, neo-Confucianism was installed as South Korea's state ideology. In more recent times, South Korean philosophers have been consistent contributors to developing New Confucianism schools of thought.

After the Asian economic crisis of the late 1990s, China's state television network began buying the rights to air Korean television shows across the country. The 2003–04 drama, *Dae Jang Geum (Jewel of the Palace)*, swept China by storm in 2005. The drama, based on a true story, features a young 16th-century chef who uses her knowledge of ancient herbs to become the Joseon king's top doctor.

Many scholars have noted how "the Confucian values embodied within Korean dramas such as harmony with community, respect for elders, filial duties, and loyalty to family and friends,"[319] resonate with Korean and Chinese audiences. *Dae Jang Geum*'s final episode was the most-watched television show in Hong Kong's history.

After the surprising success of *Dae Jang Geum*, a number of other Korean television shows flooded the Chinese market, a trend that continues to this day. Filial piety often features prominently in the shows. In one recent serial, *My Love from the Star*, the male lead is an alien from the 17th-century, trapped in a body of a university professor with a penchant for reading neo-Confucian texts.

In the wake of this television success, South Korean pop music bands started getting more airtime in China as well. **K-pop** rhythms enraptured Chinese audiences and became an international phenomenon almost overnight. Rising to the heights of K-pop stardom requires years of rigorous training. Along with studying Chinese and English, would-be stars may take 10 to 12 hours of dance and voice instruction per day, six days a week for up to seven years. Contemporary bands like **BTS** and **Girls' Generation** are known for bowing to their audience as a sign of Confucian humility.

BTS captivated North America with a whirlwind tour of the most popular television talk shows, and in 2018, became the first K-pop band to be nominated for a Grammy award. In their platinum-selling hit song "Mic Drop," they sing:

> Haters gon' hate
> Players gon' play

The songs may come with a catchy beat, but do these new mega K-pop bands spread Confucian values alongside the commercialism, plastic surgery, and mass idolatry? As is typical with everything K-pop, there are supporters and skeptics. "All the strivings to be a pop-culture star may be an expression of the new enriched and meritocratic South Korea, but it is surely opposed to the Confucian worldview," writes one South Korean sociology professor.[320]

K-pop's dance moves and rhythmic beats more closely resemble European house or American hip-hop music than any traditionally Confucian harmonies. The question for critics and superfans alike is how much of the ancient ways still amplifies the synchronized choreography, and how much of the Confucian past is inevitably drowned out by the Western beats.

Confucian Games

Every year in October, thousands of people come to the plaza outside Taiwan's Presidential Office Plaza to wash their parents' feet. This public zeal for teaching filial piety is organized by the Republic of China Sports Federation. The event highlights a longstanding connection between Confucianism and contemporary sports.

Dragon boat racing is one of the world's oldest competitive sports. Its Confucian emphasis on teamwork, harmony, and sacrifice appeals to amateurs and professionals alike. There are usually 22 athletes in a boat, including one steerer in the back and a drummer barking commands up front.

In myth, the ancient contest is attributed to the fall of the famed poet and political adviser **Qu Yuan**. Much revered by neo-Confucianists for over two thousand years, Qu Yuan was an exemplar of Confucian loyalty. Banished by his own duke for advising against an unethical alliance, Qu Yuan wandered alone, composing his most enduring poetry. In the final stanza of his famous poem, *Li Sao*, the disgraced adviser echoes Confucius' skepticism about the moral character of popular politicians. "[N]one is worthy to work with in making good government," Qu Yuan wrote, before drowning himself in China's Miluo River.

Local fishermen in dragon boats desperately tried but failed to rescue Qu Yuan on the fifth day of the fifth month of Chinese **lunar calendar**. Now an official state holiday in China, the Dragon Boat Festival is celebrated in Yueyang (Qu Yuan's hometown) and around the world with racing competitions and sticky rice dumplings wrapped in bamboo leaves.

Today, dragon boat racers "make the person beside, in front, and behind them better. The sum total of the crew is greater than the sum of its parts."[321] The sport's fast-growing popularity is a lasting tribute to Qu Yuan and this Confucian ideal.

During the opening ceremony of the 2008 Summer Olympics in Beijing, Confucian disciples chanted the famous line from the first verse of the *Analects*: "Friends have come from afar, how happy we are." After the magnificent display, the athletes marched into Beijing National Stadium. They represented over 10,000 athletes from 204 countries. Following the Confucian-inspired opening, so many different people with so many different values marched together in rhythmic harmony.

Outside of sports, many political philosophers today are starting to recognize how the Confucian ideal of harmony can help us negotiate a globalized world that is always in danger of slipping us further into the modern traps of nationalism, intolerance, and xenophobia. In contrast, Confucian harmony "is an attempt to seek common ground for different opinions, commitments, and ideological orientations. It presupposes diversity, recognizing the other and celebrating difference."[322] After thousands of years, thinking through and enacting the ancient Confucian values of humanity and harmony appears to be more urgent than ever.

Discovery Questions

1. In the *Analects* (7:20) we are told that Confucius never talked about "strange occurrences, feats of strength, rebellion, the gods." Why not? What do the subjects have in common?

2. Describe the different kinds of music you listen to at different times or in different moods (i.e., for studying, driving, dancing, times when you're feeling happy, lonely, depressed). How does the music help reorder your emotions? Would a world without music change you in any ethically meaningful way?

3. Describe a much older relative whom you respect. Which character traits of theirs do you hope to emulate? How do you express your admiration? Describe some interactions with them that you regret. What could you have done differently? Why does it matter?

4. Find an online translation of the *Mencius*. Choose one passage that speaks to a political issue today. How would you change Mencius' answer to find the best solution?

5. Watch an episode of the 2012 reality show, *K-POP: Extreme Survival*. Which interactions on the show would Confucius appreciate and which interactions would he criticize? Why?

6. Read the introduction to a cookbook you have in your home. What connections are made between good food and a good life? Are there stories in the book, or only recipes? How might personal stories change the way the food is prepared?

7. Watch a YouTube clip of the opening ceremony of the 2008 Summer Olympics. How are some features of traditional China expressed? What connections do you find between religion and sports in your own culture?

Glossary

Terms	Definitions
Amy Tan	20th-century Chinese-American novelist
Analects	Ancient compilation of Confucius' moral teaching
Ancestor worship	Prayers honoring or consulting deceased relatives
Book on Filial Piety	Treatise explaining how to respect one's elders, written by Confucius' disciple, Hsiao Xing
BTS	Contemporary South Korean boy band; abbreviation for *Beyond The Scene*
Calligraphy	Ancient style of decorative writing
Ching Ming Festival	Spring festival that celebrates and worships ancestors

Chu Hsi	12th-century Confucian philosopher
Cultural Revolution	Anti-Confucian nationalist movement led by Mao Zedong from 1966 to 1976
Dae Jang Geum	Korean drama series that first aired in 2003; translated as *Jewel of the Palace*
Dragon boat racing	Ancient competitive sport in which athletes must coordinate their movements to maximize rowing speed
Five Classics	Ancient texts containing peasant songs, etiquette instruction, and genealogies of creation
Four Books	Foundational Confucian texts: *Analects*, *Mencius*, *Doctrine of the Mean* and the *Great Learning*
Girls' Generation	Contemporary South Korean girl band
He	Confucian concept of harmony
Joseon Dynasty	Korean period of rule from the 14th to 19th century
K-pop	Korean-based genre of popular music that involves intricately choreographed modern dance moves
Kevin Kwan	20th-century Singaporean-American author
Li	A Confucian value referring to ritual action
Li Sao	Ancient Confucian poem composed by Qu Yuan
Lunar calendar	Calendar based upon the monthly phases of the moon
Mencius	Most famous ancient Confucian interpreter and philosopher
Neo-Confucianism	11th-century revival of Confucian philosophy intended to differentiate it from other Chinese religions and philosophies of the time
"Orchid Pavilion Preface"	Fourth-century poetry written by Wang Xizhi in calligraphy
Qu Yuan	Ancient Confucian poet and political adviser
Ren	Confucian value referring to humanity, harmony, and altruism
Sage	One who utilizes their knowledge to spread humanity
Sun Qianli	Seventh-century calligrapher
Wang Xizhi	Third-century calligrapher
Wok	Ancient bowl-shaped pan used for stir-fry cooking
Xu Bing	Contemporary Chinese artist
Yu Dan	Contemporary professor of media studies at Beijing Normal University
Zhu Xi	12th-century Confucian philosopher

Chapter Nine
Sikhism
Resisting Conformity

The *Koh-I-Noor* diamond (or "Mountain of Light") is not the biggest, boldest, or the shiniest jewel in the world. Yet it stands out as one of the most valuable gems in the Queen of England's collection of crown jewels, admired by millions of visitors every year. It's said the diamond was unearthed in the time of Krishna and is invested with special powers.

In the 17th century it was placed in the head of a carved peacock, atop the Shah's throne, the seat of power for the **Mughal Empire**. As the Sikhs grew in prestige, the diamond changed hands again, but not for the last time. In 1849, Britain formally annexed much of the Sikh lands and forced the 10-year old Sikh prince **Duleep Singh** to cede the diamond to Queen Victoria. His precious gem was cut to shine more brilliantly in the Queen's crown where, as Lord Dalhousie said, "it shall shine, and shine, too, with purest ray serene."

The Prince was whisked away from his home, and forcefully separated from his Sikh heritage. His fate was similar to millions of Sikhs of the 19th and 20th century, diminished and displaced. And yet, like the Koh-I-Noor diamond, so many of them aspire to shine forth sometimes far from home, "and shine, too, with purest ray serene."

Guru Nanak's Multicultural Revolution
In 1469, **Guru Nanak** was born to Hindu parents in **Punjab**, in the town of Talvandi, 80 kilometres southwest of **Lahore**. Throughout the Middle Ages, Sufi poets and Hindu mystics roamed the Punjab from village to village, communing with the householders and counseling the needy. This rich tradition of singing, dancing, and devoutly loving God would have a lasting impact on Guru Nanak.

But the Punjab was also contested ground between the Muslim Mughal Empire, Afghan warlords and Turkish Sultans. By the 15th century, Punjabis were tiring of all the political wrangling, but they were also passively succumbing to intolerance, self-aggrandizement, and petty fears. The powerlessness and passivity so deeply ingrained in his community weighed heavily on Guru Nanak.

While working for a Muslim landowner in **Sultanpur**, Guru Nanak had a mystical experience. He was bathing in a river when he was carried off to the Divine Court to drink the nectar of the Holy Name. Given up for dead, Guru Nanak emerged from the water three days later, with a deeper understanding of the unity of the one God.

After his brief union with God, the first thing Nanak said was, "There is no Hindu and there is no Muslim." It was a controversial claim. Instead of conforming to one side or the other, Guru Nanak was preaching the spirit of God in all people. Humanity is not divided. But when we choose to pick one side and turn our backs on all others, we become less than what we ought to be. Instead, Guru Nanak preached resistance to such cowardly conformity and encouraged the building of spiritual strength that comes with building something together. Wherever Guru Nanak went, he noticed people blindly following religious precepts without the passion for becoming better people that would make them stand out uniquely from one another.

A story from the ***Janamsākhīs*** tells of the pilgrimage Guru Nanak made to Mecca. One day he fell asleep with his feet disrespectfully pointing to the Holy Kaaba. When a well-intentioned man angrily woke him up, Guru Nanak asked the man to help him turn his feet to a place God wasn't. When the man moved Nanak's legs, the *Mihrab* moved too, definitively proving that God is everywhere. The story also shows us that Guru Nanak liked to needle religious people who took themselves too seriously, emphasizing their showy outward displays in place of a quieter inner development. "Contrary to the prevailing notion of piety, the emphasis was not on turning away from reality but on a willing, even joyous, acceptance of it."[323]

Once, when Guru Nanak was traveling through Punjab, he stayed at **Lalo the carpenter**'s home. There he ate a simple but generous dinner. The next day he was invited to a feast from a wealthier but more selfish host. To prove a point, Guru Nanak took the rich food, but also brought along some simpler food from Lalo's home. When he squeezed Lalo's food, milk miraculously dripped out. But when he squeezed the food of his wealthy host, only blood dripped down. The story shows us that people who live with anger, instilling fear in others, feed only their own violence. It also expresses the fundamental Sikh theme of **Kirat Karo**, dedicating oneself selflessly to honest work and only eating what you've worked for.

Guru Nanak eventually settled in the town of Kartarpur. There he founded the first assembly of Sikhs (from the Sanskrit, meaning "learners"). Muslims, Hindus, and people from all walks of life could pray and study together in what would become the basis for the first **Gurdwaras**. After the meeting, everyone would be treated to a meal. These meals were revolutionary because throughout Punjab, it was not common for men and women, the poor and the rich to sit side by side, preparing and eating the same meal at the same time. The free and open kitchen initiated by Guru Nanak is still practiced today in *Gurdwaras* around the world.

On his deathbed, Hindus and Muslims alike came together to pay their respects to Guru Nanak and to decide how he should be buried, and therefore remembered. Was he a Hindu or a Muslim? Nanak told followers of each religion to place fresh flowers by his bedside. After he died, whichever side still had fresh flowers could claim him as their own. Of course, when he died the flowers stayed fresh on both sides. As the first Guru of Sikhism once said, "God is said to be permeating each and every heart. He looks alike upon the high and the low, the ant and the elephant. Friends, companions, children and relatives are all created by Him."[324]

The Gurus and the *Khalsa*: Building Community

After Guru Nanak died his followers kept a written record of his many hymns, sayings, and philosophies. As the succession of **Gurus** passed from one to another, **Guru Arjan Dev** began collecting the wisdom of his predecessors. In the late 17th century, **Guru Gobind Singh**, the tenth Guru, had amassed a collection of over 2,400 hymns dating back over 200 years. To this work, he added works of non-Sikh poets and singers from as far back as the 12th century. Upon its completion the ***Adi Granth*** (or "Original Book") became the definitive collection in Sikh religious life.

Guru Gobind Singh also changed forever the role of the Gurus in Sikhism by abdicating his authority. In keeping with the Sikh message of equality for all, Guru Gobind Singh brought an end to propping up leaders above the community. "Guru Gobind Singh, by stepping down, became part of the community, and once and for all dissolved the hierarchy that existed between the guru and his Sikhs."[325]

Instead of a person, he elevated the *Adi Granth* as the one and only Guru for the Sikh community. To this day Sikhs revere the **Guru Granth Sahib** as the living Guru, placing the book on a pedestal under a canopy in the most central locations.

In 1699, in order to help establish a tighter solidarity, Guru Gobind Singh founded the ***khalsa***, a community of committed men and women (given names of Singh and Kaur, or "Lion," and "Lioness") who were willing to defend the rights of all people against religious persecution. These followers agreed to a dress code involving the **five Ks**: *kesh* (uncut hair), *kirpan* (a sword), *kangha* (a comb), *kara* (a bracelet), *kachera* (undergarments). Of the five Ks, the hair and the sword continue to be particularly noticeable symbols of Sikhism around the world.

Kesh (Hair)

In the 18th century, long braided hair was more than a fashion statement for Sikh women. It symbolized "the central scriptural message that the relationship between the individual and the Divine is tightly braided."[326]

By requiring men to wear their hair uncut, Guru Gobind Singh was asking Sikh men to make a more radical change. Wearing their hair long became a source of pride for Sikhs and a sign of stubborn rebellion to their enemies. In 1745, **Taru Singh**, a heroic farmer who aided Sikh warriors, was forced to cut his hair as a pledge to leave the *khalsa* and convert to Islam. Singh refused and was therefore executed by Mughal soldiers. There are many stories about Singh's execution in what is now Lahore, Pakistan. In one story the Mughal executioner chops off his head only to learn that like Sikhism, Singh's hair proves to be too tough to cut or divide.

Today for Sikh men living abroad, their long hair, protected by a **turban**, connects them to their homeland. In Western countries such hairstyles can make young men stand out in sometimes uncomfortable ways. It is also time-consuming to care for. Sikh poet **Puran Singh** was not sympathetic to such excuses for cutting one's hair. He wrote, "People say it is difficult to keep hair, but a life devoid of any source of inspiration is all the more difficult to live."[327]

Kirpan (Sword)

Whoever wields the *kirpan* is expected to do so with courage and compassion. Guru Arjan Dev wore two swords: one for justice, the second for spiritual strength. He understood that political reform, social justice and spiritual enlightenment must work together in equal measure.

In 1704, Guru Gobind Singh was in Anandpur when the Mughal army lay siege to the city. After eight months, the Sikh army was out of food, subsisting on leaves and bark from the trees. A group of 40 men deserted the *khalsa* to return home to their villages in the **Amritsar** district. But in the village of Jhabal, the defiant **Mai Bhago** wielded her *kirpan*. She insisted the cowards return to their Guru and with Bhago at their side, they fought to the death, defeating the Mughal army in the **Battle of Muktsar**. Guru Gobind Singh forgave their desertion and released the *Chali Mukte* (**Forty Liberated Ones**) from their past indiscretions. Only the heralded warrior Mai Bhago survived, becoming one of the Guru's five bodyguards who stood beside him while he slept and watched over him when he died. Mai Bhago's legendary *kirpan* is still on display at her *Gurdwara* in Nanded, India.

But the *kirpan* isn't only used to violently repel enemies. The word's root is the Punjabi word *kirpa*, meaning compassion. More than a sword of combat, the *kirpan* symbolizes the cutting down of our egos, which prevent us from doing the right thing. By slicing through our own violent attachments, "the sword is in fact a medium for grasping the One Reality of the universe."[328]

During the same siege of Anandpur, the soldier **Bhai Kanhaiya** wielded his *kirpan* in battle. But he was more often seen offering water to both sides of the standoff. As he told Guru Gobind Singh, "I do not see the other, the foe. I only see that the light in me is in all beings alike and my service is rendered unto that source of life." Impressed, the Guru offered his disciple medicine and bandages so the next time Kanhaiya could do more than simply quench the enemy's thirst.

The Lions of Punjab

On a windy day in Amritsar, you can see the unfurling ***Nishan Sahib***, the Sikh triangular flag, inviting, the hungry, the homeless, and the casual traveler to seek inspiration and guidance in the **Harmandir Sahib** (the Golden Temple). The Temple is surrounded by a giant pool that invites introspection. In 1830, at the height of the Sikh empire, the entire temple was plated in gold. "The shining and intricate surface of gold on the temple's upper storey creates the impression of an elegant jewelry box floating on the water and rising into the air."[329]

The temple can be entered through four doors that are open to each direction, welcoming all, regardless of religion, nationality, or social status. The Golden Temple's *Guruka Langar* is said to have the largest free kitchen in the world, feeding up to 100,000 visitors every day.

Throughout the 18th century, Sikh warriors and martyrs helped instill a sacred and successful foundation for the fighting spirit of the *khalsa,* emanating out from Amritsar. They fought off the

Mughal Empire in the east and the Afghan army in the west. Maharaja **Ranjit Singh** is credited with finally turning the tide of war, creating and expanding the Sikh Empire in the first half of the 19th century. The stories of daring and sacrifice continue to give spiritual strength to Sikhs today. "This is the destiny of the Khalsa, fulfilled in the time of Maharaja Ranjit Singh yet never laid to rest. Whenever tyrants arise, whenever injustice reigns, whenever the **Panth** is threatened, then must the Khalsa prepare again for struggle. The call to duty may come to any generation. The destiny is eternal."[330]

Ranjit Singh was able to take advantage of declining Mughal power in the West while warily negotiating with the British colonies in India. His empire would prove to be short-lived, however. After Singh's death in 1839, the British East India Company began its advance on the Punjab. The Company had already annexed most of the Indian sub-continent by that time. And after the devastating loss in the **Battle of Gujrat**, the Sikhs were forced to lay down their swords, sadly proclaiming, "Today Ranjit Singh has truly died."

More than the empire was broken up after the Sikhs were forced to abide by the **Treaty of Lahore**. The Sikh way of life, the very spirit of resistance was fractured. Under British control, Westernization proved to be a debilitating counterforce to the centuries-old call of the Gurus. To combat the tide of Western modernity and bureaucratic conformity, the Lions of the Punjab struck back.

At the turn of the twentieth century, **Vir Singh**, the saint poet of Punjab, wrote stories that took readers back to a distant time when brave Sikhs battled enemies though outnumbered at nearly every confrontation. Singh reminded his readers that Sikhs had many times before risen to resistance when "petty local governors became aggressive and daring; the country was subject to subversion and confusion, and arrogant rulers committed atrocities as they liked."[331]

In Singh's 1898 novel, *Sundari*, his titular character joins renegade Sikhs in the forest, risking their lives to stand up for justice and equality. Singh writes, "Firm belief or staunch faith is a great power in itself and when it is nourished, it becomes unshakeable like a rock." Sundari's heart is "soft like wax and also hard like a stone." When she emerges from the forest on horseback, her kirpan brandished and ready to defend the *Khalsa*, "none can shake her resolve."

In Vir Singh's novel, Sundari eventually falls in battle, but Sikh faith is rejuvenated through this fearless female warrior who appears to them as a goddess. Though the community mourns Sundari's death, they return to the hard work ahead, because no matter how bleak things may appear on the horizon, Singh writes, "One should live in the world of action and play one's part dispassionately."

This message to live in the world we find ourselves is a recurring theme in Sikhism. It helps explain why for nearly 100 years, the Sikhs cultivated a tense but productive relationship with their colonial rulers. The British were careful to harness the fearless fighting spirit of the *khalsa*. In World War I, for example, over 100,000 Punjabi Sikhs enlisted to fight in the British army. Known as the "**Black Lions**," the Sikhs often fought with swords in their traditional garb, sometimes carrying a copy of the *Guru Granth Sahib* into battle.

Performing our everyday job responsibilities need not conflict with our spiritual development. One of the most influential Sikh intellectuals in the 20th century, **Kirpal Singh**, worked for 37 years as a civil servant in charge of military pensions. Singh awoke every day at 4 a.m. so he could meditate for five hours before arriving at his desk job. He understood that the fruits of religious seeds might take years to ripen. "It is a very odd outlook that some have," Singh mused, "to expect God and self-realization in a short time and with little labor, while the same people are willing to toil for years to obtain the pot of porridge that is all this world has to offer."[332]

Kirpal Singh

Where the attention is, there you are. Through putting your attention wholeheartedly on physical exercises, with a little training you can be a wrestler of powerful strength. With your attention directed on scholastic subjects, you can become an intellectual giant. If you put all your attention on the Greater Attention (God), you will grow in spiritual stature. On the spiritual health depends the health of mind and body both. This teaching is for all, but most of us are still playing with toys.

Under British rule, Singh's religious education included instruction in a Christian missionary school. All religions, Singh realized, argued against the unequal treatment of the disempowered. As Sikh philosophers have long insisted, tough times can also provide healing. In the most desperate situations, Sikhs reach out to God all the more urgently. "*Whosoever got Him, did so with tears,*" Singh wrote. "*Could He be got with laughter and joy, none would be without Him.*"[333]

Simply turning within, however, couldn't possibly improve the desperate situation Sikhs faced under British control. Resisting conformity meant speaking out against injustices and working toward freedom and equality, core Sikh philosophies. As Singh explained, Sikhs needed to take action, but not with hatred or anger. "I am not saying that you should leave your life in the world and take the road to the lonely forests," Singh wrote.[334] Helping others and growing spiritually should go hand in hand. "A man without love will never realize the Lord," Singh wrote, "so make this body a cage of love, and then talk."[335]

Partition: Facts and Fiction

In 1919, Sikhs gathered for a peaceful protest in a walled-in garden in Jallianwala Bagh, in Amritsar. British troops ended the protest by firing live ammunition into the crowd, killing upwards of 500 people and injuring over a thousand more. The **Jallianwala Bagh Massacre** became the turning point for India's move to independence from British colonial rule.

Before Indian independence in 1947, British lawyer Cyril Radcliffe was tasked with drawing up new borders that would allow the minority Muslim population their own land in a new country to be called Pakistan. The **Radcliffe Line** cut Punjab in two; the land of five rivers became the land of two-and-a-half rivers. The holy city of Amritsar was awarded to India, the Sikh cultural center of Lahore awarded to Pakistan.

In the summer and fall of 1947, the Punjab **Partition** was home to the largest migration movement in human history. Most of the Sikhs who were living in the West Punjab were effectively forced to move east into India, while the Muslims in East Punjab moved west into the new Pakistan. Violence in Sikh and Muslim communities quickly led to the deaths of over one million

Sikhism: Resisting Conformity • 143

people. Over 12 million people were permanently displaced.

In the Rawalpindi District of the Punjab, over 4,000 Sikh villagers were killed in one week of violence. In the village of **Thoa Khalsa**, 90 Sikh women committed mass suicide by jumping into a well only moments before attackers pillaged the town.

Bhisham Sahni, a lecturer at Khalsa College in Amritsar, was working for the Rawalpindi Relief Committee at that time. He saw firsthand the bodies floating in the Thoa Khalsa well. In 1974, Sahni wrote a short novel, *Tamas* (or *Darkness*), detailing the horrors and the emptiness Punjabi Sikhs faced during Partition. He wrote about "the tragedy that occurs in the loss of faith in the ability (or will?) of neighbors, people one grew up with, to protect each other when the familiar spaces of home and neighborhood turn menacing—truly, the loss of one's home."[336]

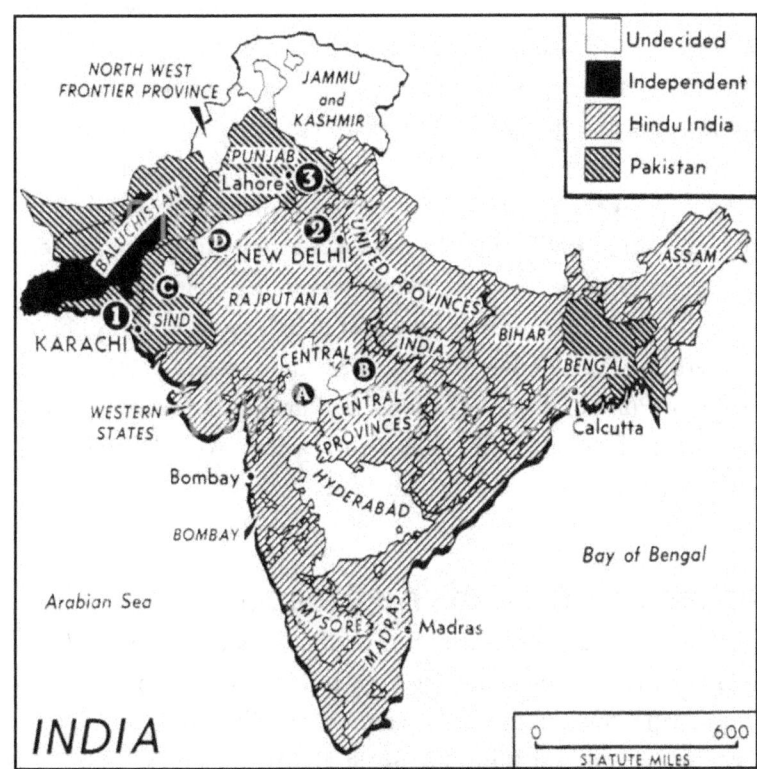

This 1947 map from the Chicago *Sun-Times* shows the partition of British India between the newly independent dominions of India and Pakistan in 1947. Punjab (the area surrounding the numeral 3 on this map) was divided between the two new states, an arrangement which remains the source of unrest today, more than seven decades later. At the point this map was created, the ultimate fate of some regions, such as Baluchistan and Hyderabad, remained uncertain. East Bengal, initially a geographically separated part of Pakistan, ultimately formed the independent state of Bangladesh in 1971.

In 1988, Sahni's *Tamas* was adapted into a six-part television series that was shown across India. The Sikhs of Partition were heroically imprinted on the television audience, none more so than the women of Thoa Khalsa. Their refusal to give in to their attackers is still a point of pride for Sikhs and Hindus across India. In Dehli, today, a small Sikh community of Partition survivors continues to honor the women in a yearly ceremony.

From 1948 to 1956, India and Pakistan initiated a joint mission to rescue kidnapped and abused Sikh and Muslim women stuck on the wrong side of the border. However, because of forced conversions and fear of reprisals when the women returned "home," it was often difficult to determine who still identified themselves as Sikh.

In the 2003 award-winning film ***Khamosh Pani*** (or *Silent Waters*), Punjabi director Sabhia Sumar tells the story of a Sikh woman named Veero who refuses to jump into the well with the other villagers. For feminist artists like Sumar, the decision not to capitulate to male-dominated honor codes is also revolutionary. After suffering indignities, including rape and sexual assault, Veero converts to Islam and changes her name to Ayesha. Though she stays on in her hometown, now in Pakistan, Ayesha is spiritually without home or community. Cast out by her Sikh community, now in India, and never fully accepted in the Muslim community, Ayesha chooses to take her life in the well years after walking away from it. Films like *Khamosh Pani* show us the complexity of determining who best represents the future of Sikhism. In fiction and film, Sikh women are challenging traditional notions of Sikh identity. Any modern-day discussion of Sikhism will have to take into account the many people, women in particular, who, through forced conversion or tragic circumstances, are reluctant to call themselves Sikh at all.

Partition was, and continues to be, a devastating blow to the Sikh communities historically rooted in Punjab. "Yet, for many of Partition's refugees, while the physical relationship with land/place was irrevocably lost, their 'Punjab' would live on in their imaginaries, and in the new worlds they constructed for themselves."[337]

Defiant Women of the Diaspora

Over 70 years after the drawing of the Radcliffe Line, Sikh scholars observe, "A resounding silence surrounds the question of women and Partition."[338] And yet, despite the silence, Sikh women often played critical roles in rebuilding their lives and religious culture. In their fiction, **Amrita Pritam** and **Shauna Singh Baldwin** depict the complexities of identifying with Sikh culture in the modern age.

Amrita Pritam

Pritam was born into a Sikh family in Lahore. As a child, Pritam used to dream of the Gurus while running her fingertips over the portrait of Guru Gobind Singh: "the horse he rode on, the sword he carried, the falcon he held in his hand, anything."[339] This need to touch something, whether relics or flowers, was Pritam's way of making abstract ideas real. Like her father, a poet, she learned to bridge empty chasms through words. Her faith in God was shattered at age 11, when her mother died of natural causes.

When Partition forced her from her home in what was to become Pakistan, she took a train through India, looking for work. Outside the train, she noted, the night wind was "wailing at the sorrows the Partition had brought." Inside the train, Pritam penned her popular "Ode to Waris Shah," a poetic plea to the beloved 18th-century Sufi poet. In the opening verse, she writes:

> Waris Shah I call out to you today to rise from your grave
> Rise and open a new page of the immortal book of love
> A daughter of Punjab had wept and you wrote many a dirge
> A million daughters weep today and look at you for solace

Pritam's 1950 novel *Pinjar* was adapted into an award-winning film in 2003. The story covers the trials of an abducted Hindu woman who remains with her adopted family on the Pakistani side. The book, and the film, have been praised for depicting the complexities behind religious identity. Growing up with a Sikh father helped force Pritam to confront these religious shifts firsthand.

Time and again, Pritam returned to the Sikh women divided in their faith, their politics, and their relationships. When asked to write a poem in honor of Guru Nanak's 500th birthday, Pritam wrote in praise of the Guru's mother, **Mata Tripta**, and her "cravings of unripe pregnancy: the restless heart."[340]

Throughout her life, Pritam was also guided by a restless heart. Her "Travelogue of Thirst" stretched "From the Ganges to vodka." For many Sikhs, Pritam's bohemian lifestyle was seen as a departure from the ethical code of conduct laid out by the Gurus. It's true that Pritam often distanced herself from many of the formal trappings of organized religion. Even so, this distinctly Sikh philosophy of "longing for the One, and respect for the Word" grew deep inside her, like seeds for her soul. "They just cannot be uprooted," she wrote.[341]

After her death in 2005, an obituary in *The Hindu* newspaper observed how Pritam "lived two lives.... From the mundane to the sublime. Even divine."[342] As Imroz, her lover of 40 years said definitively, "Beautiful words take the form of a beautiful body once in a while and Amrita was an example of such a blend."[343]

> ## Amrita Pritam
>
> *Life and Times*
> I am a chain-smoker. I love a drop of whisky too, occasionally.... When a plate of sweet, semolina halwa is placed in offering before the great Sikh book *Guru Granth Sahib* the blade of a sword is passed through it. Thereupon, the simple halwa becomes kraah prasad which is distributed to the congregation. Similarly, the cigarette between my fingers or the glass of drink in my hands transform themselves into something infinitely purer. The intensity of my thoughts is cut through as with the blade of a sword: and my thoughts, like the halwa that is transformed into prasad, are then ready for distribution.
>
>

Shauna Singh Baldwin

Baldwin was born in Canada five years after Partition. From her grandmother's memoirs she crafted her most famous book, *What the Body Remembers*. In the story Singh depicts the teenager Roop as a coquettish girl more interested in her looks than her spiritual development. "Roop is a new Sikh," Baldwin writes, "an uncomprehending carrier of the orthodoxy resurging in them all."[344] Though the family rituals are influenced by Sikhs, Hindus, and Muslims, after her mother dies, Roop's father chooses the more orthodox Sikh path. No longer will the family "walk the border between one faith and another … this one in the morning, that one in the evening."[345]

Roop is betrothed to Sardar, a well-respected bureaucrat in the Indian Irrigation Department. His mind is colonized by the British and, as his first wife cautions, Roop's mind will be colonized by her husband.

During Partition, the family finds itself on the wrong side of the Radcliffe Line. Sardar's flour mill is overrun, his businesses gutted. The sharp line drawn between Sikhs and Muslims "has severed ties, severed all pretensions to culture, informed everyone of the savagery of which neighbors are capable."[346] A witness to some of the atrocities committed on both sides, Roop barely escapes to India.

In Delhi, on the other side of Punjab, Roop is forced to start anew. As mother of the household, Roop is charged with the day-to-day tasks of keeping what's left of her family and culture intact. The fictional Roop is a symbol of displaced Sikh women, in India and around the world, with the courage and conviction to start over, leaning on their religion to help find their strength. "And maybe Roop is, now, finally, a Sikh. For it's only when a fish is pulled from water that it truly understands it is not fowl."[347] Living away from one's ancient homeland, Singh notes, leads some Sikhs to strengthen their religious faith.

In Baldwin's short story "Montreal, 1962," a young Sikh man who emigrated to Montreal is told he must take off his turban and cut his hair before he is offered a job in the new Canada. His wife, however, won't let him sever the deep ties to their ancestral homeland. Instead, she lays his bright red turban on their bed, "and it seemed as though I'd poured a pool of the sainted blood of the Sikh martyrs there."[348]

More than an article of clothing, the turban symbolizes a meaningful tie to an older world. Singh ends her story defiantly. The young Sikh woman confidently asserts, "One day our children will say, 'My father came to this country with very little but his turban and my mother learned to work because no one would hire him.' Then we will have taught Canadians what it takes to wear a turban."

Bowlers of the *Panth*: Sikhs and Cricket

Since Partition, identifying a specific Sikh culture has become even more complicated. Though most Sikhs still trace their roots back locally, to Punjab, many Sikhs are also closely allied with the larger nationalities of India or Pakistan. Since the time of British colonialism many of these same Sikhs share strong cultural ties with the English. Nowhere do we see these overlapping identities more clearly than in the international sport of cricket.

When the British colonized India in the 19th century, they introduced cricket to Southern Asia. The prevailing belief was that "cricket typically nourished British virtues and the spread of cricket would promote, albeit indirectly, Britain's civilizing mission."[349] But it wasn't long before Indian cricket became of symbol of resistance to colonial servility. In more recent times, Indian cricketers are "expected to recover the self-esteem of 800 million Indians and undo—in both the everyday and psychoanalytic senses of the term—colonial history in the southern world."[350]

In the popular 2001 Indian film *Lagaan*, a game of cricket decides just how much tax an Indian village will owe the British rulers. The Sikh character from Punjab, Deva Singh Sodhi, joins the team because, as he tells the captain, "Whether with sticks and spears or bat and ball, I want to be in every battle against the British." The Indian team learns to play cricket and even makes the sport its own.

In 1983, when the great Sikh cricketer **Kapil Dev** made his legendary running catch against the West Indies' stalwart Vivian Richards, India had all but secured its first-ever World Cup championship. But already in the previous decade, the bowlers of the Spin Quartet, led by an Amritsar-born Sikh, **Bishan Singh Bedi**, had helped establish the foundations of Indian cricket that would eventually topple the English giants.

Bedi comes from a long line of Punjabi Sikhs. His father founded a girls' secondary school and helped instill Sikh values in his son. In the third grade, after his friend was struck down by polio, Bedi used to lead him around school in his wheelchair. The story goes that Bedi built his strong wrists by washing his own clothes as a child, wringing out the family towels with his little hands. In the Sikh tradition, who you are is as important as what you do. "A spinner must have the right temperament," Bedi once said, "a big heart, loads of patience and an ability to stay switched on."[351]

At the age of 25, Bedi left his home in Punjab to compete with India on his first world tour. He had to promise his Sikh mother he'd come back home. Equally important, he assured her that he would not return home clean-shaven. Bedi's roommate reported, "He would retire to the room after play and keep writing letters to his family—to his parents, cousins, uncle. He also prayed a lot."[352]

Between 1971 and 1973, India came of age in the international cricket scene, defeating England at home and away. Known for his colorful **patkas** that he changed for every session, Bedi relished "the art of spin bowling, with the bland smile of the 'villain' that goes with it."[353] Bedi's spin bowling was villainous because it could frustrate the batsmen, more so than the fast-pitching of the shorter modern game. Bedi would never give in to the modern speeds. He "abhorred brutality,"[354] preferring the artistry of the illusive spins. Bedi "was a throwback to the Golden Age, a reminder of the essentially romantic nature of cricket, where beauty sometimes overrode effectiveness, but, at its best, was essential to it."[355]

When a batsman would hit Bedi for a six (the equivalent of a home run in baseball), Bedi would clap along with the crowd in an uncommon sign of sportsmanship. By the time Bedi became captain of the Indian side, "the basic lessons he taught were philosophical rather than cricketing: Learn to respect the game. Work hard."[356]

After Bedi retired, he fulfilled his dream, managing Punjab to its first-ever Indian title in 1992–93. He succeeded in typical Sikh fashion, scorning authorities by helping "a player to develop his own strength instead of imposing rules from the outside."[357]

Frustrating the hypocrites and equivocators is a tradition that Bedi has passed down to Sikh bowlers today. Harbhajan Singh, or the "Turbanator," as he calls himself on his Facebook and Twitter accounts, was India's first-choice spinner in the 2003 and 2007 World Cup. He credits his father for ensuring he holds on to Sikh values amidst the money and fame that comes with cricket success. "My father used to cite the example of a tree that, as it keeps growing taller, droops closer to the ground because of the fruit it bears," the Turbanator once said. "Similarly, the more you achieve in life, the more humble you should be."[358]

If it's true that cricket in India has its own unique qualities that make it different from the English brand, some of that credit should go to the Sikh bowlers after Bedi, who refuse to blindly follow everybody else. By resisting hegemony, demanding equality, and retaining their unique individuality, Sikhs have offered much to the sport of cricket, and even more to the world outside the pitch.

Discovery Questions

1. Read an online translation of the opening to *Guru Granth Sahib* (known as the "Mool Mantra"). How does the hymn advance a sense of community and inclusivity? Can it be made more practical today?

2. On YouTube, watch a *kirtan* recorded from the Golden Temple with translations. How does it make you feel? What effect does the singing with accompanying instruments add to the recitation?

3. Visit a local *Gurdwara* off campus. How did you feel? How do the practises or initiatives at the temple contribute to advancing a sense of inclusiveness in Western societies?

4. Sit with your family or friends on the ground to have a meal together, with you as the server. What changes did you notice in the group dynamic from your usual meals?

5. Describe any articles, symbols, or keepsakes that you carry on your body. How do they inspire you toward seeking betterment in yourself and others?

6. Watch Ravi Singh's TED Talk entitled "Cause beyond Causes." What does it mean to "be unconditional" when you help someone? When have you helped someone conditionally, and when have you helped someone unconditionally?

7. Flip through some of Rupi Kaur's contemporary Instapoetry online. What Sikh themes can you find in her short poems? Which themes can you apply to your own life?

Glossary

Terms	Definitions
Adi Granth	Sikhism's foundational text by Guru Arjan Dev, the fifth guru of Sikhism
Amrita Pritam	Influential 20th-century poet and writer
Amritsar	City of Golden Temple in the state of Punjab, India; holy pilgrimage destination
Battle of Gujrat	Battle in 1849 between the British and Sikhs
Battle of Mukstar	Battle in 1705 between Sikhs and Mughals
Bhai Kanhaiya	17th-century Sikh disciple distinguished by his selfless service
Bishan Singh Bedi	20th-century Indian cricket star
Black Lions	Punjabi Sikhs who enlisted to fight in the British army in the First World War

Duleep Singh	19th-century Sikh prince
Five Ks	*kesh* (uncut hair), *kirpan* (sword), *kangha* (comb), *kara* (bracelet), *kachera* (undergarment)
Forty Liberated Ones	Martyred 18th-century fighters defending Guru Gobind Singh against the Mughal army
Gurdwaras	Holy places where Sikhs gather and pray
Guru Arjan Dev	The fifth Guru
Guru Gobind Singh	The 10th Guru and founder of the *Khalsa*
Guru Granth Sahib	Foundational text of Sikhism, revered as the Living Guru
Guru Nanak	The first Guru and founder of Sikhism
Gurus	Spiritual leaders of Sikhism
Harmandir Sahib	*Gurdwara* located in Amritsar
Jallianwala Bagh Massacre	Square in Amritsar where British Indian Army fired into a crowd of Indian civilians, killing hundreds
Janamsākhīs	Stories of Guru Nanak Dev's childhood, accomplishments and travels
Kapil Dev	20th-century Indian cricket star
Khalsa	Community of initiated Sikhs
Khamosh Pani	20th-century Indo-Pakistani film that outlines the atrocities of Partition
Kirat Karo	Sikh principle of dedicating oneself selflessly to honest work and only eating what one's worked for
Kirpal Singh	20th-century Sikh spiritual leader
Kraah Prasad	Offering given to attendees of *Gurdwara* services
Lahore	Capital city of the Pakistani province of Punjab
Lalo the carpenter	A poor commoner who invited Guru Nanak Dev to visit his home
Mata Tripta	Mother of Guru Nanak Dev
Mughal Empire	16th- to 19th-century Imperial rule in South Asia
Nishan Sahib	Sikh triangular flag
Panth	Path founded by a spiritual preceptor or learned master
Partition	British-led division and creation of India and Pakistan in 1947
Patkas	Cloth worn by Sikh men to cover their hair
Punjab	Spiritual home of Sikhism in northern India
Puran Singh	20th-century Sikh poet
Radcliffe Line	Partition border dividing the state of Punjab
Ranjit Singh	19th-century ruler of Sikh empire
Shauna Singh Baldwin	20th-century Canadian-American novelist of Sikh origin
Sultanpur	A city in the Indian state of Uttar Pradesh

Sundari	19th-century novel written by Vir Singh
Tamas	20th-century novel written by Bhisham Sahni, later made into a television film
Thoa Khalsa	Pakistani town in city of Islamabad
Treaty of Lahore	19th-century peace treaty marking the end of the first war between the British and Sikhs
Turban	Sikh headdress tying and safeguarding one's hair
Vir Singh	Prominent 19th-century Sikh novelist and poet

Chapter Ten
Navajo
Land of the People

On Arizona's *Dook'o'oosłiid* ("Shining on Top") the Snowbowl welcomes skiers and snowboarders from November to April. It boasts the longest ski season in the state, thanks in part to a "state-of-the-art" snowmaking machine that covers 65 percent of its trails. The snow is made from reclaimed water, piped in from the city of Flagstaff, 14 miles away. One of the ski resort investors claimed that building the artificial snow machine should be guided by one sole mission: "Skiing First."

In the American courts, the Navajo vainly argued against this development. The summit is located in the **San Francisco Peaks,** one of six sacred mountains that enclose Navajo land. In Navajo stories, "Shining on Top" is fastened by a sunbeam and enveloped by yellow clouds. The mountain is a sacred place to heal one's body and restore the natural harmony that gets damaged from precisely this kind of industrial and recreational development. According to the Navajo court of law, "Mother Earth and Father Sky is part of us," and we "must treat this sacred bond with love and respect without exerting dominance for we do not own our mother or father."[359]

While the American courts ultimately decided in favor of the ski resort, one still unanswered question revolves around how we ought to use the land we all call home. The Navajo see their guiding mission as a duty "to protect and preserve the beauty of the natural world for future generations."[360] It's a philosophy that has served them well for hundreds of years and continues to inform their decisions in the face of colonization and environmental dangers.

Blessings of Home

The Navajo origin stories tell of four previous worlds in which people lived and above which they would eventually rise. In the Fourth World, the **Holy People** are described as "people who can travel far by following the path of the rainbow. And they can travel swiftly by following the path of the sunray."[361] They created **First Man and First Woman** from two ears of **corn** placed on **eagle** feathers, covered with dried buckskin and blown by the **White Wind**.

With the help of tireless digging by a locust and a badger, First Man and First Woman emerged from a hole in the ground, leading other Holy People into the **Fifth World**. It is this world they helped fashion into the place we live in today. "As such their creation was an Emergence *from* the earth, much like a corn plant pushes forth from the earth as it grows, with deep roots stretching back and connecting it to the memory and power of its origins."[362]

The Navajo call themselves the ***Diné*** ("the people"), descendants of First Man and First Woman. The land bequeathed by the Holy People is bounded and defined by six sacred mountains: *Sisnaajiní* (**Blanca Peak**) in the east, *Tsoodził* (**Mount Taylor**) in the South, *Dook'o'oosłííd* (San Francisco Peaks) in the west, *Dibé Nitsaa* (**Mount Hesperus**) in the north, *Dziłná'oodiłii* (**Huerforno Mountain**) representing the central lungs, and *Ch'óol'í'í* (**Gobernador Knob**), the chimney carrying prayers up to the sky.

> ### *Diné Bahane'* (Story of the People)
>
> It was the wind that had given them life: the very wind that gives us our breath as we go about our daily affairs here in the world we ourselves live in!
> When this wind ceases to blow inside of us, we become speechless. Then we die.
> In the skin at the tips of our fingers we can see the trail of that life-giving wind.
> Look carefully at your own fingertips.
> There you will see where the wind blew when it created your most ancient ancestors out of two ears of corn, it is said.

The connections between *Diné* families and their homeland run deep. In formal introductions, the Navajo begin with naming their mother's clan and end with the place where they live. The land has a kind of sacred beauty. ***Hózhó*** is the Navajo word for walking in beauty. "A Navajo uses this concept to express his happiness, his health, the beauty of his land, and harmony of his relations to others."[363] *Sạ'áh Naagháí Bik'eh Hózhó* means joining one's personal quest for beauty with the larger natural world.

Walking in beauty begins in the home. The traditional Navajo family lived in a ***hogan*** made from natural elements like wood, mud, and bark. The most mundane object can partake in the beauty of the natural world. It might be "a pair of moccasins, a rug, a child, the sheep, the day, an idea, a person's appearance, the sky, the stars, a way of speaking...."[364] After a baby is born, the umbilical cord is buried in a carefully chosen place to forever bind the child to the land near their home.

When *hózhó* is disrupted, the Navajo rely on any number of highly ritualized ceremonies, led by **medicine men**, and most often taking place in a specially prepared *hogan*. In ceremonies like the **Blessingway**, ancient stories are recited and enacted through ritualistic practices that have been orally transmitted from generation to generation. Over the last hundred years, many of these stories have been written down, translated, and collected in volumes known as ***Diné Bahane'***, or the Story of the People. Such stories recall "a time when the Animal People—the furred, feathered, and scaled other nonhuman beings—walked the Earth together and shared a common language and experience."[365]

Roaming Coyote

Often called "Little Trotter" or "First Scolder," **Coyote** is the consummate trickster. His whimsical decisions unpredictably tip the balance of the cosmos, causing chaos. But Coyote's ill-advised adventures also push other life forms to ingenuity and compassion. "Without question, Coyote is

the most enigmatic, controversial, mystifying, and versatile figure in the Navajo stories."[366]

It was Coyote who gave us the mystery of the night sky. First Man was carefully placing the constellations in the sky according to a rationally ordered plan, when Coyote lost his patience. He grabbed the magical mica and chucked it into the sky at random, giving us the beautiful mess of stars we can see today on clear desert nights.

It was Coyote who convincingly argued that all animals, including five-fingered people, should not stay in this world forever. "Isn't it better that each of us should live here for just a while," he argued. "Leave everything behind for the young. Make room for the next generation."[367] Because of Coyote, the rationally ordered cosmos is infused with creativity, originality, and constant change.

While our current world was still under construction, Coyote served as the eyes and ears for First Man and the Holy People. In the assembly of Holy People, the good ones are on the south side, the bad ones congregate on the north side. Only Coyote is by the door, "so that he may ally himself with either side according to his whim."[368]

In one well-known Navajo story, Coyote steals Water Monster's baby (in some versions, two babies), inciting her anger and causing a devastating flood. Only when the baby is returned does the water finally recede to where it currently resides out in the distant blue horizon.

Stories of Coyote's adventures and mishaps teach us about the dangers of wanting more than our share. Coyote is constantly coveting fancy robes and newer skins, trying the patience of an otherwise sympathetic community. In one story he gambles away his own skin in a contest with the beavers and has to jump into the water naked. One of the beavers finally gives him new clothes for his trouble.

Other stories lay out a hunting ethos where fast-thinking trickery and subterfuge are values that can tip the scale between life and death. In one story Coyote catches a deer by first warning her about hunters in the area. After establishing the doe's trust, Coyote hides and shoots her himself. Pretending then to nurse the fallen doe, Coyote prepares a mixture that will help subdue the deer for his next meal.

In another story, the son of Coyote remembers how Owl raised him "by spreading darkness upon me, by spreading skyblue upon me, by spreading evening twilight also upon me, by spreading dawn, too, upon me."[369] He experiences sensations in his throat, nose, and skin, and recalls bad dreams that carried warnings. Paying close attention to the language of the land can keep us away from danger. Sticks, broken pots, old brooms, even his buried placenta that marked his birthplace arise from the ground to help Coyote find his way. The son of Coyote reminds us that separating ourselves from the land can prevent us from noticing the "unusual happenings Earth Surface People should believe!"[370]

Ignoring the warnings is bad enough. For the Navajo, the bigger fear is that if we become too distant, the land may stop talking to us altogether.

Changing Woman and Gender Fluidity

Changing Woman, "the most highly revered of all Navajo Holy People,"[371] directed the Holy People to the sacred land between the six sacred mountains. Changing Woman is given the name because she is ever aging in the winter, and showing youthful buoyancy in the spring. "Restoration to youth is the pattern of the earth, something for which the Navaho lives."[372]

Youth and transformation continue to be great causes for joy in Navajo Nation. After a young woman's first menstruation, her closest friends of the family hang a blanket on the door to the *hogan* and begin a sacred ritual known as the **Kinaaldá**. Like most Navajo traditions, the ritual looks forward and backwards at the same time. "When it is time for a grandmother to direct her granddaughter through the transition from childhood to womanhood, she turns for guidance to the Changing Woman stories and the rules governing performance of the *Kinaaldá* ceremony."[373] Changing Woman returns from the ancient world to check up on her newest proteges during the *Kinaaldá*.

The *Kinaaldá* is a sacred space for females to sing together all night long in honour of the Holy People and in praise of their newest Navajo woman. At dawn, the young woman sets out on a long run in which she breathes in the crisp air and uses her newfound reproductive powers to bless the earth. Her special powers will last a full month, until her second period.

From mountains to homes, male and female categories are sharply delineated in the Navajo cosmos. However, neither category is dominant or more valued than the other. The universe requires both sexes to succeed, alternating back and forth to keep our world in balance.

Men who dress as women, women who dress as men, or anyone who takes on gender roles traditionally taken up by the opposite sex are known as **nádleehí**. In Navajo culture, "there is no basis for determining whether the individual has the personality aspects, occupations, attire, and other features of only one gender or of both."[374] Therefore, there is room, and even encouragement, for people of multiple, or alternate genders. The *nádleehí* often bring good luck and are blessed with special abilities to reach the Holy People.

For hundreds of years, "representatives of gender diversity were among those who took strong stands on behalf of their tribes, who sought and found creative strategies by which their people could survive."[375] Like Changing Woman, Navajo men, women, and *nádleehí* must constantly change to adapt to modern pressures. We should "emulate the values of Changing Woman," Navajo activist **Annie Wauneka** said, "integrating the role of traditional and modern values and the importance of Navajo men and women working together."[376]

As progenitors of the people, Navajo women have always enjoyed a privileged status. The Navajo have traditionally been a matrilineal society, meaning the family's wealth is passed from mother to daughter. The high status of women came as a surprise to the European colonists who came to Navajo Nation in the 17th century. "The social universe of native North America was nowhere more at odds with that of Europe and Anglo-America than in its diverse gender roles."[377]

Monster Slayers: Confronting Colonialism

When First Man and First Woman were unable to resolve their differences, they separated. Because of this separation of the sexes, abnormal babies were born. They became monsters. In the Navajo creations stories these monsters quickly overran the world. "Soon they would begin to lurk under rocks and along cliff-paths.… And because of all those monsters the people would live in daily fear, it is said."[378]

Changing Woman knew such a vicious world was no place to introduce **five-fingered people**. She therefore became impregnated with sunlight so she could give birth to twins who would defeat these monsters and spawn the human race. The twins were named **Monster Slayer** and **Born from Water**. When they were old enough to save the world, they set off to find their father, the Sun. **Talking God** helped them on their journey by dropping a rainbow onto the ground for them to walk on.

When they reached the Sun, the twins were given magical armor, arrows, and potions. But their true strength lay in their courage and religious faith his sunlight instilled. "That is why I did it," he told his twins. "Although the flint armor is good, that which stands inside you will conquer the fierce monsters which now exist and even those which may come into being in the future."[379]

The twins took the advice to heart and courageously defeated the most dangerous monsters. But some monsters survived. Monsters representing Poverty and Hunger, for example, were spared because Changing Woman convinced her sons to let them live. "They are not altogether good or entirely bad," she argued. "Poverty and hunger meet somewhere between that which causes satisfactions and that which causes pain."[380]

The monsters that can help us grow and become stronger were allowed to roam free so that we can all fight them like Monster Slayer and Born from Water. This story remains a central rallying point for the Navajo people in dark times.

When the Americans annexed Santa Fe in 1846, the Navajo were forced to confront outright extinction for the first time in their long history. After a series of violent skirmishes, the Ameri-

This photograph of Sacred Spider Rock was taken around the year 1900. Rising 750 feet (229 metres) above the canyon floor, Spider Rock is located where Canyon de Chelly and Monument Canyon meet. Canyon de Chelly National Monument is owned by the Navajo Tribal Trust and managed in cooperation with the U.S. National Park Service.

cans launched a calculated campaign to wipe out the Navajo or force them into assimilating into Christian America.

Beginning in 1862, over 11,000 Navajo were rounded up and forced to walk up to 300 miles hundred miles to **Bosque Redondo** where they were held captive. During the time of the **Long Walk**, as it came to be called, at least 1,000 Navajo people lost their lives. Some died from preparing foods they were unfamiliar with, by frying and eating coffee beans or boiling bacon. Others died of starvation. Warriors like **Manuelito** and **Barboncito** held out longer than most, and in the end, proved helpful for getting the two sides to end the violence.

In 1868, the Navajo were released from captivity and allowed to return home, but not before signing away a large swath of their sacred land to the American government. The **Treaty of Bosque Redondo** also compelled the Navajo to send all of their children, ages 6 to 16, to American boarding schools where Navajo religion and culture could be expunged. One result of relocation and subsequent Indian boarding schools is that generations of Navajo youth still feel uprooted from their homeland and unwelcome in the new America. Other Navajo children returned from their boarding schools, like their parent's generation returned from Bosque Redondo, with a renewed purpose. Instead of fracturing, "the stories tightened the fiber that held the culture together."[381]

The Navajo Long Walk and forced relocation teach us that the ancient command to fight monsters is as relevant today as it was with Changing Woman and the twins. "Now the landscape is dotted with a new class of Alien Monsters: oil rigs, coal drag lines, power plants, logging trucks and uranium names, to name but a few." In 2020, COVID-19 hit Navajo Nation especially hard. Approximately five percent of Navajo Nation tested positive for the virus which was a higher number per capita than any state in the USA. This newest monster required the ***Diné*** to work together as never before. As Navajo activist **John Redhouse** said, "This resistance has been part of our lives since the Monster Slayers, since the time of Changing Woman."[382]

Weaving Stories and Rugs

In ancient times, some Navajos struggled to get by on the hard land. Under duress, a party of women set out through **Canyon de Chelly** to seek the assistance of **Spider Woman**. At the foot of Spider Rock, Spider Woman gave the women invaluable instructions: the secrets of weaving rugs. Since then, the *Diné* have kept a bustling trade alive with rugs for lining their *hogans*, softening their saddles, or covering their bodies for warmth.

Weaving Navajo blankets and rugs involves a highly specialized ability to intertwine the tightly stretched yarns into one coherent design. One word for their rugs is *Dah'iiistlo*, or "progressing from the ground up." The weaving process begins with **shearing** sheep and washing the wool. Then the strands of wool are stretched and straightened in a process known as **carding**. After that, **spinning** the yarn involves twisting the strands around a wooden stick for strengthening the wool. The wool is then stretched on a **loom** that is built with a series of log posts dug into the ground. As "homologues of the Navajo world,"[383] the logs point upward to the sky, downward to the earth, and support an opening in the middle so the weaver always has a spiritual way out and won't therefore succumb to madness.

The Navajo artist sits on the ground and sets their fingers to working the longitudinal **warp** strands into one foundational background. To make her patterns she must also be adept at weaving the **weft** yarn through the warp. The patterns, along with the colors, often symbolize particular stories and practices in the Navajo religion. "An entire culture might be woven into a single textile: its mythic and historical associations, its ceremonial practices, its need for balance and order, its sense of place."[384] Common themes include creation stories, animal stories, and the sacred mountains.

The Long Walk and subsequent incarcerations nearly "destroyed the old unthinking freedom, killed the joyous, prideful spirit in which fine blankets were woven…"[385] But even then, the Navajo went back to their yarn. This time, along with the joyous stories of the past, new patterns emerged symbolizing the suffering and displacement of the *Diné*. "To weave in the present is to summon the past."[386]

Towards the end of the 19th century, trading posts began dotting the Navajo land. White traders came in to barter canned food, flour, sugar, and coffee for Navajo blankets and other hand-made artwork. These trading posts became central economic nodes in which Navajos could socialize and exchange goods. Weavers would bring in their blankets and show off their work in the backroom. There would follow some haggling over price until an agreement was reached. Today the international demand for Navajo rugs keeps weavers in business. Since the time of Spider Woman, the act of weaving is a religious act that, like all rituals, helps to keep alive the old stories and values. Selling the rugs to traveling tourists is one of the many ways Navajo traditions have bequeathed beauty to people around the world. "Navajos have not simply responded to outside influences, nor have they relinquished their culture. Instead, they

> **Christine Martin, Navajo weaver**
>
> When the fire began to blaze, elders would tell of the ancient times while the young people listened in wide-eyed wonder until they fell asleep. Then the grown-ups' stories would begin. Eventually those stories found their way into the rugs….

This photograph, taken in what was then the New Mexico Territory by Timothy H. O'Sullivan in 1873, shows a Navajo family with their loom.

have struggled, and continue to struggle, to maintain their cultural traditions as they create and sell their products."[387]

American Heroes: The Code Talkers

One of the stiffest tests for American soldiers in World War II came in the pitched fighting on the Japanese island of Iwo Jima. The bloody battle for the island in the winter of 1945 helped set the stage for the Allies' victory in the Pacific theatre later that year. As we now know, the Americans won the island with the help of a top secret weapon: radios manned by Navajo soldiers.

The Japanese were experts at cracking English codes, and could easily decipher commands for American military troop movements. Furthermore, Japanese linguists could also interrupt messages by imitating American accents from Dallas, Texas to Brooklyn, New York. But once the Navajo took over the radios, the Japanese were flummoxed. In one critical two-day operation on Iwo Jima, the Navajo used their own language to send over 800 coded messages between the American officers and the soldiers on the ground. As Sgt. **Philip Johnston** proclaimed, "Were it not for the Navajos, the Marines would never have taken Iwo Jima."[388]

It was Sgt. Johnston who first came up with the idea to use the Navajo language to create a military code. Although not Navajo by birth, Johnston grew up in Navajo Nation, where he "learned songs and ceremonials by the flickering light of many a *hogan* campfire."[389]

What started with 29 soldiers learning 211 words ended with over 300 Navajo soldiers memorizing over 600 coded words and their meanings. Before long, the progress of the war was being tracked with Navajo words steeped in an ancient worldview. Enemy fighter planes were called "hummingbirds," the bombs they dropped were "eggs." Neighboring platoons were called "clans."

The Navajos proved to be hearty soldiers. As one American general observed, "The ability of these Indians to receive and transmit under battle conditions and noises is good, if not better, than their English-speaking fellow soldiers."[390] Many of the soldiers credited their upbringing on the Navajo land as inspiration. It wasn't uncommon, for example, for Navajo mothers to force their children out to freeze in the snow in the early morning, before returning home for a hot bath and a long run. From their previous battles with American settlers and other Native American communities, Navajos learned the importance of hardening their bodies and sharpening their readiness to run at a moment's notice. In one training mission, a Navajo detachment defeated an all-white Marine troop in a 25-mile race, because when the water ran low, the Navajos knew how to drink sap from cactus-like plants.

Navajo soldiers also drew courage from their religion. Code talker **Samuel Holiday**, for example, used the story of Monster Slayer and Born from Water to help survive the maddening gunfire. He said, "It is only when a person believes in the spiritual way that he will be guided and shielded by prayer. In the ceremony I had the words of the prayer said that the spirit of Monster Slayer would be with me as if I was a person who could not be harmed by dangers in my path."[391]

Throughout the brutality of the Japanese island-hopping campaign, the Navajos were remarkably well-prepared to apply their ancient cosmology to the war's swiftly changing fortunes, all the while operating previously unfamiliar technologies. In the Navajo language, the radios used in World War II were called *nílch'i báyaa'ahi*, or "wind that sings." It recalled the four primordial winds that blew at the beginning of all creation. "Suffusing all of nature, Holy Wind gives life, thought, speech, and the power of motion to all living things and serves as the means of communication between all elements of the living world. As such, it is central to Navajo philosophy and world view."[392]

In the year 2000, the original 29 Navajo code talkers were awarded American Congressional Medals of Honor. The following year, American President George W. Bush handed out the medals to the surviving soldiers. "It is a story of ancient people, called to serve in a modern war," he said. "Above all, it's a story of young Navajos who brought honor to their nation and victory to their country."[393] An American corporal who fought on Iwo Jima said it in even simpler terms. "My life," he said, "belongs to those Navajos."[394]

The Navajo Go Hollywood: Monument Valley in John Ford's Westerns

Nearly broke after the Great Depression, Harry Goulding left his Trading Post in Monument Valley where he had done business with the Navajos for years. He had heard a little-known Hollywood director, John Ford, was looking for locations to shoot a Western. Armed with photos of Navajo country and his last $60, Goulding set out for California. At Ford's studio in Burbank, Goulding was promptly dismissed by the receptionist. "I've lived among the Navajos so long that I don't get so busy that I can't wait," he said defiantly. "I've got a bedroll. I've got plenty of time, so I'll just stay right here."[395]

Goulding's perseverance won the day, and soon after Ford saw the photographs, he and his equally unknown lead actor named John Wayne were on their way to Monument Valley to shoot the award-winning film ***Stagecoach***. The film was the first of twelve westerns Ford would shoot at Monument Valley. "My favorite location is Monument Valley," Ford later said. "I feel at peace there. I have been all over the world, but I consider this the most complete, beautiful, and peaceful place on Earth."[396]

Headquartered at **Goulding's Trading Post**, thousands of Navajo actors were used for extras and occasionally speaking parts throughout the films. In Ford's 1950 Western *Wagon Master* (filmed in Utah), the uncredited **Lee Bradley** plays a Navajo who believes "all white men are thieves," but nevertheless agrees to take in a weary Mormon wagon train.

For the Navajos who participated in the filming, these were memorable times. Along with the free meals, the Navajos were paid between five and twenty dollars a day. Camped alongside the Hollywood actors, they spent the days filming, and the nights playing cards and singing English and Navajo songs by campfire. There were wrestling matches, horse races, and constant, good-natured teasing.

While filming ***The Searchers*** in 1956, the Navajos held an adoption ceremony to make Ford (known as "Tall Leader") an honorary member of the Navajo people. For his "courtesy and friendship," they gave Ford a deer hide inscribed with the words, "In your travels may there be beauty on both sides of you, and beauty ahead of you."[397] Years after Ford's death, the 96-year old Navajo Billy Yellow traveled to Portland, Maine to help dedicate a statue in Ford's hometown.

Not everyone was enamored with the roles the Navajo portrayed. Racial stereotypes in many of the films painted Native Americans as Romantic savages, clinging to an untenable life with the coming of the railway and 19th-century Western civilization. In Ford's films, the Navajos were cast according to what Native Americans "should look like," the wilder the better. No distinctions were made between Native American peoples. The Navajo might be called on to play Comanche or Apache without anyone in Hollywood bothering to learn their languages or customs.

The filming was done on sacred land, a point some elders angrily pointed out. Hastiin Tso, a respected Navajo medicine man, could make $100 for getting the rain clouds to dissipate before a day's filming. But when a drought afflicted Navajo country some years later, Tso was blamed for having tampered with the Holy People just to help Hollywood make a movie.

In the Navajo worldview, symbols are animated with real life. "Some of the medicine men and elders did not like all this pretend killing," said one of the Navajo actors.[398] The line between acting and reality is always porous. "Navajo actors feared that what they did on the screen was a foreshadowing of what they could expect in the future."[399] Pretending to die on sacred land was serious business. It could have grave consequences long after the film crews packed their camera bags and headed back home to Hollywood.

Though he worked with John Wayne, Shirley Temple, and Henry Fonda, Ford always credited the Navajo Valley as the source of his inspiration. "I think you can say that the real star of my Westerns has always been the land," he said.[400] In Ford's classic American Westerns, the beautiful and rugged Navajo landscape serves as the backdrop for a lonely, nostalgic, and fiercely independent myth of the American dream.

As an outsider to the Navajo traditions, does John Ford present Monument Valley to "invoke too much meaning or rather the loss of meaning?"[401] To put it another way, when today's global tourists take photographs on John Ford Point in Monument Valley, does the land of the Navajo still speak the ancient stories of their connections to the land, or do the awe-inspiring spires merely "serve as monuments, memorials, to a relationship of affinity that has been lost forever"?[402]

Leaving the "Rez"

In the 1960s, outside interest in the Navajo worldview was at an all-time high. Anthropologists and knowledge seekers came to the reservation (or the "rez" as it is referred to more colloquially) to learn from Navajo medicine men, weavers, and philosophers. Some Navajo artists also began the challenging experiment of living and working outside Navajo Nation.

Carl Gorman was the eldest member of the original 29 code talkers. Steeped in Navajo tradition, Gorman was an artist who incorporated modern philosophies into traditional ceremonial patterns and paints. When he and his son, **R.C. Gorman**, held their first father-son art exhibit off the reservation in Phoenix, Arizona, the local newspaper dubbed them "Rebels in Indian Art." The elder Gorman later left Navajo Nation to help found the Native American Studies Department at the University of California, Davis.

The younger Gorman grew up on the reservation too poor to have pencils and paper. Instead, Gorman used sticks and charcoal to perfect his art. "I would lay on the soft red earth of Canyon de Chelly," he recalled, "looking up at the stars and my grandmother would tell me the Navajo name for each star."[403]

In his small one-room school, Gorman was punished for drawing pictures of naked women. He was later expelled from his Catholic junior high school for being "too difficult." In the early 1960s he left the reservation to live with other hippies and artists in the now legendary Castro section of San Francisco. Gorman's basement apartment was a place for intellectual conversation, artistic experimenting and raucous parties where everybody danced, "girls with boys, boys with boys."[404]

By 1968, he had made enough money from his paintings to buy a successful art gallery in Taos, New Mexico. Gorman's new **Navajo Gallery** quickly became a hotspot for artists and socialites across the country. American celebrities were buying his Navajo-inspired paintings for upwards of $10,000 apiece. Gorman was traveling across the country, hanging out with Andy Warhol in New York and hosting celebrities when they came through Taos.

In 1971, Gorman's "Homage to Navajo Women" series was an immediate success. The colorful lithographs showed traditional Navajo women with mysterious expressions that turned inward. "I deal with the common woman who smells of the fields and maize," he explained. "She lives and breathes. She's earthy. My women work and walk the land. They have big hands, strong feet. They are soft and strong like my mother and grandmother who gave me life."[405]

Though Gorman was off the reservation, the hill country of Taos is still within range of the six sacred mountains. When today's Navajos go further away, some find their new lives disorienting. Like other religious groups in diaspora, many Navajos struggle to assimilate into a New World American melting pot, while still keeping their traditions as a sometimes secret reserve for strength in tough times.

> ### Esther Belin
>
> That is what I like to leave with my Indian audiences, a yearning to search for their place in the Indian diaspora.
>
> There is so much written on Indian, on being an Indian, defining an Indian, on the genocide of the Indian. I want the focus to be on life. The Indian that lives and loves the creation on this planet. The Indian that births Indian babies capable of enjoying the culture that makes us survivors, interpreters, artists.

In her poem, "Blues-ing on the Brown Vibe," poet **Esther Belin** tells the story of a Navajo named Coyote who struts down the street "feeling good/looking good." He leaves Navajo Nation on a Greyhound bus to California, befriending other Native Americans along the way. In Belin's poem, Coyote, like so many others, is reduced to "blues-ing on the urban brown funk vibe." Not quite as confident or secure as he appears, Coyote embarks on a wandering life, "tasting the brown/rusty at times/worn bitter from relocation."

As the Navajo join the wider world at the edges of their ever-shrinking borders, new challenges await. The land that once called the Holy People now calls out to others as well. More than ever, tourists come from around the world to visit Monument Valley and Canyon de Chelly on road trips through some of America's most beautiful national parks. They come because of old stories, old movies, or hoping to learn something of the old religious rituals. To such wisdom seekers, the **Navajo Nation Museum** gives us an important reminder. "*T'ahdii kǫ́ǫ́ honiidlǫ́,*" it boldly proclaims at the end of one exhibit. "We are still here."

Discovery Questions

1. Describe a story that helped you through a difficult time in your life. What strength did you draw from it? Why?

2. Research how tourism and digital culture are changing the Canyon de Chelly. What can digital culture add to the way we understand ourselves and our environment, and what does it take away?

3. Describe a time in your life when you felt like you were "walking in beauty." What steps can you take to feel that way again?

4. Go online and read different versions of the Navajo creation story. What differences do you find in the many versions? What is it about verbal storytelling that is different from reading or writing?

5. Given the contemporary debates on climate change, what potential solutions can Navajo stories and philosophies offer us?

6. Find and select one painting of R.C. Gorman on the Internet. What does it say about beauty or the relationship between humans and nature?

7. Visit an art gallery and choose a work that says something about the natural world. What new perspective is being offered? Why?

Glossary

Terms	Definitions
Annie Wauneka	Civil activist and member of the Navajo Nation Council
Barboncito	19th-century Navajo political and spiritual leader
Blanca Peak	One of six sacred mountains that enclose the land of the Navajo
Blessingway	Recital and re-enactment of ritualistic practices transmitted orally from generation to generation
Born from Water	One of two twins tasked to defeat monsters and spawn the human race in the Navajo creation story
Bosque Redondo	Place of 1864 deportation and attempted socio-ethnic cleansing of the Navajo people by the US government
Canyon de Chelly	National park in the northeastern region of Arizona.
Carding	Weaving process in which strands of wool are stretched and straightened
Carl Gorman	20th-century Navajo artist and World War II code talker
Changing Woman	One of the Holy People who directed the Navajo People to the sacred land between the six sacred mountains
Corn	Sacred Navajo food; its pollen is regularly used in religious rituals. Also called maize
Coyote	The consummate trickster in Navajo legend
Diné	Meaning "people," refers specifically to the Navajo
Diné Bahane'	The Navajo creation story
Eagle	Sacred animal; its feathers are regularly worn for protection
Esther Belin	Contemporary Navajo poet
Fifth World	Present world in the Navajo creation story
First Man and First Woman	First human beings created from corn
Five-fingered People	Human beings
Gobernador Knob	One of six sacred mountains that enclose the land of the Navajo
Gouding's Trading Post	Trading post and museum located in Monument Valley
Hogan	A traditional Navajo home made of wood, mud and bark
Hózhó	Navajo word for walking in beauty
Holy People	Creators and protectors of the natural world
John Redhouse	Contemporary environmental activist
Kinaaldá	A sacred Navajo ritual marking the coming of womanhood

Lee Bradley	Uncredited actor appearing in and facilitating many of John Ford's Western films
Long Walk	Refers to the 1864 forced exodus and relocation of the Navajo people
Loom	A ritualistically constructed contraption used to weave blankets
Manuelito	19th-century Navajo leader and warrior
Medicine men	Communally accredited performers of traditional ceremonies
Monster Slayer	One of two twins tasked to defeat monsters and spawn the human race in the Navajo creation story
Mount Hesperus	One of six sacred mountains that enclose the land of the Navajo
Mount Huerforno	One of six sacred mountains that enclose the land of the Navajo
Mount Taylor	One of six sacred mountains that enclose the land of the Navajo
Nádleehí	People who take on multiple or alternate gender roles
Navajo Gallery	Art gallery in Taos, New Mexico, once curated by artist R.C. Gorman
Navajo Nation Museum	Library and museum on Navajo grounds located in Window Rock, Arizona
Philip Johnston	Organized the Navajo code talkers during World War II
R.C. Gorman	20th-century Navajo artist; son of Carl Gorman
Samuel Holiday	Navajo code talker during World War II
San Francisco Peaks	One of six sacred mountains that enclose the land of the Navajo
Shearing	Cutting the wool off sheep
Spider Woman	One of the Holy People from Canyon de Chelly who gifted the Navajo the knowledge of weaving
Spinning	Strengthening wool by twisting it around a wooden stick
Stagecoach	A 1939 western filmed in Monument Valley
The Searchers	A 1959 Hollywood western filmed in Monument Valley
Treaty of Bosque Redondo	19th-century treaty compelling the Navajo to surrender their sacred land to the American government, forcing their children into Christian boarding schools
Warp	Weaving technique in which longitudinal lines are drawn by threads of wool
Weft	Weaving technique in which yarn is threaded into a warp by using an under-and-over pattern
White Wind	Ancient life-giving wind

Chapter Eleven
Shintoism
One with Nature

If we want to understand who we are and where we're going, we need to learn our place in the natural world. Ancient Shinto stories teach us how to rediscover and reconnect with other living beings.One profound and popular story beings in the simplest manner, with a goddess calmly weaving.

The ancient story of **Amaterasu** (Heaven Shining) and her brother **Susanoo** (Rushing Raging Man) does more than shed light on a loving but turbulent brother-sister relationship. Susanoo had good reason to be jealous of his sister. She ruled the Heaven with foresight and love. But down below, Susanoo was making a bit of a mess of his own divinely inherited world. While he appeared to visit his sister with the best intentions, his anger soon got the best of him. He defecated inside the pure hall where Amaterasu held the sacred feast for the new rice harvest. Later he cut a hole in the roof and dropped a badly skinned pony into the holy weaving room where his sister was loyally threading garments for the gods.

After covering for her disruptive brother all her life, Amaterasu finally had enough. Disgusted, she ran away to hide in a cave, far away from an ungrateful world that had clearly taken her for granted. "And so the high plains of heaven were cast into utter darkness and the central realm of reed plains was filled with gloom. Because of this, endless night came to cover the world."[406]

Realizing their mistake, the gods approached Amaterasu's cave in a spirited effort to lure her out. Their dubious plan involved a sacred mirror, an impromptu drum kit, and a bawdy dance scene more typical of a modern-day cabaret than a watershed moment to save creation. Amazingly, the plan worked.

Like a caterpillar that morphs into a butterfly, Heaven Shining metaphorically finished her weaving, retreated into her cocoon, and emerged from the darkness stronger, more dazzling than ever before. There was no more turning back for the Sun Goddess, and from then on, "the high plains of heaven and central realm of reed plains were lit up with her radiance."[407]

Shrine and State

The story of Shintoism is inseparable from the more than 6,000 islands that make up modern-day Japan. The word "Japan" means "Land of the Rising Sun." The Shinto connection between the

Japanese people and their natural environment is emblazoned on their national flag and portrayed over the years in festivals, art, and popular stories.

Many of these early stories were collected and codified in the eighth-century editions of the ***Kojiki*** and the ***Nihongi***. Infused with the cross-currents of Confucianism and Buddhism, the books recount how heaven and earth were separated, how the islands of Japan first emerged from the primordial sea, and how a people sustained life from the deadly and delicate balance of natural phenomena. A famous Japanese folklorist called Shintoism "the unifying principle of an ancient lifestyle founded on religion."[408]

The word "Shintoism" means "the way of the ***kami***." The *kami*, gods or spirits of Japan, are one with the natural landscapes of the country. They are the life forces that infuse us with vitality, courage, and willpower. The *kami* are the "innate powers of renewal within the world,"[409] revealing themselves through natural events: through wind, rain, sun, growth and decomposition. For thousands of years the Japanese people have offered food and gifts to particular *kami* in order to gain confidence in future decisions, to soften everyday hardships, and to feel more at home in their natural environment.

Shrine culture is one of Shintoism's most visible legacies in contemporary Japan. *Kami* dwell in over 80,000 shrines across Japan. A large majority of Japanese people still attend shrines throughout the year for good luck, health, or money, regardless of whether they consider themselves Shinto or not. Many Shinto shrines are now cared for by Buddhist monks, which in itself shows the elasticity of Shintoism throughout the years.

Because the *kami* are so deeply entwined with nature, Shinto shrines are generally built with natural wood; their grounds offer the ancient and modern-day city-dweller a quiet refuge for philosophical reflection. The enduring symbol of a Shinto shrine is a ***torii***, a tall wooden gate that serves as a portal for us to leave behind our daily stress and enter into the realm of the sacred.

The **Ise Shrine**, sometimes called "the soul of Japan," is one of the country's most sacred Shinto shrines. Amaterasu was enshrined in Ise over 2,000 years ago. The wooden sanctuary that houses Amaterasu's secret mirror is torn down and rebuilt every 20 years to keep it pure for the revered *kami*. Ritualistically chopped down in the forest, the wooden logs symbolize sustainability and the passing on of traditional skills to the next generation.

One novelist has described the "melody of the echoing axe blows" that marks the tree-cutting as "a very ancient art," and cuts close to "the very essence of Shintō."[410] In 2016, Prime Minister Shinzo Abe hosted the Group of Seven world leaders at the Ise Shrine because he believed that the Shinto shrine was the "most suited to get in touch with the Japanese spirit."

Kojiki

Now the spirits of heaven all commanded the mighty one He Who Beckoned [Izanagi] and the mighty one She Who Beckoned [Izanami] with mighty words, proclaiming:

"Make firm this drifting land and fashion it in its final form!"

And so proclaiming, they gave them a jeweled halberd of heaven to aid them in this undertaking.

So the two spirits stood on the floating bridge of heaven, and when they lowered the jeweled spear to stir the sea below, its brine sloshed and swished about as they churned it. When they pulled it up, clumps of salt dripped down from its tip to pile up into an island.

This is the Self-Shaped Isle.

For much of Japan's history there has been little separation between religion and government. The country's emperors were seen as heavenly-blessed descendants from the land's founders, **Izanagi** and **Izanami**. For hundreds of years, the chief priest or priestess of the Ise Shrine has been chosen from the **Imperial House of Japan**. In the late 19th century, the Japanese government took full administrative control of many Shinto shrines, a move that further blurred the distinction between Shintoism and the Japanese State.

Since the end of World War II, Shinto shrines are no longer fully controlled by government officials, but paying respects to the *kami* of old is as popular as ever. For example, millions of people attend shrines on New Year's Eve to celebrate *Hatsumode*, the first Shrine visit of the year.

In Tokyo, the Shinto shrine honoring the *kami* of **Emperor Meiji** and his wife, **Empress Shōken**, is one of most popular tourist sites throughout the year. On weekends there may be 15 weddings a day, where the bride and groom still exchange ceremonial sake drinks and sip cherry blossom tea.

Japanese high school students still flock to **Tenjin Shrines** in January and February to give gifts before embarking on the final steps of "exam hell." At some Tenjin shrines students can also buy lucky pencils or "Pass the Exam" headbands to help motivate them while studying. Like the fragrance from the plum trees, the sweetness of ancient history may come again if one studies patiently and diligently. In the words of **Sugawara no Michizane,** the scholar-*kami* honored in Tenjin shrines:

> In a roadside field stands
> A leafless willow tree-
> Spring will come, and then
> The wonders of long ago,
> Will all return.[411]

Masks of Longing: Zeami's Noh Theatre

First popularized in the Middle Ages, Noh theatre features a lead actor whose every movement has been lovingly handed down from teacher to student. The dramas are filled with poetry recitals and carefully choreographed dance moves to the beating of drums, the sounds of flutes, and sometimes jarring human wails.

"The aesthetic of the dance is correct for a god,"[412] wrote **Zeami**, the pre-eminent Japanese playwright of the 15th century. Zeami claimed that the first Noh dance was performed to lure Amaterasu out of her cave. The theatrical tradition therefore emerges directly from these sacred Shinto roots.

Some plays, often performed on New Year's Day, portray Shinto *kami* directly. In the days before "becoming a god," the lead actor would be expected to go through a number of rituals designed to purify the body and soul for the task ahead. Because the acting is "like praying to the god,"[413] the performance takes religious discipline to pull off effectively.

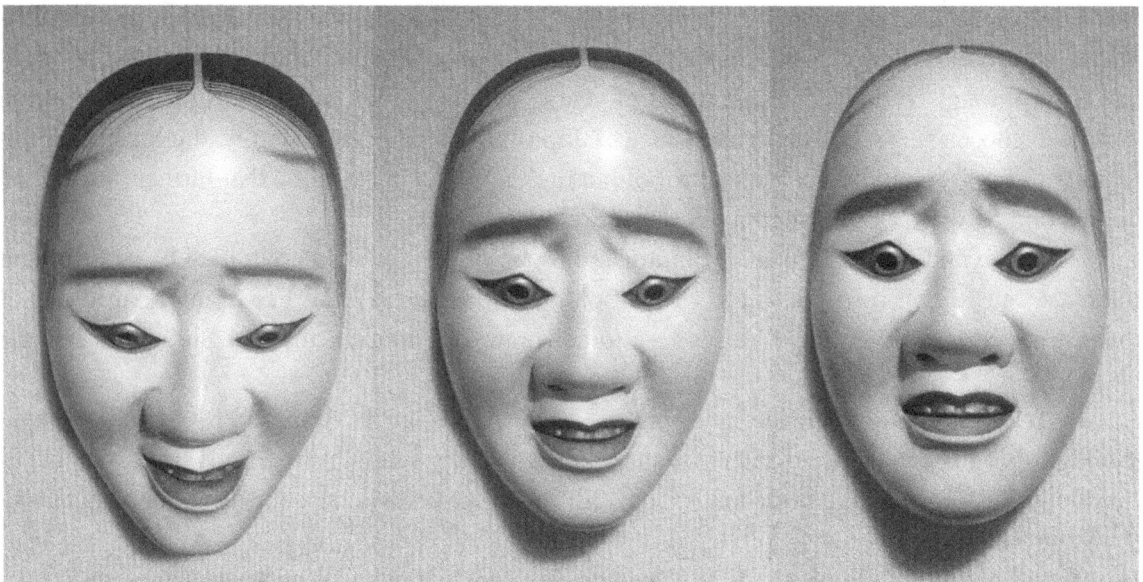

These three photographs of the same female Noh mask show how actors, simply by tilting their heads, can display significant changes of expression and emotion. The artistic intention behind the use of masks in Noh theatre is to encourage the audience to use their imaginations to engage with the play, as well as to codify and stylize facial expressions.

Zeami insisted that the essence of the gods could be made manifest in the costumes and masks the actor dons. It's critical that actors lose themselves in order to transform into something higher. The moment an actor puts on the mask in the **mirror room** backstage is as important as anything that is presented on stage. It is while alone with the mask that the best actor is imbued with the spirit of longing, requiring "the total transformation of self which is the basic intent of Noh."[414]

A dedicated Buddhist, Zeami nonetheless invoked Shinto elements, drawing on ancient stories that depict the longing for constancy behind the chaotic natural world. We see this dramatized in two of Zeami's most popular plays, *Hagoromo* and *Izutsu*.[415]

Hagoromo

The play opens with an ordinary fisherman stumbling upon an angel's feather robe hanging from a tree. The fisherman only recognizes its earthly value. He takes it for himself because he cannot fathom the pain he is causing the angel, who is now condemned to the ordinary world.

"Without my feather mantle, the pathways of flight are closed to me," the angel wails. "Never again will I return to Heaven! Please, please, give it back!"

Touched by the angel's suffering, the fisherman reluctantly agrees to return the robe, but only if the angel will dance for him. His deal is accepted. "And in thanks," sings the angel, "I will gladly dance, for those who inhabit this sad, lower world, a dance to commemorate my visit among them."

Binding Heaven and earth, the beauty of the dance links the simple fisherman with another more perfect world. The angel commands the fisherman to remember the Ise Shrine where the "Gods' offspring will rule our moon-illumined land, source of the sun!" Like the celestial dance that lures Amaterasu out of the cave, the angel's dance reminds all who witness it that otherworldly enchantments are never far from view.

"Ah, beautiful! Although not Heaven, the earth is lovely too," the angel concludes. And with that, she departs. Her feather robe floats in the wind high above

> Mount Ashitaka,
> Fuji's soaring peak,
> and, mingling with the mists,
> fades into the heavens,
> lost forever to view.

Izutsu

Long before Zeami, Japanese poets set to work collecting and editing traditional poems of the ancient tradition. Such poetry "without the slightest effort, moves Heaven and Earth," and "stirs the unseen gods and spirits to feelings of pity."[416] Medieval playwrights like Zeami were especially attracted to the verses collected in the eleventh-century **The Tales of Ise** that addressed love and longing in elegantly simple language.

In *Izutsu*, Zeami draws on a set of *Ise* poems written by lovers who recall playing by a well as children. The woman, older now, writes of her hair growing long as she waits to marry her childhood sweetheart. "For whom shall it be put up if not for you," she pines. Happily, they marry.

But in Zeami's drama, the pure and innocent love cannot survive the worldly challenges all lovers face. As children, the lovers came to the well "cheek to cheek and sleeve to sleeve." But at the ancient temple site years later, Zeami shows us only the ghost of the long-haired lover still sadly longing for a happier time. Under a wistful mask, she sings of how "the old days, once forgotten, flood a troubled mind."

In the play, a Buddhist monk is attracted to the site because the religious pining for something more is shown to be universal. The weary long-haired ghost welcomes all visitors.

> Yes it is true, a loneliness
> pervades the autumn nights,
> and at this ancient temple,
> callers are rare

One theme of the Noh play is that ancient religious stories, like the flowering passions of first love, are too easily forgotten. Zeami's monk will guard the well, keeping the spirit of love alive, while the actors on stage will keep the story from oblivion. Today's Noh spectators still leave the theatre with the chorus plaintively singing of the old temple bell:

> an ancient bell tolls in the dawn:
> an ancient temple, loud with pines
> where the wind sighs.

It's a temple that no longer stands in modern-day Japan. Today's pilgrims can still find a pillar marking the ancient love in front of a croquet ground for the elderly. The inspirational well was recently removed to make room for a large-scale construction project.

Kurozumi Munetada's Healing Rituals

In the Shinto tradition, the lessons of the Sun Goddess Amaterasu are not just for emperors or dancers. **Kurozumi Munetada** was a Shinto priest from Okayama who was famous for healing sicknesses of the body and soul in the early 1800s. In his practice of *majinai*, Munetada combined medical practice with philosophical wisdom. He believed his unique *majinai* ritual was "the action that mediates our prayers and carries them to Amaterasu."[417]

> ### Kurozumi Munetada
>
> Although your situation is understandable and reasonable, gloominess is taboo for one who is devoted in faith. Vitalizing your life is the divine way of things. Enjoying your life is the divine way, so practice complying with the holy heart of Great Kami. Please try to get a spark of cheerfulness into yourself. The first thing you should do is to laugh. It looks like you have not laughed for years. From this very day try to laugh as much and as often as possible.

Munetada noticed that people were no longer getting along with each other. Community spirit was fracturing as the people of Okayama frequently argued, wearied from work, wearied from life. Sickness and death were inevitable, no high priest could change that. But Munetada believed that if people were able to access just a small part of the light of the Sun God, they could fight their ailments and live out their lives with more vitality.

One story tells of a religious man, Ogata, who had a particularly nasty case of tuberculosis. He prayed and prayed to no avail. The sickness left him tired and bitter. Finally, Munetada sternly said to the broken man, "Ogata san, do you mean to say you have been defeated by the illness?"[418] At that moment Ogata understood what it means to be pure in the body and the mind. Munetada helped his patients turn their attention to the ways they confronted and negotiated the sufferings of the world.

Another story tells of Munetada watching children fly their kites through the trees. The kites that got stuck on living branches were easily pulled free. But the kites that hit upon the dead branches seemed to get more and more tangled. The lesson was simple. When you lose your vigor and happiness, your relationships get caught. "Everything gets all tangled up," Munetada said, "going haywire and causing a big commotion, all confused. What a mess it all becomes!"[419]

The Shinto *kami* of the Sun exhorts us to shine more radiantly by cultivating our inner joy and spontaneity. Only when we learn to

Amaterasu

revive our deadened vitality can we begin to repair our relationships with others. "With Sincerity alone," Munetada wrote, "the Earth can be a family."[420]

In another story, Munetada healed a shunned patient with a disfiguring skin condition. Inviting him into his Amaterasu shrine room, Munetada went right to work, covering his own hands and face "with the man's ugly, bloody pus." Why would Munetada risk defiling himself in such a sacred place? As the Shinto priest later explained to his wife, "If we are to fear diseases and feel that such things are dirty and polluting, how could we pray for those who are suffering?"[421]

For Munetada, religious faith in the Sun Goddess and hands-on aid to his fellow humans were intimately woven into his famous healing rituals.

Sumo wrestlers get ready for a match.

Sumo Wrestling: Grappling with the *Kami*

The *Kojiki* tells of an ancient wrestling match, a story of Amaterasu sending Brave Mighty Thunderbolt Man (*Takemikazuchi*) on an important mission to clear the land for the Japanese people. The mission seems destined to fail when Brave Southward Smelter (*Takeminakata*) appears, "carrying by his fingertips a boulder that it would take a thousand men to pull." But Brave Mighty Thunderbolt Man is not deterred and wrestles with his rival, crushing his opponent's arm "as though it were a young reed."[422]

Since that ancient battle, Sumo wrestling matches have been performed at Shinto shrines to honor the *kami*. The matches, rarely lasting more than two minutes, end when a wrestler is forced out of a ring or taken down to the ground. Traditionally, such contests of strength have helped the faithful interpret the will of the *kami*.

Ancient Shinto practices are still in place in modern-day contests. Today, Sumo matches begin and end with the throwing of rice, harkening back to celebrations of the harvest when the *kami* were called on to bless the newest crop. Modern day referees still wear costumes that are meant to resemble the colorful garb of Shinto priests. Above the ring hangs a pointed structure that recall the roof of a Shinto temple.

For three days, dedicated workers build the wrestling ring in a circle of clay and sand to exact specifications. After the work is completed, the **ring ceremony** can begin. The ceremony is over 250 years old and is traditionally held the day before a Sumo wrestling tournament to draw attention to the physical and spiritual strength of the wrestlers.

Three men dressed in ceremonial white robes consecrate the ring by calling the *kami* to intervene and protect the faithful participants. "Everlasting life to heaven, long life to earth, and may the wind and rain faithfully follow the seasons," they chant. Musicians holding lacquered drums hanging from ritualistic poles march around the circle three times, concluding the Shinto service.

When a Sumo wrestler reaches ***yokozuna***, the highest rank, he must first participate in a religious ceremony at the Tomioka Hachiman Shrine in Tokyo. At the Shinto shrine stands the Yokozuna Stone, a memorial to Japan's finest wrestlers.

Today, ritualistic Sumo wrestling is still performed in Shinto shrines across Japan. They also take place at Tokyo's more secular Ryōgoku *Sumo* Hall that seats over 11,000 spectators. Still, even in modern-day Tokyo, many Shinto elements of Sumo wrestling are practiced and respected. "It is the constant interplay of a heritage intrinsically both sacred and profane ... that makes this indigenous wrestling form the national sport of Japan."[423]

Mount Fuji: Power and Passion

Standing 3,776.24 metres (12,389 feet) tall, Mount Fuji is the highest peak in Japan and one of its most enduring national symbols. The story of Mount Fuji, like the stories behind so many natural wonders in Japan, has its roots in Shintoism.

Mount Fuji is an active volcano. The fires of destruction and creation have long excited the religious imagination of Japan. Shintoism is replete with examples of *kami* that inspire beauty and *kami* that inspire dread. The scorching lava that bubbles deep within Mount Fuji has been feared and revered since ancient times.

Konohana Sakuya (Lady Blooming Tree Blossoms) is the *kami* most often associated with caring for Mount Fuji. Sakuya is the *kami* for all delicate living things. Her symbol is the

From mouth to mouth will pass the word,
Travelling and speaking
Of the peak of Fuji.

—Yamabe no Akahito

cherry tree, famous in Japan for its fragility, fragrance, and short blossoming life. To the outsider, entrusting the full force of Mount Fuji to a waifish and gentle goddess may seem imprudent. But Sakuya is portrayed with an inner strength that rivals nature's fiercest volcanic eruptions.

In the *Kojiki*, Sakuya is the prized daughter of Great Mountain Majesty (*Ōyamatsumi*). Sakuya tells her husband that she is pregnant with "a mighty child of heaven's spirits." Her husband suspects Sakuya was unfaithful and therefore the child will be born weak, without the vitality that surges from the *kami*. In defiant response, Sakuya locks herself in a room and lights an unchecked fire. "While the flames burned the fiercest," she gives birth to three heavenly children, before calmly walking them out of the flames. If any *kami* could tame the fires of Mount Fuji it would surely be Lady Blooming Tree Blossoms.

In classical Japanese writing, Mount Fuji can be spelled in different ways that highlight varying philosophical traits the mountain inspires: "immortal," "unequaled," "inextinguishable." Like the sun and the sea, Mount Fuji is more than a natural wonder; it is a sacred place where the *kami* reside and renew. Since ancient times, gazing at the mountain was therefore treated as an awe-inspiring religious moment that deepened one's spiritual connections to the natural world. Such forms of ritualistic gazing encourage "the poetic dimension of praise, appreciating and expressing through language and emotion the enjoyment of Fuji and nature."[424]

For over one thousand years, Japanese **Waka** poetry has captured profound natural philosophies in simple, everyday language. In the seventh and eighth centuries, the *Man'yōshū* poets were renowned for their *Waka* verses that showed reverence for nature. Poet **Yamabe no Akahito** held a special veneration for Mount Fuji. In one of his most famous poems, still recited today, he writes:

> From the bay at Tago
> I see, when gazing out,
> Pure white—
> On the heights of Fuji's peak—
> The snow has fallen.

In the later Middle Ages, poets inspired by the inner fires of Mount Fuji turned their attention to the passionate stirrings of romantic love. They wrote of the heat and explosive power of the volcano as mirrors to their own carnal passions and spiritual restlessness.

Once poets began to climb to the volcano's peak in the 1700s, the praise took on loftier dimensions. Upon making the rigorous journey, one Shinto priest from **Kyoto** wrote "As I gaze far out from Fuji's summit, there across the blue-green sea plain is the light of heaven's sun rising in the distance."[425]

Soon a number of new religions and sects, some of them direct offshoots of Shintoism, began to emerge around Mount Fuji. All of them encouraged practitioners to make pilgrimages to the mountain and complete a hike to the summit. For such religious pilgrims today, "completing the ascent is not as crucial as looking inward and achieving a spiritual goal."[426]

Seitō's "New Women"

Many traditional Shinto followers were surprised and offended when a new magazine hit the Japanese newsstands in 1911. The magazine was called *Seitō*, named after England's 18th-century Blue Stockings Society feminist salon. But while the all-female editors and contributors shared much with their Western sisters, their challenging, revolutionary writing also drew from classic Shinto sources.

Raichō

In the beginning, Woman was truly the Sun. An authentic person.

Now, Woman is the Moon. A sickly, pale-faced moon, living off another, reflecting another's brilliance.

We must now recapture our hidden Sun.

"Let us reveal our hidden Sun and our dormant Genius." This is the cry we ceaselessly turn toward ourselves, the craving so hard to suppress, so difficult to extinguish. This is the sole instinct toward the ultimate completion of character, the unification of all fragmented instincts.

It is this cry, this craving, this ultimate instinct that embodies a passionate spiritual focus.

Thus it is at the peak of this spiritual focus that the proud throne of Genius shines.

Yosano Akiko

"Mountain Moving Day"
The day when mountains move has come.
Or so I said. But no one believed me.
The mountains have simply been asleep for a while.
In their ancient past,
the mountains blazed with fire and they moved.
If you don't believe that either, fine.
But trust me when I tell you this -
all the women who were sleeping
are awake now and moving.

The founder of the magazine, Hiratsuka Haru, adopted the pen name **Raichō** after graduating from Japan's Women's College. Raichō began the first magazine with her famous **Seitō Manifesto** in which she makes allusions to Amaterasu, with passionate writing that "restored the goddess and other mythic images of productive female energy to a new generation of women."[427]

The Manifesto began with the now famous opening, "In the beginning, Woman was truly the Sun. An authentic person." But such brilliant light had been steadily receding from the world, as women were being forced into subservient roles in 20th-century Japan. As Raichō plaintively writes in her Manifesto, realizing one's authentic self is not something to be learned from a book. "It is the Sun, before sunset, burning with a scorching heat above the Japan Alps, circling round and round. It is my hushed sobbing as I stand by myself at the summit of a lone peak."

The magazine featured young, unknown writers like **Itō Noe** alongside more popular poets like **Yosano Akiko**. *Seitō* would go on to cover a wide range of personal and political topics, from chastity to abortion, marriage to prostitution. But before the magazine ended its run, its articles would always return to the ancient Shinto longing for self-discovery, using traditional symbols to help awaken female vitality.

Yasunari Kawabata's "Elegies"

In 1968, **Yasunari Kawabata** was awarded the Nobel Prize in Literature for his poetic depictions of Japan's decaying (but still enduring) attachment to nature's cycles in the de-spiritualizing rush of the modern world. The Swedish Nobel committee commented specifically on Kawabata's description of the ancient holy city of Kyoto, "with its Shinto and Buddha temples, its old artisan quarters and botanical gardens."

In his novel, *The Old Capital*, Kawabata makes a point of noting how some camphor trees appear displaced outside a Buddhist temple. "Isn't that the way it is with Kyoto? Isn't it the same with mountains and rivers … and the people too?" a young girl asks her father.

The old man has lost his vitality in the new Japan, but he can't quite accept his daughter's sadness. "That's not always true with people," he argues unconvincingly.

To his surprise, his young daughter hasn't entirely lost touch with an ancient philosophy that looks to nature for understanding of the human condition. "Father," she says, "if you look closely at the trunks of those trees and the strangely spreading limbs, don't they seem frightening, as though they possess some great power?"

"They do, but does a young girl like you think of such things?"[428]

Though never an avid follower of Shintoism, Kawabata always held reverence for its philosophies that he found still embedded in Japanese life. After the destruction of World War II and the arrival of American occupation forces, Kawabata claimed he would only write elegies for Japan's old, enchanted ways.

His restless, alienated characters recall a richly evocative world while negotiating the new realities of their everyday life. In the novel *Snow Country*, the hollowed-out character, "who lived a life of idleness, found that he tended to lose his honesty with himself, and he frequently went out alone into the mountains to recover something of it."[429] The mountains, like the flowers and the trees, held ancient spirits to those who listened.

Kawabata introduces us to a sick old man spitting up blood in his novel, *The Sound of the Mountain*. The old man begins to hear the rumblings deep within the mountain outside his window.

"The sound stopped," Kawabata writes, "and he was suddenly afraid. A chill passed over him, as if he had been notified that death was approaching…. It was as if a demon had passed, making the mountain sound out."[430] But despite the mountain's profound beckoning, life continues to move along pleasantly enough for the old man. The novel ends with the playful chatter of family life and the superficial sound of his daughter-in-law doing the dishes.

This persistent interplay between modern living and ancient religion informs many of Kawabata's stories. It also highlights the challenge that Shinto beliefs present Japan and the modern world.

> ## Yasunari Kawabata
>
> *1968 Nobel Prize Acceptance Speech*
> When we see the beauty of the snow, when we see the beauty of the full moon, when we see the beauty of the cherries in bloom, when in short we brush against and are awakened by the beauty of the four seasons, it is then that we think most of those close to us, and want them to share the pleasure. The excitement of beauty calls forth strong fellow feelings, yearnings for companionship… The snow, the moon, the blossoms, words expressive of the seasons as they move one into another, include in the Japanese tradition the beauty of mountains and rivers and grasses and trees, of all the myriad manifestations of nature, of human feelings as well.

Studio Ghibli and the Wonder of Anime

"In the past this land was covered with deep forests and *kami* from ancient times lived there."

So begins the Japanese version of the 1997 blockbuster film **Princess Mononoke**. In the words of the film's renowned director, **Hayao Miyazaki**, *Princess Mononoke* depicts "an epic battle" between "the encroaching civilization of man and the gods of the forest."[431]

Mononoke, or "evil spirits," speaks to the human desire to use the natural world for our own selfishly destructive purposes. In the film, the ancient *kami* that fill the land are disregarded and under persistent attack. "But even in the midst of hatred and slaughter there is still much to live for," Miyazaki proclaimed. "Wonderful encounters and beautiful things still exist."[432]

Many Japanese filmgoers agreed. After eight months the film had already grossed over $150 million, a remarkable sum that means, on average, one out of every 10 people in Japan saw the film in the first year.

In Japan and abroad, the popularity of *Princess Monokoke* helped launch the success of its production company, **Studio Ghibli**. The studio is famous for its **anime** films that blend adult themes with childlike characters in the tradition of Japanese **manga** comics.

Miyazaki is the studio's most popular director and animator, owing a large portion of his success to how he redraws ancient Shinto themes for a modern movie-going audience. "I do not believe in Shinto," Miyazaki has claimed, "but I do respect it, and I feel that the animism origin of Shinto is rooted deep within me."[433]

"The animism origin of Shinto" is especially prevalent in his 2001 anime film **Spirited Away**, which won Miyazaki an Oscar for the Best Animated Feature. Until 2016, the film was the world's highest grossing animated film of all time. The Japanese title, *Kamikakushi*, literally means "Hidden by the *Kami*."

The Shinto-inspired film opens with the words, "Beyond the tunnel is a town of wonder." The tunnel leads to a world of *kami*, where a 10-year-old child must enter in order to find her parents and break a curse.

In *Spirited Away* Miyazaki creates many images from Japan's Shinto sources. For example, the paper faces of the *kami* who are seen purifying themselves in a bathhouse were inspired by masks used in a real-world Shinto ritual at the Kasuga Shrine in the city of Nara.

There are many such examples of Shinto traditions reinterpreted and sometimes exploited in Japanese anime. Popular Nintendo video games, like **Pokémon** and **Ōkami**, for example, reference traditional *kami* and a reverence of nature for a new generation of youth in and out of Japan.

But, more effective than any other medium, Miyazaki's films at Studio Ghibli have thoughtfully developed ancient Shinto themes "to offer the same values in the new context of post-industrial, globalised Japan."[434]

As one American cultural critic writes, Miyazaki always seems to "appreciate flaws, find wonder in unusual places, and understand the importance of balancing contrasts."[435] If that turns out to be Studio Ghibli's greatest gift to the modern world, then we might also say the same for Shintoism.

For centuries, forests have been sacred sites for many of the world's religions.

Discovery Questions

1. Watch a YouTube video on the ritualistic construction of the Ise Shrine. What forms of reverence do you witness in the volunteers? What community values are exhibited?

2. Describe your ritual for studying for a test, what you listen to, wear, eat, etc. How does it put you in the best position to do well on the exam? Would you consider these preparations religious, spiritual, or something else?

3. This weekend, spend an afternoon walking through a forest. Describe the different kinds of trees. What animals did you see or hear? What happened in the forest after you went home for the night? Imagine and describe it.

4. Watch the documentary film *Grand Sumo: The Beauty of Tradition* (Marty Gross Film Productions). Which elements of Sumo wrestling address core Shinto religious beliefs? What are the connections between sports and religion in your own culture?

5. Read Satō Kinko's short story, "The Scar," published in *Seitō* magazine (October 1915). The story is reproduced in the journal *Monumenta Nipponica*, vol. 58, no. 2 (Summer 2003), pp. 181–188. Describe the character Sakae's "loneliness and sense of isolation." Can Shintoism provide comfort for such loneliness or is the religion part of the problem?

6. Describe, in some detail, some of the different life forms you journeyed past on your way home from class. What did you notice for the first time? What does it say about the potential variety of your days?

7. Watch a clip from a Studio Ghibli film. What Shinto themes do you see depicted? How are they modernized or reinterpreted? Does the animation make the religious themes more or less mysterious?

Glossary

Terms	Definitions
Amaterasu	The Sun *kami*; born from Izanagi and Izanami
Anime	A Japanese style of animation featuring natural wonders
Cherry tree	Shinto symbol of brevity and fragility of life
Emperor Meiji	Japanese emperor from 1868 to 1912
Empress Shōken	Revered spouse of Emperor Meiji
Hatsumode	A Japanese tradition to welcome the new year
Hayao Miyazaki	Contemporary anime director and co-founder of Studio Ghibli
Imperial House of Japan	The familial house of the reigning emperor of Japan
Ise Shrine	Holiest Shinto shrine, dedicated to Amaterasu
Itō Noe	20th-century social activist and poet
Izanagi no Mikoto	Male primordial spirit; father of the kami and creator of Japan
Izanami no Mikoto	Female primordial spirit; mother of the kami and creator of Japan
Kami	Shinto spirits, or nature gods
Kojiki	Oldest text of Japan detailing Shinto mythology and ancient Japanese history
Konohana Sakuya	Daughter of mountain *kami* and symbol of material fragility
Kurozumi Munetada	19th-century founder of Shinto sect Kurozumi-kyō
Kyoto	Sacred Japanese city known for its abundance of Buddhist temples and Shinto shrines
Majinai	A series of words said to ward off misfortune
Manga	Japanese style of animation in comic book form
Man'yōshū	Ancient compilation of Japanese *waka* poetry
Mirror room	Noh theatre backstage room where actors mentally prepare for wearing their masks
Mount Fuji	Highest mountain and spiritual landmark of Japan
Nihongi	Chronicles of Japan detailing early histories and myths
Ōkami	2006 Sony Entertainment video game
Pokémon	Nintendo game created by Satoshi Tajiri in 1995

Princess Mononoke	Animated film produced by Studio Ghibli in 1997
Raichō	Pen name of Hiratsuka Haru, 19th-century feminist writer
Ring Ceremony	Ceremony performed before sumo wrestling competitions in which the *kami* are invoked to bless the participants
Seitō	Japan's first women's magazine
Seitō Manifesto	Seitō's statement of purpose written by Raichō
Spirited Away	2001 animated feature film written and directed by Hayao Miyazaki and produced by Studio Ghilbi
Studio Ghibli	Animation studio in Japan co-founded by Hayao Miyazaki
Sugawara no Michizane	Ninth-century poet and scholar
Susanoo	*Kami* of storms; sibling of the sun and the moon
Tenjin Shrines	Shrines where students come seeking good results in their studies
The Tales of Ise	11th-century Japanese stories addressing love and longing
Torii	Iconic Shinto gateway that serves as an entrance into a sacred space
Waka	Ancient style of short Japanese poetry
Yamabe no Akahito	Eighth-century Japanese poet
Yasunari Kawabata	20th-century Nobel laureate
Yokozuna	Highest rank in sumo wrestling
Yosano Akiko	19th-century writer and poet
Zeami	15th-century playwright who developed modern Noh Theatre

Acknowledgements

Today, just as in Ancient Greece, there is a kind of person so confident in their abilities they choose to go it alone, not needing the help of others and not troubling themselves with others' problems. The Greek word for such a self-made man was "ιδιώτης," literally translated as "an idiot." The Greeks understood that the best things in life are created and shared with others.

It takes a village to write a book, and I'm relieved to have such a good one. First off, I'd like to thank my editor David Stover who appreciated the need to expand our discipline's outdated views on what it means to be religious. With his constant encouragement, David nudged us down non-traditional paths, in a stubborn effort to make religious philosophies more inclusive and wide-reaching. I thank him especially for taking a chance on this ambitious project, guiding it out of the darkness and into the light.

This textbook could not have come together were it not for Nishan Kaushall's tireless research and his philosophical integrity. Nishan's persistent insistence on making simple ideas more nuanced and complex philosophical arguments more relatable enlivened each chapter with new directions and endless possibilities. I only hope that the conclusion of our work does not bring an end to our stories, our arguments, and above all, our friendship.

At York University, I'd like to thank Tony Burke for his patient, unwavering support, and his inclusive and welcoming leadership in York's Religious Studies program. I am also indebted to my students of the Gods and Humans course in York's Humanities Department. Confucius was right: when the students are passionate and creative, it is a pleasure to study and practice what we learn.

In Navajo Nation, I am grateful for the generous assistance of Herman Peterson, librarian and keeper of the archives at Diné College. I'd also like to thank Nancy Brown-Martinez for her help at the Center for Southwest Research at the University of New Mexico.

There are many paths up the mountain, though none of them easy. This book is meant for Casley Rose Matthews, Meaghan Hart and everyone who seeks ancient wisdom in the hard-to-find spaces of the modern world. Back home I raise a glass to Aaron Duncan, Stewart McDonough, and the three sisters of Sunny Acres who interrupted the writing process at every opportunity. For that I can't thank them enough.

Finally, I am in never-ending gratitude to Aryn Martin who showed me the deeper meaning of Platonic love. Let the Greek god Hephaestus come down to us, and ask his pointed question: "Do you desire to be wholly one; always day and night to be in one another's company … and after your death in the world below still be one departed soul instead of two?" My answer is yes.

Notes

1. Martianus Capella, "The Marriage of Philosophy and Mercury," in *Martianus Capella and the Seven Liberal Arts*, vol. 2, translated by William Harris Stahl (New York: Columbia University Press, 1977), p. 16.
2. Max Weber, "Science as a Vocation," reprinted in *Daedalus*, vol. 87, no. 1 (Winter 1958).
3. Weber, "Science as a Vocation": 117.
4. Charles Taylor, *A Secular Age* (Cambridge, MA: The Belknap Press of Harvard University Press, 2007), p. 433.
5. Sean Murphy, *One Bird, One Stone: 108 American Zen Stories* (New York: Renaissance Books, 2002), p. 78.
6. P. Hefner, *Technology and Human Becoming* (Minneapolis: Fortress Press, 2003), p. 88, quoted in George Pattison, *Thinking about God in an Age of Technology* (Oxford: Oxford University Press, 2005), p. 51.
7. Taylor, *Secular Age*, pp. 429–430.
8. William James, "Mysticism," in *The Varieties of Religious Experience: A Study in Human Nature*, ed. Martin E. Marty (New York: Penguin, 1982), p. 388.
9. Derek Walcott, "A Sea-Chantey," *In a Green Night: Poems, 1948–1960* (London: J. Cape, 1962).
10. Proverbs (English Standard Version), 1:20.
11. G.U. Thite, *Music in the Vedas: Its Magico-Religious Significance* (Delhi: Sharada, 1997), p. 71.
12. *Rigveda* 10.72.6 (Sharma, 2013), p. 774.
13. Sarvepalli Radhakrishnan, *A Sourcebook in Indian Philosophy*, ed. Sarvepalli Radhakrishnan and Charles A. Moore (Princeton: Princeton University Press, 1967), p. xxiv.
14. Robert Kaplan, *The Nothing that Is: A Natural History of Zero* (Oxford: Oxford University Press, 2000), p. 1.
15. Charles Seife, *Zero: The Biography of a Dangerous Idea* (New York: Penguin, 2000), p. 65.
16. Seife, *Zero*, pp. 208–9.
17. Fritjof Capra, *The Tao of Physics* (Boulder, CO: Bantam, 1975), p. 233.
18. *The Bhagavad Gita*, tr. Gavin Flood and Charles Martin (New York: W.W. Norton & Company, Inc., 2015), 3.37.
19. *Bhagavad Gita*, 5.12.
20. *Bhagavad Gita*, 6.8.
21. *Bhagavad Gita*, 2.71.
22. *Bhagavad Gita*, 6.13.
23. *Yoga Philosophy of Patañjali*, ed. Swāmi Harihārananda Āraṇya, tr. P.N. Mukerji (Albany: SUNY Press, 1983), 1.33.
24. Ian Whicher, "The Integration of Spirit (*purusa*) and Matter (*prakrti*) in the Yoga Sūtra," in *Yoga: The Indian Tradition*, eds. Ian Whicher and David Carpenter (NY: Routledge, 2003), p. 63.
25. Valmiki, *The Ramayana of Valmiki,* tr. P. Lal (Delhi: Vikas Publishing, 1981), p. 55.
26. *Ramayana*, p. 59.
27. *Ramayana*, p. 243.
28. Vikas Bajas, "Anant Pai, 81, is Dead; Comics Told Indian Children their Country's Stories," *New York Times*, February 28, 2011, https://www.nytimes.com/2011/03/01/world/asia/01pai.html.
29. Tania Roy, "Mallika Sarabhi, Sita's Daughters," Accessed, March 4, 2019. http://taniarhea.blogspot.com/2009/10/mallika-sarabhai-sitas-daughters.html.
30. *The Bhāgavata Purāṇa*, eds. Ravi M. Gupta and Kenneth R. Valpey (New York: Columbia University Press, 2017), book 10, 29.2.

31. *Bhāgavata Purāna,* book 10, chp. 29.3.
32. *Love Song of the Dark Lord: Jayadeva's Gita Govinda,* tr. Barbara Stoler Miller (New York Columbia University Press, 1977), 6.18.
33. *Gita Govinda,* 11.16.
34. *Gita Govinda,* 12.10.
35. Mirabai, *Mirabai: Ecsataic Poems,* eds. Robert Bly and Jane Hirshfield (Boston: Beacon Press, 2004), p. 13.
36. *Mirabai,* p. 60.
37. *Mirabai,* p. 36.
38. Jeffrey J. Kripal, *Kāli's Child: The Mystical and the Erotic in the Life and Teachings of of Ramakrishna* (Chicago: University of Chicago Press, 1995), p. 88.
39. *Mahābhāgavata Purāna,* 23.22b–25, quoted in Patricia Dold, "Kālī the Terrific and her Tests: The Śākta Devotionalism of the *Mahābhāgavata Purāna,*" in *Encountering Kālī: In the Margins, at the Center, in the West,* eds. Rachel Fell McDermott and Jeffrey J. Kripal (Berkeley: University of California Press), p. 50.
40. Carl Olson, *The Mysterious Play of Kāli: An Interpretive Study of Rāmakrishna* (Atlanta: Scholars Press, 1990), pp. 44-45.
41. *The Gospel of Sri Ramakrishna,* tr. Swami Nikhilananda (New York: Ramakrishna-Vivekananda Center, 1973), p. 632.
42. *Gospel of Sri Ramakrishna,* p. 752.
43. *Gospel of Sri Ramakrishna,* p. 572.
44. Rita M. Gross, "Is the Goddess a Feminist?" in *Is the Goddess a Feminist?: The Politics of South Asian Goddesses,* eds. Alf Hiltebeitel and Kathleen M. Erndl (New York: New York University Press, 2000), p. 105.
45. Lina Gupta, "Kali, the Savior," in *After Patriarchy: Feminist Transformations of the World Religions,* eds. Paula M. Cooey, et al (Maryknoll, NY: Orbis Books, 1997), p. 37.
46. Mahatma Gandhi, *Hind Saraj,* quoted in Arvind Sharma, *Modern Hindu Thought: The Essential Texts* (Oxford: Oxford University Press, 2002), p. 265.
47. Gandhi, *Hind Saraj,* p. 261.
48. Gandhi, *Hind Saraj,* p. 265.
49. Martin Luther King, Jr., "My Trip to the Land of Gandhi," *Ebony Magazine,* accessed March 7, 2019, https://kinginstitute.stanford.edu/king-papers/documents/my-trip-land-gandhi#ftnref10.
50. Tiruvalluvar, *Kural,* ed. P.S. Sundaram (New York: Penguin, 1990), p. 318.
51. Christopher Key Chappelle, "Indic Traditions and Animals," in *Call to Compassion: Religious Perspectives on Animal Advocacy,* eds. Lisa Kemmerer and Anthony J. Nocella II (NY: Lantern Books), p. 25.
52. Rachel Dwyer, *Filming the Gods: Religion and Indian Cinema* (New York: Routledge, 2006), p. 163.
53. Karen Armstrong, *Buddha* (New York: Penguin, 2001) pp. 22–23.
54. *Dhammacakkappavattana-Sutta,* "Setting in Motion the Wheel of Truth," Buddhist Studies, accessed April 13, 2019, http://www.buddhanet.net/e-learning/buddhism/bp_sut17.htm.
55. Candrakīrti, *Four Illusions: Candrakīrti's Advice to Travelers on the Bodhisattva Path,* tr. Karen C. Lang (Oxford: Oxford University Press, 2003) 80:1.
56. "The Three Refuges (Saranattayam)," tr. Bhikku Nānamoli, in *Buddhist Scriptures,* ed. Donald S. Lopez, Jr. (London: Penguin, 2004), p. 103.
57. Quoted in Susan Murcott, *First Buddhist Women: Poems and Stories of Awakening* (Berkeley, CA: Parallax Press, 2006), p. 79.
58. *The Lotus Sutra,* tr. Burton Watson (New York: Columbia University Press, 1994), p. 305.
59. *Buddhist Scriptures,* p. 527.
60. Sulak Sivaraksa, "Mindful Communication for Sustainable Development," in *Mindful Communication for Sustainable Development: Perspectives from Asia,* ed. Kalinga Seneviratne (Los Angeles: Sage, 2018), p. 32.

61. Thich Nhat Hanh, *The Heart of the Buddha's Teaching: Transforming Suffering into Peace, Joy, and Liberation* (New York: Penguin, 2015), p. 113.
62. *Satipathāna Sutra,* in *Buddhist Scriptures*, p. 345.
63. Kirk Warren Brown et al, "Mindfulness: Theoretical Foundations and Evidence for its Salutary Effects, *Psychological Inquiry* 18 (2007): 212.
64. Brown, et al, "Mindfulness."
65. John Wellwood, *Toward a Psychology of Awakening: Buddhism, Psychotherapy, and the Path of Personal and Spiritual Transformation* (Boston: Shambhala, 2000), p. 177.
66. Kirk Warren Brown and Richard M. Ryan, "The Benefits of Being Present: Mindfulness and Its Role in Psychological Well-Being," *Journal of Personality and Social Psychology* 84, no. 4 (April 2003): 832.
67. Dogen, *Treasury of the True Dharma Eye: Zen Master Dogen's* Shobo Genzo, tr. Kazuaki Tanahashi, (Boulder, CO: Shambala, 2013), p. 42.
68. Dogen, *True Dharma Eye*, p. 297.
69. T. Griffith Foulk, "The Form and Function of Koan Literature: A Historical Overview," in *The Koan: Texts and Contexts in Zen Buddhism*, eds. Steven Heine and Dale S. Wright (New York: Oxford University Press, 2000), p. 38.
70. Matsuo Basho, *Narrow Road to the Interior*, in *Basho's Narrow Road: Spring & Autumn Passages*, tr. Hiroaki Sato (Berkeley, CA: Stone Bridge Press, 1996), p. 95. In its original Japanese, the poetry conforms to the classic Haiku structure.
71. Basho, *Narrow Road*, p. 47.
72. Basho, *Narrow Road*, p. 89.
73. Daisetz T. Suzuki, *Zen and Japanese Culture* (Princeton: Princeton University Press, 1959), p. 228.
74. Soyen Shaku, "Spiritual Enlightenment" in *Zen for Americans* (New York: Metro Books, 2002), p. 136.
75. Shaku, "Spiritual Enlightenment," p. 136.
76. D.T. Suzuki, *An Introduction to Zen Buddhism* (New York: Grove Press, 1964), p. 111.
77. Gary Snyder, *The Selected Letters of Allen Ginsberg and Gary Snyder*, ed. Bill Morgan (Berkeley, CA: Counterpoint, 2009), p. 63.
78. Shunryu Suzuki, *Zen Mind, Beginner's Mind: Informal Talks on Zen Meditation and Practice*, ed. Trudy Dixon (Boston: Weatherhill, 2000), p. 138.
79. Tenzing Norgay and James Ramsey Ullman, *Tiger of the Snows: The Autobiography of Tenzing of Everest* (New York: G.P. Putnam's Sons, 1955), p. 106.
80. Norgay, *Tiger of the Snows*, p. 8.
81. Edmund Hillary, "The Summit," in John Hunt, *The Conquest of Everest* (New York: E.P. Dutton & Company, 1953), p. 205.
82. Norgay, *Tiger of the Snows*, p. 99.
83. Norgay, *Tiger of the Snows*, p. 8.
84. Mary Craig, *Kundun: A Biography of the Family of the Dalai Lama* (London: HarperCollins, 1997), p. 23.
85. Dalai Lama and Desmond Tutu, with Douglas Abrams, *The Book of Joy: Lasting Happiness in a Changing World* (New York: Penguin, 2016), p. 254.
86. David A. Palmer and Elijaho Siegler, *Dream Trippers: Global Daoism and the Predicament of Modern Spirituality* (Chicago: University of Chicago Press, 2017), p. 53.
87. Lao Tzu, *The Old Master: A Syncretic Reading of the* Laozi *from Mawangdui Test A Onward*, tr. Hongkyung Kim (Albany, NY: SUNY Press, 2012), ch. 1.
88. Wing-Tsit Chan, *A Source Book in Chinese Philosophy* (Princeton: Princeton University Press, 1969), p. 266.
89. Catherine Despeux and Livia Kohn, *Women in Daoism* (Cambridge, MA: Three Pine Press, 2003), p. 1.
90. *Old Master*, p. 175.

91. Lao Tzu, ch. 78.
92. Lao Tzu, ch. 30.
93. Richard Wilhelm, *Lectures on the I Ching: Constancy and Change*, tr. Irene Eber (Princeton: Princeton University Press, 1979), p. 30.
94. Lao Tzu, ch. 78.
95. *Chuang-Tzŭ: The Inner Chapters*, tr. A.C. Graham (Indianapolis: Hackett, 2001), ch. 2.
96. *Chuang-Tzŭ*, ch. 1.
97. Stephen Eskildsen, *The Teachings and Practices of the Early Quanzhen Taoist Masters* (Albany, NY: SUNY Press, 2004), p. 23.
98. Joanna Yang Liu, "Songs of Her Spirit: Poetic Musings of a Song Daoist Nun," *Journal of Song-Yuan Studies* 44 (2014): 191.
99. Li Po, "Long Yearning (Sent Far)," http://www.chinese-poems.com/lbe.html.
100. *The Seven Taoist Masters: A Folk Novel of China*, tr. Eva Wang (Boston: Shambala, 1990), p. 52.
101. *Seven Taoist Masters*, p. 123.
102. *Women in Daoism*, p. 147.
103. *Journey to the West*, vol. 1, tr. Anthony C. Yu (Chicago: University of Chicago Press, 1977), p. 75.
104. *Journey to the West*, p. 81.
105. Richard Mather, *A New Account of Tales of the World*, ch. 23, reprinted in *Classical Chinese Literature: An Anthology of Translations*, vol. 1, eds. John Minford and Joseph S.M. Lau (New York: Columbia University Press, 2000), p. 473.
106. "Letter to Shan Tao," tr. J.R. Hightower, in *Classical Chinese Literature*, p. 464.
107. *Chuang-Tzu*, chp. 6
108. Liu Yanchi, *Essential Book of Traditional Chinese Medicine*, vol. 1, trs. Fang Tingyu and Chen Laidi (New York: Columbia University Press, 1988), p. 9.
109. Zhanwen Liu and Liang Liu, *Essentials of Chinese Medicine*, vol. 1 (London: Springer, 2009), p. 10.
110. Yanchi, *Traditional Chinese Medicine*, p. 21.
111. Liu, *Essentials of Chinese Medicine*, p. 425.
112. Yang Jwing-Ming, *Essence of Tai Chi Chi Kung: Health and Martial Arts* (Jamaica Plain, MA: YMAA Publication Center, 1990), p. 55.
113. Tsung Hwa Jou, *The Tao of Tai-Chi Chuan: Way to Rejuvenation*, ed. Shoshana Shapiro Warwick (New York: Tai Chi Foundation, 1981), p. A29.
114. *Tao of Tai-Chi Chuan*, p. 95.
115. *Laozi*, ch. 64.
116. *Bruce Lee: Words from a Master*, ed. John R. Little (Lincolnwood, IL: Contemporary Books, 1999), p. 64.
117. Charles Russo, *Striking Distance: Bruce Lee and the Dawn of Martial Arts in America* (Lincoln, NE: University of Nebraska Press, 2016), pp. 113–14.
118. Raymond Zhou, "Abing: The Most Celebrated Musician in Wuxi," accessed February 21, 2019, http://en.chinaculture.org/chineseway/2013-06/20/content_464302.htm.
119. Jacob K. Olupona, *City of 201 Gods: Ilé-Ifè in Time, Space, and the Imagination* (Berkeley, CA: University of California Press, 2011), p. 5.
120. Jacob K. Olupona and Terry Rey, *Òrìṣà Devotion as World Religion: The Globalization of Yorùbá Religious Culture*, eds. Jacob K. Olupona and Terry Rey (Madison, WI: University of Wisconsin Press, 2008), p. 16.
121. John Ayotunde Isola Bewaji, "Èsù and Liminality in the Yoruba Thought System: A Leadership Perspective," in *Èsù: Yoruba God, Power, and the Imaginative Frontiers*, ed. Toyin Falola (Durham, NC: Carolina Academic Press, 2013), pp. 143–144.
122. Nathaniel Samuel Murrell, *Afro-Caribbean Religions: An Introduction to their Historical, Cultural, and Sacred Traditions*, (Philadelphia: Temple University Press, 2010), p. 30.
123. Bewaji, "Èsù and Liminality," in *Èsù*, ed. Falola, p. 144.

124. Omotade Abegbindin, *Ifá in Yorùbá Thought System* (Durham, NC: Carolina Academic Press, 2014), p. 70.
125. E. Bolaji Idowu, *Olódùmarè: God in Yoruba Belief* (London: Longmans, 1962), p. 6.
126. Diedre Badejo, *Osun Seegesi: The Elegant Deity of Wealth, Power, and Femininity* (Trenton, NJ: Africa World Press, 1996), p. 68.
127. Badejo, *Osun Seegesi*, p. 71.
128. Katherin J. Hagedorn, "Engendering Spiritual Power and Empowering Gendered Spirits," *The Yorùbá God of Drumming: Transatlantic Perspectives on the Wood that Talks*, ed. Amanda Villepastour (Jackson, MS: University Press of Mississippi, 2015), p 154.
129. Badejo, *Osun Seegesi*, p 89.
130. Badejo, *Osun Seegesi*, p. 80.
131. Cornelius O. Adepegba, "Osun and Brass: An insight into Yoruba Religious Symbology, *Osun Across the Waters: A Yoruba Goddess in Africa and the Americas*, eds. Joseph M. Murphy and Mei-Mei Sanford (Bloomington, IN: Indiana University Press, 2001) p. 104.
132. Donald Cosentino, "Who is that Fellow in the Many-Colored Cap? Transformations of Eshu in Old and New World Mythologies," *The Journal of American Folklore* 100, no. 397 (Jul.-Sep., 1987): 262.
133. dele jegede, "Convergence and Spirituality: Èsù in Lagos," in *Èsù*, ed. Falola, p. 164.
134. Bewaji, in *Èsù*, ed. Falola, p. 146.
135. Allison Sellers and Joel E. Tishken, "The Place of Èsù in the Yorùbá Pantheon," in *Èsù,* ed. Falola, p. 47.
136. Oyèrónkẹ́ Oyèwùmí, *The Invention of Women: Making an African Sense of Western Gender Discourses* (Minneapolis: University of Minnesota Press, 1997), p. 40.
137. Cheryl Johnson, "Grassroots Organizing: Women in Anticolonial Activity in Southwestern Nigeria," *African Studies Review* 25, no. 2/3 (Jun.-Sep., 1982): 138.
138. Oyeronke Olajubu, "Seeing through a Woman's Eye: Yoruba Religious Tradition and Gender," *Journal of Feminist Studies in Religion* 20, no. 1 (Spring, 2004): p. 43.
139. Wole Soyinka, "The Tolerant Gods," *Òrìṣà Devotion*, Olupona and Rey, p. 49.
140. Raul Canizares, *Walking with the Night: The Afro-Cuban World Santeria* (Rochester, VT: Destiny Books, 1993), p. 68.
141. Juan J. Sosa, "La Santería: An Integrating, Mythological Worldview in a Disintegrating Society," *Òrìṣà Devotion*, Olupona and Rey, p. 387.
142. Amanda Villepastour, "Anthropomorphizing Àyàn in Transatlantic Gender Narratives," in *Yorùbá God of Drumming*, p. 142.
143. "Strength, Perseverance, and Humanism: An Interview with Daymé Arocena," accessed May 19, 2009, https://afropop.org/articles/dayme-arocena-interview.
144. Luis Nicolau Parés, "Xangô in Afro-Brazilian Religion: 'Aristocracy' and 'Syncretic' Interactions," in *Sàngó in Africa and the African Diaspora*, eds. Joel E. Tishken, et al. (Bloomington, IN, University of Indiana Press, 2009), p. 252.
145. Barbara Browning, *Samba: Resistance in Motion* (Bloomington, IN: Indiana University Press, 1995), p. 23.
146. Yvonne Daniel, *Dancing wisdom: Embodied Knowledge in Haitian Vodou, Cuban Yoruba, and Bahian Candomblé*, (Urbana, IL: University of Illinois Press, 2005), p. 59.
147. Daniel, *Dancing Wisdom*, p 64
148. Krista White, "Espousing Ezili: Images of a Lwa, Reflections of the Haitian Woman," *Journal of Haitian Studies* 5/6 (1999-2000): 63.
149. Marc A. Christophe, Ulrick Jean-Pierre's "Cayman Wood Ceremony," *Journal of Haitian Studies* 10, no. 2, (Fall 2004): p. 55.
150. Murrell, *Afro-Caribbean Religions*, p. 59.
151. Nobel Prize award citation.

152. Wole Soyinka, *Death and the King's Horseman* (New York: W.W. Norton, 2003), p. 80.
153. *Death and the King's Horseman*, p. 22
154. *Death and the King's Horseman*, p. 43
155. *Death and the King's Horseman*, p. 36
156. *Death and the King's Horseman*, p. 51
157. *Death and the King's Horseman*, p. 62
158. Ryan Topper, "The Sacrificial Foundation of Modernity in Wole Soyinka's *Death and the King's Horseman*," *Research in African Literatures* 50, no. 1 (July 2019): 59.
159. *Death and the King's Horseman*, p. 63
160. Genesis 11:1–9.
161. Genesis 22:2.
162. S. Kierkegaard, *Fear and Trembling*, translated by A. Hannay (London: Penguin, 1985).
163. Exodus 3:14.
164. Exodus 33:20.
165. See A. Heschel, *Sabbath* (New York: Farrar, Strauss and Giroux, 2005).
166. M. Maimonides, *Guide for the Perplexed*, 2:24.
167. Psalms 34:8.
168. E. Wiesel, *Souls on Fire: Portraits and Legends of Hasidic Masters*, translated by Marion Wiesel (New York: Summit Books, 1972), p. 7.
169. K. Armstrong, *A History of God: The 4,000-Year Quest of Judaism, Christianity and Islam* (New York: Ballantine, 1993), p. 50.
170. M. Buber, *To Hallow This Life: An Anthology*, edited by J. Trapp (Westport, CT: Greenwood Press, 1974), p. 84.
171. M. Friedman, *Martin Buber: The Life of Dialogue* (New York: Routledge, 2002), p. 148.
172. Buber, *To Hallow This Life*, p. 92.
173. H. Kushner, *When Bad Things Happen to Good People* (New York: Schocken, 1989), p. 11.
174. Job 19:7.
175. D. Jacobson, *Creator, Are you Listening?: Israeli Poets on God and Prayer* (Bloomington, IN: Indiana University Press, 2007), p. 134.
176. Genesis 11:1.
177. Jeremiah 29:14.
178. D. Ben-Gurion, "Uniqueness and Destiny," in *Ben-Gurion Looks at the Bible*, translated by J. Kolatch (Middle Village, NY: Johnathan David Publishers, 2015).
179. H. Schlesinger, "Meeting my Palestinian neighbors for the First Time" (2014), accessed December 14, 2019, https://www.myjewishlearning.com/rabbis-without-borders/meeting-my-palestinian-neighbors-for-the-first-time/.
180. A. Kook, "A Call for Unity" in *The Essential Writings of Abraham Isaac Kook*, translated by B. Bokser (Teaneck, NJ: Ben Yehuda Press, 2006), p. 24.
181. S. Freud, *Jokes and Their Relation to the Unconscious*, translated by J. Strachey (New York: Penguin, 1976), p. 157.
182. L. Siegel, *Groucho Marx: The Comedy of Existence* (New Haven: Yale University Press, 2015), p. 120.
183. S. Björkman, *Woody Allen on Woody Allen* (New York: Grove Press, 1994), p. 223.
184. https://www.cbsnews.com/news/jerry-seinfeld-on-new-museum-of-jewish-history/.
185. S. Silverman, *The Bedwetter: Stories of Redemption, Courage, and Pee* (New York: HarperCollins, 2010), p. 217.
186. *The Sarah Silverman Project*, "Ah, Men," 02x05.
187. *Inside Amy Schumer*, "You would Bang Her?" 02x01.
188. J. Kalman, "Heckling the Divine: Woody Allen, the Book of Job, and Jewish Theology after the Holocaust." in *Jews and Humor*, edited by L. Greenspoon (West Lafayette, IN: Purdue University Press, 2011), p. 178.

189. Richard Swinburne, *The Resurrection of God Incarnate* (Oxford: Oxford University Press, 2003) p. 37.
190. Luke, 1:31–32.
191. Matthew 2:6, Micah 5:2.
192. Quoted in *Mary: The Complete Resource*, ed. Sarah Jane Boss (Oxford: Oxford University Press, 2007), p. 74.
193. Christopher O'Donnell OCarm, "Models in Mariology," in *Mary for Time and Eternity: Essays on Mary and Ecumenism*, eds. William McLoughlin and Jill Pinnock (Herefordshire, UK: Gracewing, 2007) p. 69
194. Giorgio Vasari, *Lives of the Most Eminent Painters, Sculptors and Architects,* vol. 9, tr. Gaston Du C. de Vere, accessed June 9, 2019, http://www.gutenberg.org/files/32362/32362.txt.
195. Chris Maunder, "Apparitions of Mary," in *Mary*, ed. Boss, p. 446.
196. Elizabeth A. Johnson, *Truly Our Sister: A Theology of Mary in the Communion of Saints* (New York: Continuum, 2003), p. 305.
197. John 1:23.
198. Luke 1:77.
199. Matthew 3:16.
200. Matthew 17:20.
201. Matthew 26:28.
202. Luke 22:42.
203. Luke 22:44.
204. John, 18:36.
205. Luke 23:34.
206. Matthew 27:46.
207. Luke 24:38–39.
208. 1 Corinthians 15:51–52.
209. Saint Augustine, *Confessions*, tr. Henry Chadwick (Oxford: Oxford University Press, 1991), 2.3.
210. *Confessions*, 10.7.
211. St. Bonaventure, "The Life of St. Francis," in *Bonaventure*, tr. Ewart Cousins (New York: Paulist Press, 1978), p. 104.
212. Roger D. Sorrell, *St. Francis of Assisi and Nature: Tradition and Innovation in Western Christian Attitudes toward the Environment* (Oxford: Oxford University Press, 2009), p. 146.
213. St. Teresa, *The Life of Teresa of Jesus: The Autobiography of Teresa of Avila,* tr. E. Allison Peers (Grand Rapids, MI: Generic NL Freebook Publisher), p. 30.
214. St. Teresa, *Interior Castle* (Grand Rapids, MI: Generic NL Freebook Publisher), 6.2.
215. Solrunn Nes, *Mystical Language of Icons* (Grand Rapids, MI: William B. Eerdmans, 2004), p. 20.
216. Oleg Tarasov, *Icon and Devotion: Sacred Spaces in Imperial Russia*, tr. Robin Milner-Gulland (London: Reaktion Books, 2002), p. 12.
217. Nes, *Mystical Language*, p. 16.
218. Robert Bird, "Tarkovsky and the Celluloid Icon," in *Alter Icons: The Russian Icon and Modernity*, ed. Jefferson J.A. Gatrall and Douglas Greenfield (University Park, PA: Penn State University Press, 2010), p. 235.
219. Andrey Tarkovsky, *Sculpting in Time: Reflections on the Cinema,* tr. Kitty Hunter-Blair (London: Bodley Head, 1986), p. 36.
220. Matthew, chapters 5–7.
221. Leo Tolstoi, *My Religion*, tr. Huntington Smith (New York: Thomas Y. Crowell, 1885), pp. ix–x.
222. Tolstoi, *My Religion*, pp. 181–182.
223. Tolstoi, *My Religion*, p. 4.
224. Quoted in Nadejda Gorodetzky, *Saint Tikhon of Zadonsk: Inspirer of Dostoevsky* (Crestwood, NY: St. Vladimir's Seminary Press, 1976), p. 223.
225. Fyodor Dostoevsky, *Crime and Punishment*, tr. Constance Garnett (Grand Rapids, MI: Generic NL Freebook Publisher), p. 329.

226. Gorodetzky, *Saint Tikun*, p. 154.
227. Fyodor Dostoyevsky, *The Brothers Karamazov*, tr. Constance Garnett (Grand Rapids, MI: Generic NL Freebook Publisher), Book 6, ch. 1.
228. *The Brothers Karamazov,* Book 5, ch. 5.
229. *The Brothers Karamazov,* Book 5, ch. 5.
230. Martin Luther, "The Grievances of the German People," Thesis 31, *The Protestant Reformation*, ed. Hans J. Hillerbrand (New York: HarperPerennial, 2009), p. 6.
231. Max Weber, *The Protestant Ethic and the Spirit of Capitalism*, tr. Talcott Parsons (New York: Routledge, 2001), p. 40.
232. John Winthrop, "A Model of Christian Charity (1630)," Hanover Historical Texts Collection, accessed June 11, 2019, https://history.hanover.edu/texts/winthmod.html.
233. Letter to John Warren, October, 1780, in *The Writings of Samuel Adams*, vol. 4, ed. Harry Alonzo Cushing (New York: Octagon Books, 1968).
234. Anthony Heilbut, *The Gospel Sound: Good News and Bad Times* (New York: Limelight Edition, 2002), p. 57.
235. Heilbut, *Gospel Sound*, p. 65.
236. *Qur'an*, translated by M.A.S. Abdel Haleem (Oxford: Oxford University Press, 2004), 57:4.
237. Abdulaziz Sachedina, *The Islamic Roots of Democratic Pluralism* (Oxford: Oxford University Press, 2004), p. 113.
238. *Qur'an,* 16: 123.
239. *Qur'an*, 9: 60.
240. Sahih al-Bukhari 6416, Book 81, Hadith 5, https://sunnah.com/bukhari/81/5.
241. Mona Siddiqui, *Hospitality and Islam: Welcoming in God's Name* (New Haven: Yale University Press, 2015), p. 15.
242. Qur'an, 93: 6–7.
243. Karen Armstrong, *Muhammed: A Prophet for Our Time* (New York: HarperCollins, 2006).
244. Lara Deeb, *An Enchanted Modern: Gender and Public Piety in Shi'i Lebanon* (Princeton: Princeton University Press, 2006), p. 207.
245. Qur'an, 2: 62.
246. Anne-Marie Edde, *Saladin*, translated by Jane Marie Todd (Cambridge, MA: Harvard University Press, 2011), p. 402.
247. Edde, *Saladin*, p. 2.
248. Qur'an, 109: 2–6.
249. Quoted in *Rābi'a: The Life and Work of Rābi'a and Other Women Mystics in Islam*, ed. Margaret Smith (Oxford: Oneworld Publications, 1994), p. 21.
250. Quoted in *Rābi'a*, p. 122.
251. Al Ghazali, "Deliverance from Error," translated by W.M. Watt (London: George Allen and Unwin, 1951), reprinted in *Philosophy in the Middle Ages*, 2nd ed., edited by Arthur Hyman and James J. Walsh (Indianapolis: Hackett, 1973), p. 277.
252. Ibn al'Arabi, *The Bezels of Wisdom*, translated by R.W.J. Austin (Mahwah, NJ: Paulist Press, 1980), p. 137.
253. Jalal al-Din Rumi, "The Songs of the Reed," in *The Masnavi: Book One*, translated by Jawad Mojaddedi (Oxford: Oxford University Press, 2004), p.4.
254. Jalal al-Din Rumi, "In Baghdad, Dreaming of Cairo: In Cairo, Dreaming of Baghdad," *The Essential Rumi*, translated by Coleman Barks (New York: HarperOne, 1994), p. 211.
255. Seyyed Hossein Nasr, "The Spiritual Needs of Western Man and the Message of Sufism," in *Sufism: Love and Wisdom*, ed. Jean-Louis Michon and Roger Gaetani (Bloomington, IN: World Wisdom, Inc., 2006), p. 199.
256. Nobel Prize lecture. https://www.nobelprize.org/prizes/literature/1988/mahfouz/lecture.
257. Haim Gordon, *Naguib Mahfouz's Egypt: Existential Themes in His Writings* (New York: Greenwood Press, 1990), p. 130.

258. Naguib Mahfouz, *Cairo Trilogy*, translated by William Maynard Hutchins, Lorne M. Kenny, and Olive E. Kenny (New York: Alfred A. Knopf, 2001), p. 70.
259. Mahfouz, *Cairo Trilogy*, p. 39.
260. Mahfouz, *Cairo Trilogy*, p. 288.
261. Mahfouz, *Cairo Trilogy*, p. 588.
262. Mahfouz, *Cairo Trilogy*, p. 587.
263. Mahfouz, *Cairo Trilogy*, p. 747.
264. Mahfouz, *Cairo Trilogy*, p. 743.
265. Mahfouz, *Cairo Trilogy*, p. 892.
266. Mahfouz, *Cairo Trilogy*, p. 930.
267. Mahfouz, *Cairo Trilogy*, p. 1112.
268. Mahfouz, *Cairo Trilogy*, p. 1116.
269. Gordon, *Mahfouz's Egypt*, p. 93.
270. Manning Marable, *Malcolm X: A Life of Reinvention* (New York: Penguin, 2011), p. 96.
271. Marble, *Malcolm X*, p. 411.
272. Alex Haley, *Autobiography of Malcolm X* (New York: One World, 1965), p. 361.
273. *Autobiography*, p. 370.
274. *Autobiography*, p. 371.
275. *Autobiography*, p. 372.
276. Benazir Bhutto, *Reconciliation: Islam, Democracy, and the West* (New York: HarperCollins, 2008), p. 19.
277. Brooke Allen, *Benazir Bhutto: Favored Daughter* (Boston: New Harvest, 2016), p. 86.
278. *Reconciliation*, p. 18.
279. *Reconciliation*, p. 20.
280. *Reconciliation*, p. 18.
281. Yu Dan, *Confucius from the Heart: Ancient Wisdom for Today's World* (New York: Atria Books, 2013), p. 11.
282. Confucius, *Analects*, translated by Burton Watson (New York: Columbia University Press, 2007), 2.11.
283. *Analects*, 13.5
284. Daniel K. Gardner, *Zhu Xi's Reading of the* Analects: *Canon, Commentary, and the Classical Tradition* (New York: Columbia University Press, 2003), p. 31.
285. *Analects*, 5.20.
286. Wing-Tsit Chan, *A Source Book in Chinese Philosophy* (Princeton: Princeton University Press, 1969), p. 104.
287. Zhu Xi, in Gardner, *Zhu Xi's Reading*, p. 54.
288. David T. Hall and Roger T. Ames, *Thinking Through Confucius* (Albany, NY: State University of New York Press, 1987), p. 64.
289. *Book of Rites,* 17.iii.23, quoted in "Confucian Moral Cultivation," Karyn Lai, in *The Moral Circle and the Self: Chinese and Western Approaches*, ed. Kim-chone Chong, Sor-hoon Tan, and C.L Ten (Chicago: Open Court, 2003), p. 107.
290. *Doctrine of the Mean*, in *Source Book*, Chan, p. 98.
291. Confucius, *Analects*, 3.23.
292. Chou Lien-hsi, in *Source Book*, Chan, p. 472.
293. Henry Rosemont, Jr., *Against Individualism: A Confucian Rethinking of the Foundations of Morality, Politics, Family, and Religion* (Lanham, MD: Lexington Books, 2015), p. 123.
294. Confucius, *Analects*, 2.17.
295. Confucius, *Analects*, 3.15.
296. Hsiao Xing, *Book on Filial Piety*, in *Source Book*, Chan, p. 102.
297. Anna Sun in *Confucianism and Spiritual Traditions in Modern China and Beyond*, ed. Fenggang Yang and Joseph Tamney (Boston: Leiden 2012), pp. 323–24.

298. Confucius, *Analects*, 1:2.
299. Confucius, *Analects*, 1:11.
300. Confucius, *Analects*, 13:18.
301. Mencius, *Mencius*, translated by D.C. Lau (Toronto: Penguin, 1970), 7A:15.
302. Sin Yee Chan, "Gender and Relationship Roles in the Analects and the Mencius," *Asian Philosophy* vol. 10, no. 2 (2000): 115–132.
303. A. T. Nuyen, "Love and Respect in the Confucian Family," in *The Moral Circle and the Self: Chinese and Western Approaches*, ed.. Kim-chong Chong et al. (Chicago: Open Court, 2003), p. 93.
304. Hahm Chaibong, "Family Versus the Individual," in *The Politics of Marriage Laws in Korea*, in *Confucianism for the Modern World*, ed. Daniel A. Bell and Hahm Chaibong (Cambridge: Cambridge University Press, 2003), p. 358.
305. Eileen Yin-Fei Lo, *The Chinese Kitchen: Recipes, Techniques, Ingredients, History and Memories from America's Leading Authority on Chinese Cooking* (New York: William Morrow Cookbooks), p. 218.
306. Eileen Yin-Fei Lo, *Chinese Kitchen*, p. 1.
307. Roel Sterckx, *Food, Sacrifice, and Sagehood in Ancient China* (New York: Cambridge University Press, 2011), p. 1.
308. Grace Young, *The Wisdom of the Chinese Kitchen: Chinese Recipes for Celebration and Healing* (New York: Simon and Schuster, 1999), p. 101.
309. Francis Halvorsen, *The Food and Cooking of China: An Exploration of Chinese Cuisine in the Provinces and Cities of China, Hong Kong, and Taiwan* (New York: John Wiley & Sons, 1996), p. 2.
310. *Mencius*, 7B11.
311. Roel Sterckx, "Food and Philosophy in Early China," in *Of Tripod and Palate: Food Politics and Religion in Ancient China*, ed. Roel Sterckx (New York: Palgrave Macmillan, 2005), p. 54.
312. Chu His, *The Complete Works of Chu Hsi*, in *Source Book* Chan, p. 610.
313. Liu Yeudi, "Calligraphic Expression and the Contemporary Chinese Art: Xu Bing's Pioneer Experiment," in *Subversive Strategies in Contemporary Chinese Art*. ed. Mary Bittner Wiseman and Liu Yuedi (Boston: Leidl, 2011), p. 87.
314. Peimin Ni, *Confucius: The Man and the Way of Gongfu* (Lanham, MD: Rowman and Littlefield, 2016), p. 116.
315. Richard Curt Kraus, *Brushes with Power: Modern Politics and the Chinese Art of Calligraphy* (Berkeley: University of California Press, 1991), p. 7.
316. "Treatise on Calligraphy," in *Two Chinese Treatises on Calligraphy, Sun Qianli*, Chang Ch'ung-ho and Hans H. Frankel (New Haven, CT: Yale University Press, 1995).
317. Kuan-Hung Chen, "Seriousness, Playfulness, and a Religious Reading of *Tianshu*," in *Xu Bing and Contemporary Chinese Art*, ed. Hsingyuan Tsao and Roger T. Ames (Albany, NY: SUNY Press, 2011), p. 72.
318. Stanley K. Abe, "No Questions, No Answers: China and a Book from the Sky," *Modern Chinese Literary and Cultural Studies in the Age of Theory: Reimagining a Field* 25, no. 3: 171.
319. Sujeong Kim "Interpreting Transnational Cultural Practices: Social Discourses on a Korean Drama in Japan, Hong Kong, and China," *Cultural Studies*, vol. 23, no. 5–6 (2009): 736–755.
320. John Lie, "What Is the K in K-pop? South Korean Popular Music, the Culture Industry, and National Identity," *Korea Observer*, vol. 43, no. 3 (2012): 360
321. Arlene Chan and Susan Humphries, *Paddles Up! Dragon Boat Racing in China* (Toronto: National Heritage Books, 2009), p. 130.
322. Tu Weiming, "Confucian Spirituality in Contemporary China," in *Confucianism and Spiritual Traditions in Modern China and Beyond*, ed. Fenggang Yang and Joseph B. Tamney (Boston: Brill, 2012), p. 78.
323. Harbans Singh, *Guru Nanak and the Origins of the Sikh Faith* (Bombay: Asia Publishing House, 1969), pp. 204–205.
324. *Sri Guru Granth Sahib Ji*, 319, accessed August, 10, 2019, https://www.sikhitothemax.org/ang?source=G&ang=321.

325. Gurinder Singh Mann, *The Making of Sikh Scripture* (Oxford: Oxford University Press, 2001), p. 130.
326. Nikky-Gunninder Kaur Singh, *The Birth of the Khalsa: A Feminist Re-Memory of Sikh Identity* (Albany, NY: SUNY Press, 2005), p. 106.
327. Quoted in Sarup Singh Alag, *Hair Power* (Ludhiana, India: Alag-Shabad-Yug, 1998), p. 131.
328. Singh, *The Birth of the Khalsa*, p. 117.
329. Henry J. Walker, "Golden Temple, Marble Forum: Form and Meaning in Sacred Architecture," in *Sikh Art and Literature*, ed. Kerry Brown (London: Routledge, 1999), p. 112.
330. W. H. McLeod, "The Sikh Struggle in the Eighteenth Century and Its Relevance for Today," *History of Religions* 31, no. 4 (1992): 361.
331. Vir Singh, *Sundari*, translated by G. S. Mansukhani, accessed August 27, 2019, https://www.sikhmissionarysociety.org/sms/smspublications/sundri/.
332. Kirpal Singh, "Self-Introspection and Man-Making," in *The Teachings of Kirpal Singh,* Vol. 2, ed. Ruth Seader (Bowling Green, VA: Sawan Kirpal Publications, 1981), p. 7.
333. "Love," *Teachings of Kirpal Singh*, Vol. 3, p. 102.
334. "Simran," *Teachings of Kirpal Singh*, Vol. 3, p. 116.
335. "Love," *Teachings of Kirpal Singh*, Vol. 3, p. 105.
336. Purnima Mankekar, *Screening Culture, Viewing Politics: An Ethnography of Television, Womanhood, and Nation in Postcolonial India* (Durham, NC: Duke University Press, 1999), p. 307.
337. Anshu Malhotra and Farina Mir, "Punjab in History and Historiography: An Introduction," in *Punjab Reconsidered: History, Culture, and Practice*, eds. Anshu Malhotra and Farina Mir (Oxford: Oxford University, 2012).
338. Urvashi Butalia, "Community, State and Gender: On Women's Agency during Partition," *Economic and Political Weekly*, vol. 28, no. 17 (Apr. 24, 1993): 13.
339. Amrita Pritam, *Life and Times* (New Delhi: Vikas Pub. House, 1989), p. 7.
340. Amrita Pritam, "Nine Dreams and the Annunciation" in *Alone in the Multitude: Selected Poems*, translated by Suresh Kohli (New Delhi: Indian Literary Review Editions, 1979).
341. David Gilmartin, "The Historiography of India's Partition: Between Civilization and Modernity," *The Journal of Asian Studies* 74, no. 1 (2015): 37.
342. "Juggling Two Lives," *The Hindu*, accessed on August 25, 2019, https://www.thehindu.com/thehindu/mag/2005/11/13/stories/2005111300030100.htm.
343. Manoj Kumar, "Imroz, the Abiding Love in Amrita Pritam's Life," *Hindustan Times*, accessed August 25, 2019, https://www.hindustantimes.com/punjab/imroz-the-abiding-love-in-amrita-pritams-life/story-e8JajaDuE724oFbYPFmcUM.html
344. Shauna Singh Baldwin, *What the Body Remembers* (New York: Random House, 1999), p. 3.
345. Baldwin, *Body*, pp. 43–44.
346. Baldwin, *Body*, p. 430.
347. Baldwin, *Body*, p. 435.
348. Shauna Singh Baldwin, "Montreal, 1962," in *English Lessons and Other Stories* (Fredericton, NB: Goose Lane, 1999), p. 15.
349. Ashis Nandy, *Tao of Cricket: On Games of Destiny and the Destiny of Games* (Oxford: Oxford University Press, 2000), p. 5.
350. Nandy, *Tao of Cricket*, p. 108.
351. "Chucking is a Bigger Threat than Bribing or Betting," ESPN Cricinfo, accessed August 20, 2019, http://www.espncricinfo.com/wac/content/story/225767.html.
352. Suresh Menon, *Bishan: Portrait of a Cricketer* (Haryana, India: Penguin, 2011), p. 56.
353. David Frith, *Slow Men* (London: George Allen & Unwin, 1984), p 11.
354. Frith, *Slow Men*, 172
355. Menon, *Bishan,* p. 9.
356. Menon, *Bishan*, xii
357. Menon, *Bishan*, p. 183
358. "I'll Eat Anything," ESPN Cricinfo, http://www.espncricinfo.com/wac/content/story/224663.html.

359. "The Judicial Branch of the Navajo Nation," accessed on October 10, 2019, http://www.navajocourts.org/dine.htm.
360. "The Judicial Branch of the Navajo Nation," accessed on October 10, 2019, http://www.navajocourts.org/dine.htm.
361. Paul G. Zolbrod, *Diné Bahane': The Navajo Creation Story* (Albuquerque, NM: University of New Mexico Press, 1984), p. 48.
362. Kelli Carmean, *Spider Woman Walks this Land: Traditional Cultural Properties and the Navajo Nation* (Walnut Creek, CA: AltaMira Press, 2002), p. 57.
363. Gary Witherspoon, *Language and Art in the Navajo Universe* (Ann Arbor, MI: University of Michigan Press, 1997), p. 18.
364. John Farella, *The Main Stalk: A Synthesis of Navajo Philosophy* (Tuscon, AZ: University of Arizona Press, 1984), p. 35
365. Steve Pavlik, *The Navajo and the Animal People: Native American Traditional Ecological Knowledge and Ethnozoology* (Golden, CO: Fulcrum Publishing, 2014), p. 35.
366. Pavlik, *Animal People*, p. 123.
367. Zolbrod, *Diné Bahane'*, p. 82.
368. Gladys A. Reichard, *Navaho Religion: A Study of Symbolism* (Princeton: Princeton University Press, 1950), p. 423.
369. Father Berard Haile, *Navajo Coyote Tales: The Curly Tó Aheedlíinii Version* (Lincoln, NE: University of Nebraska Press, 1984), p. 58.
370. Haile, *Coyote Tales*, p. 58.
371. Maureen Trudelle Schwarz, *Molded in the Image of Changing Woman: Navajo Views on the Human Body and Personhood* (Tuscon, AZ: University of Arizona Press, 1997), p. 17.
372. Reichard, *Navaho Religion*, p. 21.
373. Schwarz, *Changing Woman*, p. 33
374. Carolyn Epple, "Coming to Terms with Navajo Nádleehí: A Critique of Berdache, 'Gay,' 'Alternate Gender,' and 'Two-spirit,' *American Ethnologist*, vol. 25, no. 2 (1998): 279.
375. Will Roscoe, *Changing Ones*, p. 5.
376. Carolyn Niethammer, *I'll Go and Do More: Annie Dodge Wauneka, Navajo Leader and Activist* (Lincoln, NE: University of Nebraska Press, 2001), p. 245.
377. Will Roscoe, *Changing Ones: Third and Fourth Genders in Native North America* (NY: St. Martin's Griffin, 1998), p. 4.
378. Zolbrod, *Diné Bahane'*, p. 97
379. Gladys A. Reichard, *Spider Woman: A Story of Navajo Weavers and Chanters* (Glorieta, NM: Rio Grande Press, 1968), p. 177.
380. Reichard, *Spider Woman*, p. 179.
381. Lawrence Cheek, *The Navajo Long Walk* (Tuscon, AZ: Rio Nuevo Publishers, 2004), p. 57.
382. John W. Sherry, *Land, Wind, and Hard Words* (Albuquerque, NM: University of New Mexico Press, 2002), p 9.
383. Schwarz, *Changing Woman*, p. 48.
384. Paul G. Zolbrod and Roseann S. Willink, *Weaving a World: Textiles and the Navajo Way of Seeing* (Santa Fe, NM: Museum of New Mexico Press, 1997), p. 4.
385. Charles Avery Amsden, *Navaho Weaving: Its Technic and its History* (Glorieta, NM: Rio Grande Press, 1982), p. 170.
386. Zolbrod and Willink, *Weaving a World*, p. 19.
387. Erika Marie Bsumek, *Indian-Made: Navajo Culture in the Marketplace, 1868–1940* (Lawrence, KS: University Press of Kansas, 2008), p. 219.
388. "Indian Jargon Won our Battles!" Northern Arizona University Digital Collections, accessed on October 3, 2019, http://archive.library.nau.edu/digital/collection/cpa/id/39510
389. "Indian Jargon Won our Battles!" Northern Arizona University Digital Collections, accessed on October 3, 2019, http://archive.library.nau.edu/digital/collection/cpa/id/39510

390. Samuel Holiday and Robert S. McPherson, *Under the Eagle: Samuel Holiday, Navajo Code Talker* (Norman, OK: University of Oklahoma Press, 2013), p. 23.
391. Holiday and McPherson, *Under the Eagle*, p. 93.
392. James Kale McNeley, Holy Wind in Navajo Philosophy (Tuscon, AZ: University of Arizona Press, 1981), p. 1.
393. "Remarks by the President in a Ceremony Honoring the Navajo Code Talkers," The White House Archives, https://georgewbush-whitehouse.archives.gov/news/releases/2001/07/20010726-5.html
394. "Indian Jargon Won our Battles!" accessed on October 3, 2019, http://archive.library.nau.edu/digital/collection/cpa/id/39510
395. Ronald L. Davis, "Paradise among the Monuments: John Ford's Vision of the American West," *Montana: The Magazine of Western History*, vol. 45, no. 3 (Summer 1995): 52.
396. Robert S. McPherson, *Navajo Land, Navajo Culture: The Utah Experience in the Twentieth Century* (Norman, OK: University of Oklahoma Press, 2001), p. 146.
397. McPherson, *Navajo Land*, p. 150.
398. John Holiday and Robert S. McPherson, *A Navajo Legacy: The Life and Teachings of John Holiday* (Norman, OK: University of Oklahoma Press, 2005), p.155.
399. McPherson, *Navajo Land*, p. 155.
400. Davis, "Paradise among the Monuments," p. 57.
401. Richard Hutson "Monument Valley in *The Searchers*" in *The Searchers: Essays and Reflections on John Ford's Classic Western*, ed. Arthur M. Eckstein and Peter Lehman (Detroit: Wayne State University Press, 2004), p. 107.
402. Hutson, "Monument Valley," p. 103.
403. *Journey to Taos* film script, Center for Southwest Research Special Collections, University of New Mexico.
404. R.C. Gorman diary (1964), Center for Southwest Research Special Collections, University of New Mexico.
405. *Journey to Taos* film script.
406. *The Kojiki: An Account of Ancient Matters*, translated by G. Heldt (New York: Columbia University Press, 2014), p. 23.
407. *Kojiki*, p. 24.
408. Orikuchi Shinobu, "Study of Life in Ancient Times," quoted in H. Saitō, "Orikuchi Shinobu and the Sea as Religious Topos: *Marebito and Musubi no kami*" (2018) and in E. Simpson, translator, *The Sea and the Sacred in Japan: Aspects of Maritime Religion*, ed. F. Rambelli (London: Bloomsbury, 1995), p. 172.
409. I. Reader, *Religion in Contemporary Japan* (London: Macmillan, 1991), p. 25.
410. L. Krasznahorkai, *Seiobo There Below*, translated by O. Mulzet (New York: New Directions, 2008), pp. 395–397.
411. Sugawara no Michizane, "Willow," accessed on January 17, 2019, http://www.wakapoetry.net/tag/sugawara-no-michizane/.
412. Zeami, *The Flowering Spirit*, translated by W. Wilson (Tokyo: Kodansha International, 2006), p. 79.
413. Kanze Hideo in interview with author, W. Vollmann, *Kissing the Mask* (New York: HarperCollins, 2010), p. 41.
414. K. Komparu, *The Noh Theater: Principles and Perspectives*, translated by J. Corddry (N.p.: Floating World Editions, 2005), p. 8.
415. The following excerpts from *Hagoromo* and *Izutsu* can be found in R. Tyler, *Japanese No Dramas* (London: Penguin, 2002).
416. K. Tsurayuki, quoted in B. Earhart, *Mount Fuji: Icon of Japan* (Columbia, SC: University of South Carolina Press, 2011), p. 8.
417. T. Kurozumi and Kohmoto, *The Living Way: Stories of Kurozumi Munetada, a Shinto Founder*, ed. W. Stoesz (Lanham, MD: Altamira Press, 1999), p 67.
418. Kurozumi and Kohmoto, *Living Way*.

419. Kurozumi and Kohmoto, *Living Way.*
420. Kurozumi and Kohmoto, *Living Way.*
421. Kurozumi and Kohmoto, *Living Way.*
422. *Kojiki*, p. 46.
423. P.L. Cuyler, *Sumo: From Rite to Sport* (New York: Weatherhill, 1979), p. 14.
424. Earhart, *Mount Fuji*, pp. 11–12.
425. K. Suetaka, quoted in K. Tashiro, "Mt. Fuji and *waka* Poetry," in *Multidisciplinary Studies of the Environment and Civilization: Japanese Perspectives,* Y. Yasuda and M. Hudson (eds.) (London: Routledge, 2018), p. 73.
426. Earhart, *Mount Fuji,* p. 143.
427. R. Copelan, "Mythical Bad Girls: The Corpse, the Crone, and the Snake," in *Bad Girls of Japan*, L. Miller and J. Bardsley (eds.) (New York: Palgrave Macmillan, 2015), p. 28.
428. Yasunari Kawabata, *The Old Capital*, translated by J. Holman (San Francisco: North Point, 1987), p. 115.
429. Yasunari Kawabata, "Snow Country," in *Snow Country and Thousand Cranes,* translated by E. Seidensticker (New York: Alfred A. Knopf, 1978), pp. 16-17.
430. Yasunari Kawabata, *The Sound of the Mountain*, translated by E. Seidensticker (New York: Berkley Medallion Books, 1970), p. 13.
431. Quoted in D. Cavallaro, *The Animé Art of Hayao Miyazaki* (Jefferson, NC: McFarland & Company, 2006), p. 122.
432. Cavallaro, *Animé Art*, p. 123
433. "Spirits, Gods and Pastel Paints: The Weird World of Master Animator Hayao Miyazaki," *The Independent*, accessed January 27, 2019, https://www.independent.co.uk/arts-entertainment/films/features/spirits-gods-and-pastel-paints-the-weird-world-of-master-animator-hayao-miyazaki-1880974.html.
434. Lucy Wright, "Forest Spirits, Giant Insects and World Trees: The Nature Vision of Hayao Miyazaki," *Journal of Religion and Popular Culture,* vol. 10, no. 1 (2005).
435. Gabrielle Bellot, "Hayao Miyazaki and the Art of Being a Woman," *The Atlantic*, accessed January 26, 2019, https://www.theatlantic.com/entertainment/archive/2016/10/hayao-miyazaki-and-the-art-of-being-a-woman/503978/.

Sources for Boxes

Laws of Manu (p. 27), *Sacred Books of the East*, vol. 25, tr. George Bühler, found at https://www.sacred-texts.com/hin/manu/manu05.htm. • *The Dhammapada* (p. 36), translated by John Ross Carter and Mahinda Palihawadana (Oxford: Oxford University Press, 1987). • Thich Nhat Hanh (p. 38), *Calming the Fearful Mind: A Zen Response to Terrorism* (Berkeley, CA: Parallax Press, 2005), p. 48. • Suzuki (p. 42), *Introduction to Zen Buddhism*, p. 95. • Jack Kerouac (p. 43), *The Dharma Bums* (London: Penguin, 1976), p. 5. • Norgay (p. 44), *Tiger of the Snows*, p. 98. • Ruan Ji poem (p. 54) in *Songs of My Heart: The Chinese Lyric Poetry of Ruan Ji*, tr. by Graham Hartill & Wu Fusheng (London: Wellsweep), 1988. • Liu Ling (p. 55), "Hymn to the Virtue of Wine" in *Classical Chinese Literature: An Anthology of Translations from Antiquity to the Tang Dynasty*, eds. John Minford and Joseph S. M. Lau (New York: Columbia University Press), p. 471. • Yellow Emperor (p. 56), *The Yellow Emperor's Classic of Medicine: A New Translation of the Neijing Suwen with Commentary*, tr. Maoshing Ni (Shambhala, 1995). • Bruce Lee (p. 59), *Tao of Jeet Kune Do* (Santa Clarita, CA: Ohara, 1975). • Osun Praise Poetry (p. 65), taken from "Invocation," tr. Jacob Olupona, in "Orisa Osun: Yoruba Sacred Kinship and Civil Religion in Osogbo, Nigeria," in *Osun across the Waters: A Yoruba Goddess in Africa and the Americas*, eds. Joseph M. Murphy, Mei-Mei Sanford (Bloomington, IN: Indiana University Press, 2001), pp. 48-49. • Oyèrónkẹ́ Oyèwùmí (p. 67), *Invention of Women*, p. 31. • Boukman's Prayer (p. 70), quoted in Margaret Mitchell Armand, *Healing in the Homeland: Haitian Vodou Tradition* (Lanham, MD: Lexington Books, 2013), p. 57. • Wole Soyinka (p. 72), *Death and the King's Horseman*, p. 11. • Book of Genesis (p. 78), https://www.chabad.org/library/bible_cdo/aid/8167/jewish/Chapter-3.htm. • Yehuda Amichai, "My Parents' Motel" (p. 79), from *Poets on the Edge: An Anthology of Contemporary Hebrew Poetry*, ed. Tsipi Keller (Albany, NY: SUNY Press, 2008), p. 6. • Moses Maimonides, *Guide for the Perplexed* (chp. LIX, tr. by M. Friedländer, 1903) at https://www.sacred-texts.com/jud/gfp/gfp069.htm. • Judith Plaskow (p. 82), *Standing Again at Sinai: Judaism from a Feminist Perspective* (New York: HarperCollins, 1991), pp. 125–26. • Elie Wiesel (p. 84), *Night* (New York: Hill and Wang, 2006), chapter 3. • Theodor Herzl (p. 86), *Old New Land*, tr. David Simon Blondheim (Federation of American Zionists, 1916), chp. 6 at https://www.jewishvirtuallibrary.org/quot-altneuland-quot-theodor-herzl. • Nicaea II (p. 98), from https://www.papalencyclicals.net/councils/ecum07.htm. • Tolstoy (p. 99), *Resurrection*, tr. Louise Maude (Champaign, IL: Project Gutenberg, 1999), p. 288. Winthrop (p. 102), "A Model of Christian Charity," https://teachingamericanhistory.org/library/document/a-model-of-christian-charity-2/. • Al-Sadr (p. 110), *Al-Hayat*, Feb. 1, 1974, quoted in Augustus Richard Norton, "Musa al-Sadr," in *Pioneers of Islamic Revival*, ed. Ali Rahnema (London: Zed Books, 1994), p. 197. • Medieval Wafa document (p. 111), quoted in David W. Tschanz, "The Islamic Roots of the Modern Hospital in *Aramco World*, March/April 2017, at https://www.aramcoworld.com/Articles/March-2017/The-Islamic-Roots-of-the-Modern-Hospital. • al Arabi (p. 113), *Futuhat* 11 111.12; cf. 11 325.13, translated in W. C. Chittick, "The Divine Roots of Human Love," *Journal of the Mubyiddin Ibn 'Arabi Society* XVII, 1995, p. 57. • Malcolm X (p. 117), in *The Autobiography of Malcolm X*, pp. 184-85. • Xunzi (p. 125), quoted in Burton Watson, *Xunzi: Basic Writings* (New York: Columbia University Press, 2003), pp. 118-119. • Yuan Mei (p. 129), *The Way of Eating: Yuan Mei's Manual of Gastronomy*, tr. Sean J.S. Chen (Great Barrington, MA: Berkshire, 2019), p. 22. • Amy Tan (p. 129), *The Joy Luck Club* (London: Penguin, 1989), p. 48. • Khoo Seow Hwa (p. 130), and Nancy I. Penrose, *Behind the Brushstrokes: Appreciating Chinese Calligraphy* (Hong Kong: Asia 2000, 2003), Author's Note, 1. • Kirpal Singh (p. 142), "It is a Noble Search," in Ruth Seader, *The Teaching of Kirpal Singh*, vol. 1 (Bowling Green, VA: Sawan Kirpal Publications, 1981), pp. 77–78. • Amrita Pritam (p. 145), *Life and Times* (New Delhi: Vikas, 1989), p. 122. • Diné Bahane' (p.

152), in Zolbrod, *Diné Bahane'*, pp. 50–51. • Christine Martin (p. 157), in Zolbrod and Willink, *Weaving a World*, p. 2. • Esther Belin (p. 162), "Contemporary Navajo Writers' Relevance to Navajo Society," *Wicazo Sa Review*, vol. 22, no. 1 (Spring, 2007), p. 73. • *Kojiki* (p. 166), from *The Kojiki: An Account of Ancient Matters*, tr. Gustav Heldt (New York: Columbia University, 2014), p. 8. • Munetada (p. 170), from T. Kurozumi and Kohmoto, *The Living Way*, p 73. • Raichō (p. 174), in "*Seitō* Manifesto," quoted in Jan Bardsley, *The Bluestockings of Japan : New Woman Essays and Fiction from Seitō*, 1911–16 (Ann Arbor: University of Michigan, 2007), p. 94. • Yosano Okiko (p. 174), "Mountain Moving Day," in Bardsley, *Bluestockings of Japan*, p. 256. • Yusunari Kawabata (p. 175), Nobel Prize Acceptance Speech, "Japan, the Beautiful, and Myself," found at https://www.nobelprize.org/prizes/literature/1968/kawabata/lecture/.

Image Credits

Part 1 Opener: The early *Upanishads*, manuscript preserved at the Lalchand Research Library, Ancient Indian Manuscript Collection, DAV College Digital Library Initiative, Chandigarh India, in association with SP Lohia and Indorama Charitable Trust. Photo: Ms. Sarah Welch (Wikimedia Commons [WMC]). Chapter 1: Shiva statue in front of CERN: Kenneth Lu (Wikimedia Commons [WMC]). Lord Shiva statue, Rishikesh: Vijay Bkn (WMC). Sunita Williams: NASA. Swami Vivekananda, Chicago, September 1893: Unknown photographer (WMC). Chapter 2: Large Gautama Buddha statue in Buddha Park of Ravangla, Sikkim: Subhrajyoti07 (WMC). Thich Nhat Hanh in Paris, 2006.: Duc (pixiduc) from Paris, France (WMC). Kerouac: 1949 Frazer automobile, Rex Gray (WMC). Dalai Lama: Unknown photographer (WMC). Chapter 3: Yin and Yang symbol: http://clipart-library.com/free/the-black-and-white-symbol.html. Li Po crater: Photo taken by the MESSENGER space probe in 2011. NASA. Seven Sages: Shinzhao (WMC). Chinese Acupuncture chart, 18th century. Credit: Wellcome Collection. Attribution 4.0 International (CC BY 4.0). Bruce Lee statue: Johnson Lau (WMC). Abing: Unknown photographer (WMC). Chapter 4: Oduduwa: (Akintoye Dekalu) Akidek (WMC). Sacred grove: Alex Mazzeto (WMC). Oyèrónkẹ́ Oyèwùmí: Courtesy Oyèrónkẹ́ Oyèwùmí (WMC). Tree on savannah: Ron-bd (Pixabay).

Part 2 Opener: The Ten Commandments. Photo: Lindert (WMC). Chapter 5: Elie Wiesel: David Shankbone, 2010, in New York City (WMC). Women at Western Wall: ChameleonsEye/Shutterstock.com. Marx Brothers poster: MGM (scan by Heritage Auctions; WMC). Chapter 6: Pieta: Stanislav Traykov (WMC). Tolstoy: Sergei Prokudin-Gorsky, 1908 (WMC). *Mayflower*: From John Clark Ridpath, *The United States: A History* (Boston, 1893) (WMC). Chapter 7: Mosque: Emre Can (Pexels). Ibn Sina (Avicenna): Banque d'images de la Bibliothèque interuniversitaire de santé (CIPB2067) (WMC). Dervishes: diaz/Flickr (WMC). Naguib Mahfouz: https://www.alaraby.co.uk/diffah/civilisation/2017/12/12/مكانة-نجيب-محفوظ-غرافيا-القاهرة-عربـ-الزمن (WMC). Macolm X: Ed Ford, *World Telegram* staff photographer, Library of Congress. New York World-Telegram & Sun Collection. http://hdl.loc.gov/loc.pnp/cph.3c15058. Bhutto: SRA Gerald B. Johnson, United States Department of Defense (WMC). Malala Yousafzai at White House: Pete Souza, White House (P101113PS-1119) (WMC).

Part 3 Opener: Annotated version of the *Book of Rites*, dating from before 907 CE (WMC). Chapter 8: Confucius: Kano Tan'yû (1602–1674), *Confucius and His Disciples Yanzi and Huizi at the "Apricot Altar"*. Mid-17th century. Ink and light color on silk, panel. Museum of Fine Arts, Boston (WMC). Female musicians: Detail from the Chinese painting *Night Revels of Han Xizai*, handscroll, ink and colors on silk. Original by Gu Hongzhong (10th century), 12th century remake from the Song Dynasty. Collection of the Palace Museum in Beijing (WMC). Wok: Cooking dumplings with a wok on an outdoor stove in Shenzhen, China. Mx. Granger (WMC). Calligraphy: Wang Xianzhi (344–386), Tang Dynasty, Taito Ward Calligraphy Museum (WMC). Chapter 9: Sikh woman: ChiccoDodiFC (Shutterstock). Kirpal Singh: Ruhani Satsang (WMC). Punjab partition: Chicago *Sun-Times*, 1947. Amrita Pritam: Photo taken in 1948. Amarjit Chandan Collection (http://theprg.co.uk/2008/08/) (WMC). Chapter 10: Coyote: Warren Metcalf (Shutterstock). Canyon de Chelly: Photograph of Sacred Spider Rock at the entrance to Monument Canyon, Canyon de Chelly, Navajo Indian Reservation, Arizona, ca.1900. California Historical Society Collection, 1860-1960. USC Libraries Special Collections (WMC). Navajo with loom: Timothy H. O'Sullivan, "Aboriginal life among the Navajoe Indians. Near old Fort Defiance, N.M./T. H." 1873. Library of Congress Call Number: LOT 4677-C, no. 7 [P&P] (WMC). Monument Valley: Moritz Zimmerman (WMC). Chapter 11: Noh masks: Wmpearl (WMC). Japanese Sun goddess Amaterasu: Utagawa Kunisada, 1856 (WMC). Sumo wrestlers: Yves Picq (http://veton.picq.fr) (WMC). Mount Fuji: Krishna. Wu (Shutterstock). Forest: Free-Photos (Pixabay).

Index

Italicized titles are literary works unless otherwise noted.

Abe, Shinzo, 166
Abing, 59–60
Abraham, 78, 80, 85, 90, 107, 108
Abu Bakr, 109, 119
Abu Talib, 109, 119
Acupuncture, 55–57, 61
Adam, 77–78, 90
Adams, Samuel, 102
Adi Granth, 139, 148
AfroCuba de Matanzas, 69, 74
Agni, 19, 31
Ahimsa, 27, 31
Akiko, Yosano, 174, 179
Al-Aqsa Mosque, 109, 119
Al-Arabi, 113, 119
Al-Ghazali, 113, 119
Al-Hussein Mosque, 115, 119
Ali, 109, 119
Alighieri, Dante, 111
Allah, 107–121
Allen, Woody, 87, 88, 91
Al-Mutawa, Naif, 112
Alternative medicine, 56, 61
Amar Chitra Katha, 23
Amaterasu, 165, 170, 171, 178
Amichai, Yehuda, 79
Amida Buddha, 38, 47
Amritsar, 140, 142, 148
Analects, 123ff.
Ancestor worship, 126–127, 134
Andrei Rublev (film), 99
Angelou, Maya, 116
Anime, 176
Anti-semitism, 85–86, 90
Arjuna, 21, 31
Ark of the covenant, 85
Arocena, Daymé, 69, 74
Ashura, 110, 119
Autobiography of Malcolm X, The, 117
Avalokiteśvara, 35, 38, 47
Avicenna, *see* Ibn Sina
Àyàn, 68–69, 74
Baal Shem Tov, 81, 90
Babalawos, 64, 74
Baghdad, 110, 112

Bahia, 69
Bakdash, 107
Baldwin, Shauna Singh, 144–146, 149
Bande Mein Tha Dum (song), 29
Baptism, 95, 104
Baptists, 103, 104
Barboncito, 156, 163
Bashō, 41, 42, 47
Batá drums 68–69, 74
Batárumba, 69
Battle of Gujrat, 141, 148
Battle of Muktsar, 140, 148
Beat Generation, 43, 47
Beatitudes, 96
Bedi, Bishan Singh, 146–147, 148
Beijing, 133
Belin, Esther, 162, 163
Bengal, 25, 31
Ben-Gurion, David, 86, 90
Benin, 69
Berlin, Irving, 87, 90
Bethlehem, 94, 104
Bhadda Kundalakesa, 37, 47
Bhagavad Gita, 21, 22, 27, 31
Bhagavata Purana, 24
Bhai Kanhaiya, 140, 148
Bhakti, 24, 31
Bhutto, Benazir, 117–118, 120
Bible (Hebrew), 15, 78, 81, 90
Bimaristans, 111
"Black Lions," 141, 148
Blanca Peak, 152, 163
Blessingway, 152, 163
Blue Cliff Record, 41, 47
"Blue-sing on the Brown Vibe," 162
Bodhidharma, 40, 41
Bodhisattvas, 37, 38, 47
Bois Caiman, 70, 74
Bollywood, 28–30, 31
"Book from the Sky, A," 131
Book of Changes (*I Ching*), 49, 50, 55, 61
Book of Songs, 125
Book on Filial Piety, 127, 134
Born from Water, 155, 159, 163
Bosque Redondo, 156, 163
Bradley, Lee, 160, 164
Brazil, 69–70

British East India Company, 141
Brothers Karamazov, The, 101
BTS, 132, 134
Buber, Martin, 83, 91
Buddha, 35–48
Buddhism, 35–48
Buonarotti, Michelangelo, *see* Michelangelo
Bush, President George W., 159
Cairo Trilogy, The, 114–116
Cairo, 114–116
Calligraphy, 130–131, 134
Canaan, 85
Candomblé dancing, 69, 74
Candrakīrti, 35, 47
Canon of Medicine, The, 111
"Canticle of the Sun," 97, 104
Canyon de Chelly, 156, 157, 163
Cao Wenyi, 52, 61
Capella, Martianus, 13
Carnival, 70
Cayman Wood Ceremony (painting), 71
CERN (European Organization for Nuclear Research), 20
Chan Buddhism, 40–41, 47
Chang San-Feng, 57, 61
Changing Woman, 154, 155, 163
Charles, Ray, 103
Cherry tree, 173, 178
China, 123–135
Ching Ming Festival, 127, 134
Christianity, 93–106
Christmas, 94, 104
Chu Hsi, 130, 135
Cidambaram Temple, 20, 31
"City of God," 97
"City of Man," 97
Cloud wandering, 52, 61
Code talkers, 158–159
Cognitive behavioral therapy (CBT), 39
Concentration camps, 85
Confessions, 98, 104
Confucianism, 123–135; gender relations and, 128; food and, 128–129; role of music in, 125–126; sports and, 132–133
Corn, 151, 163
Council of Ephesus, 94, 105
Covenant, 78, 90
Coyote, 152–154, 163
Crazy Rich Asians, 130
Cricket, 146–147
Crime and Punishment, 100–101
Cromwell, Oliver, 102
Cross, 96, 105
Crucifixion, 96, 105
Cuba, 68–69
Cultural Revolution, 128, 135
Cyril of Alexandria, 94, 105
Dae Jang Geum (television program), 131–132, 135

Dah'iiistlo, 157
Dakshineswasr Temple, 25, 26, 31
Dalai Lama, 44, 45–46, 47
Damaru, 19, 31
Damascus, 109
Dao, definition, 49, 51
Daoism, 49–62
Darwin, Charles, 115
David, King, 85, 90
David, Larry, 88, 91
Death and the King's Horseman, 71–73
Dev, Kapil, 146, 149
Devgn, Ajay, 28–29, 31
Devi Mahatmya, 25, 31
Dhammapada, The, 36, 47
Dharamsala, India, 45, 47
Dharma Bums, 43
Dharma, 22–23, 31, 37, 47
Diaspora, Jewish, 79, 90
Diaspora, Sikh, 144
Diaspora, Yoruba, 68ff., 74
Diego, Juan, 95
Diné Bahane', 152, 163
Diné, 152, 156, 157, 163
Disciples, of Jesus, 96
Disenchantment of the world, 13
Divali, 25, 31
Divine Comedy, 111
Divine right of kings, 102, 105
Dogen, 41, 47
Dook'o'oosliid, 151, 152
Dorsey, Thomas, 103
Dostoyevsky, Fyodor, 99–101, 105
Dragon boat racing, 133, 135
Duleep Singh, 137, 149
Durga, 25, 31
Dussera, 31
Dutt, Sanjay, 29
Dutty, Boukman, 70, 74
Eagle, 151. 163
Easter, 96–97, 105
Eastern Orthodox Church, 99, 105
Egypt, 114–116
"Elegies," 174–175
Emperor Meiji, 167, 178
Empress Shōken, 167, 178
Enchanted wisdom, definition, 13
Enchantment, definition, 13
Engaged Buddhism, 38, 47
Enter the Dragon (film), 58, 61
Erhu, 59, 61
Esu, 65–67, 70, 74
Eucharist, 96
Eve, 77–78, 90
Existentialist philosophers, 83, 90
Exodus, Book of, 79, 90
Favelas, 69

Fez, Morocco, 79–80
Fifth World, 151–152
Filial piety, 127–128
First Man and First Woman, 151–152, 153, 155, 163
Five Classics, 123, 135
Five Ks, 139–140, 149
Five Pillars of Islam, 107, 120
Five-fingered people, 155, 163
Ford, John, 159–161
Forty Liberated Ones, 140, 149
Foundations of Mindfulness (*Satipathāna Sutra*), 39, 47
Four Books, 123, 135
Four Noble Truths, 36, 47
Fourth World, 151
France, 70
Franklin, Benjamin, 102, 104
Freud, Sigmund, 87, 91
Fundamentalism, 117, 120
Gabriel, 94, 109, 120
Gagarin, Yuri, 14
Gandhi, Maneka, 28, 32
Gandhi, Mohandas, 27, 32
Ganges River, 25, 31
Garba (dance), 29
Garden of Eden, 77–78, 90
Gender, religious views of, 15
Gender-neutral, 82, 90
Genesis, Book of 78, 90
Gethsemane, 96, 105
Ginsberg, Allen, 43
Girls' Generation, 132, 135
Gita Govinda, 24, 31
Gobernador Knob, 152, 163
God (Christian), 93–106
God (Hebrew), 77–91; gender of, 81–82; love for, 79–80; searching for, 79; silence of, 83–84; talking to, 83
God of War (video game), 14
Golgotha, 96
Goliyon Ki Raasleela Ream-Leela (film), 29–30
Gopīs, 24, 25, 31
Gorman, Carl, 161, 163
Gorman, R.C., 161, 164
Gospel (musical genre), 103, 105
Gospels, Christian, 93, 105
Gotami, Kisa, 36–37
Goulding, Harry, 159–160
Goulding's Trading Post, 160, 163
Great Schism, 99, 105
Gurdwaras, 138, 149
Guru Arjan Dev, 139, 140, 149
Guru Gobind Singh, 139, 140, 144, 149
Guru Granth Sahib, 139, 141, 149
Guru Nanak, 137–139, 145, 149
Gurus, 139, 149
Hadith, 108
Hagar, 108, 120
Hagoromo (play), 168–169

Haiku, 41, 42, 47
Haiti, 70–71
Hajj, 108, 116, 117, 120
Handsome Monkey King, 53, 61
Hanuman, 22, 30, 31
Harmandir Sahib, 140, 149
Hasidism, 81
Hatsumode, 167, 178
Havana, 68, 74
He, 125, 135
Hermes, 13
Herzl, Theodor, 86
Hexagrams, 49, 61
Hijra, 109, 120
Hinduism, 19–33
Hogan, 152, 163
Holiday, Samuel, 159, 164
Holiness, 83
Holistic, definition, 56, 61
Holocaust, 84, 87, 90
Holy Land, 85
Holy People, 151–152, 154, 164
"Homage to Navajo Women," 161
House of Wisdom, 110, 112, 120
Householder, 25, 31
"How I Got Over," 103, 105
Hózhó, 152
Hsiao Xing, 127
Huashan Mountain, 49, 61
Huerforno Mountain, 152
Hum Dil De Chuke Sanam (film), 28–29
Humour, Jewish, 87
Hunt, John, 44
Hussein ibn Ali, 109, 120
Hymns, 103, 105
Ibn Sina, 110–111, 120
Icons, 98–99
Ifá, 64, 74
Ijapa, 63
Ila-Orangun, 65
Ile-Ife, 63, 74
Immaculate conception, 94, 105
Imperial House of Japan, 167, 178
India, 137ff.
Indra, 19, 32
Inquisition, 97, 105
Inside Amy Schumer (television program), 89
Iran, 110
Iraq, 110
Isaac, 78, 90, 108
Ise Shrine, 166, 178
Ishmael, 108
Islam, 107–121
Israel, 86–87
Iwo Jima, 158, 159
Iyá, 69, 74
Izanagi, 167, 168

Izanami, 167, 168
Izutsu (play), 168, 169–170
Jackson, Mahalia, 103, 105
Jade Emperor, 53, 61
Jade Maiden Peak, 49
Jallianwala Bagh Massacre, 142, 149
James, William, 15
Janamsākhīs, 138, 149
Japan, 165–179
Jayadeva, 24, 32
Jean-Pierre, Ulrick, 71, 75
Jeremiah, 85
Jerusalem, 86, 109, 111
Jesus Christ, 94, 95, 96, 98, 99, 101, 105
Job, 84, 90
Job, Book of, 84, 90
John Ford Point, 161
John the Baptist, 95, 105
Johnston, Philip, 158
Jordan River, 95
Journey to the West, The, 53, 62
Judaism, 77–91
Jung, Carl, 40
Kabaa, 108
Kachera, 139
Kahn, Shah Rukh (SRK), 30
Kālī, 25, 26, 32
Kami, 166, 167, 170, 171, 172, 178
Kangha, 139
Kara, 139
Karandavyuha Sutra, 38
Karbala, 109–110, 120
Kawabata, Yasunari, 174–175, 179
Kerouac, Jack, 43
Kesh, 139–140
Khadija, 109, 120
Khalsa, 139–140, 141, 149
Khama, 37, 47
Khamosh Pani (*Silent Waters*), 143–144, 149
Khoo Seow Hwa, 130
Kierkegaard, Søren, 78
Kinaaldá, 154, 163
King, Martin Luther, Jr., 27, 103, 105
Kirat Karo, 138, 149
Kirpan, 139–140
Knowledge, limits of, 77–79
Koans, 41, 47
Koh-I-Noor diamond, 137
Kojiki, 166, 171, 173, 178
Konohana Sakuya, 172–173, 178
Kook, Isaac, 87, 90
K-pop, 132, 135
Krishna, 21, 24, 25, 27, 32
Kung fu, 58–59, 61
Kushner, Rabbi Harold, 84
Kwan, Kevin, 129, 135
Kyoto, 173, 178

Lagaan (film), 146
Lage Raho Munna Bhai (film), 29
Lagos Market Women's Association, 67, 74
Lagos, Nigeria, 14, 71, 74
Lahore, Pakistan, 137, 139, 142, 149
Lalo the carpenter, 138, 149
Laozi, 49, 51, 55, 61
Laozi, 50, 61
Last Supper, 96, 105
Laws of Manu, 27, 28, 32
Lecha Dodi, 80, 82
Lee, Bruce, 58–59
Lhasa, Tibet, 45, 47
Li Po, 52, 61
Li Sao, 133, 135
Li, 126, 130, 135
Little Richard, 103
Liu Ling, 55, 61
Long Walk, 156, 164
Longstreet (television program), 58–59, 61
Lord Dalhousie, 137
Lotus Sutra, 38, 47
Love and Death (film), 88
Luke, Book of, 94
Lunar calendar, 133, 135
Luria, Isaac, 81, 90
Luther, Martin, 101, 105
Mahābhāgavata Purāna, 25, 32
Mahāyāna tradition, 38, 47
Mahfouz, Naguib, 114–116, 120
Mai Bhago, 140
Maimonides, Moses, 79–81, 91, 111
Maize, *see* Corn
Majinai, 170, 178
Malcolm X, 116–117, 120
Man'yōshū poets, 173, 178
Mandala, 35, 48
Manga, 176, 178
Manuelito, 156, 164
Mao Zedong, 45
Mara, 37, 48
Mariner 10, 52
"Marriage of Mercury and Philology," 13
Martin, Christine, 157
Martyrs, 110, 120
Marx Brothers, 87, 88, 91
Marx, Groucho, 87, 88
Mary, 93, 94, 95, 98, 105
Masks, 168–170
Matanzas, 68, 74
Mayflower, 102
Mecca, 107, 108, 117, 120, 138
Medicine men, 152, 164
Medina, Saudi Arabia, 109, 120
Meditation, 39, 48
Mencius, 127, 129, 135
Mercury (planet), 52

Mercury (god), 13, 16
Meridians, 56, 61
Messiah, 81, 91
"Mic Drop" (song), 132
Michelangelo, 94–95, 105
Middle Passage, 68, 74
Middle Way, 42, 48
Mindfulness, 39–40, 48
Mind-to-mind transmission, 40, 48
Mirabai, 25, 32
Miracles, 95–96
Miriam, Rivka, 85, 91
Mirror room, 168, 178
Miyazaki, Hayao, 176, 178
Modern Filial Piety Museum, 128
Moksha, 19, 21, 32
Mongol invasion, 112
Monotheism, in Judaism, 77ff., 91
Monster Slayer, 155, 159, 164
"Montreal, 1962," 146
Monument Valley, 159–161
Moon Reflected on the Second Springs, The, 59, 60, 62
Moses, 79, 80
Mount Everest (*Chomolungma*), 43–45, 48
Mount Fuji, 172–173, 178
Mount Hesperus, 152, 164
Mount Sinai, 79, 80
Mount Taylor, 152, 164
Mount Zion, 86
Mughal Empire, 137, 140, 149
Muhammad Ali, 116
Muhammad, 107–121
Munetada, Kurozumi, 170–171
Musa al-Sadr, Imam, 110, 120
Muslims, in India, 30
My Love from the Star (television program), 132
Nachman of Bratslav, Rabbi, 81, 91
Nádleehí, 154–155, 164
Nago, 69, 74
Nakagawa, Soen, 14
Napoleon, 70
National Nurses Day, 110
Navajo Gallery, 161, 164
Navajo Nation Museum, 162, 164
Navajo, 15, 151–164; gender fluidity among, 154–155; reservations ("rez"), 161–162; status of women among, 155; weaving by, 157–158
Nazareth, 94, 105
Negative theology, 80, 91
Neo-Confucianism, 126, 135
Nepal, 44
New Account of Tales of the World, A, 54, 61
New Orleans, 71
New York City, 87
Nicaea II, 98, 105
Nigeria, 71
Night at the Opera, A, 88 (film)

Night Journey, 109, 120
Nihongi, 166, 178
Ninety-five Theses, 101, 106
Ninety-Nine [99], The, 112, 121
Nirvana, 37, 39, 48
Nishan Sahib, 140
Noble Eightfold Path, 37, 38, 48
Noe, Itō, 174, 178
Noh theatre, 167–170
Nong Yu, 49, 61
Norgay, Tenzing, 43–45, 48
"Ode to Waris Shah," 144
Odissi dance, 24, 32
Oduduwa, 64, 74
Ogou Ferrai, 70, 75
Ogun, 70, 74
Ōkami (video game), 176, 178
Oke'badan Festival, 67, 75
Old Capital, The, 175
Old Testament, 94
Olodumare, 64, 65, 75
Olympics, 2008, Summer, 133
Om, 19, 32
Omayad Mosque, 107
"Orchard Pavilion Preface," 131, 135
Orisa, 63–76
Osama bin Laden, 117
Osogbo, 65
Ọṣun, 65, 68
Ọṣun-Osogbo Festival, 65, 75
Ouidah, 70, 75
Owl, 154
Oyèwùmí, Oyèrónkẹ́, 67
Oyo Empire, 69
Padukone, Deepika, 29, 31
Pai, Anant ("Uncle Pai"), 23, 31
Pakistan, 117–118, 137ff.
Palace of Desire, 114, 115
Palace Wall, 114–115
Palden Lhamo, 45, 48
Palestine, 86–87
Palestinians, 86–87
Pāli Canon, 35, 48
Pāṇini, 19, 32
Panth, 146, 149
Papa Legba, 70, 75
Papal infallibility, 101, 106
Parliament of World's Religions, 26, 32
Partition, of India/Punjab, 142–146, 149; women and, 144–146
Patkas, 147, 149
Paul the Apostle, 97, 106; *see also* Saint Paul
Pelewura, Alimotu, 67, 74
People for the Ethical Treatment of Animals (PETA), 97
People of the Book, 111, 120
Philology, 13, 16
Pietà, 94–95

Pilate, Pontius, 96
Pinjar, 144–145
Pipa, 59, 61
Plaskow, Judith, 82
Pokémon (video game), 176, 178
Pope Francis, 97
Potala Palace, 45, 48
"Precious Lord, Take My Hand," 103, 106
Princess Mononoke (film), 176, 179
Pritam, Amrita, 144–145, 148
Promised Land, 85
Pueblo, 15
Punjab, 137ff.
Puritans, 102, 106
Qi, 55–56, 61
Qu Yuan, 133, 135
Quanzhen School, 52, 62
Queen Mother, 53, 62
Queen Victoria, 137
Qur'an, 107, 108, 109, 110, 112, 118, 120
Rābi'a of Basra, 112–113, 120
Radcliffe Line, 142, 145, 149
Radcliffe, Cyril, 142
Rādhā, 24, 32
Rai, Aishwarya, 28–29, 31
Raichō, 174, 179
Rama, 22, 23, 32
Ramadan, 107, 120
Ramakrishna, 25–26, 32
Ramayan (television program), 23
Ramayana, 22, 29, 32
Rapture, 98, 106
Rāsa, 24, 32
Ravana, 22, 23, 30, 32
Redhouse, John, 156, 163
Reformation, Protestant, 101–102, 106
Reincarnation, 20, 32
Ren, 124–125, 127, 130, 135
Resurrection, 100
Resurrection, 96
Ring ceremony, 172, 179
Rio de Janeiro, 70
Roman Catholic Church, 97–99, 106
Rosh Hashanah, 78, 91
Rōshi, 42, 48
Ruan Ji, 54, 62
Rublev, Andrei, 99, 104
"Rules for Students and Children," 128
Rūmī, 113–114, 120
Russia, 98–100
Russian Orthodox Church, 98, 100
Sabbath, 79, 91
Sacred Spider Rock, 156
Safed, 80, 81, 91
Sage, 125, 135
Sahni, Bhisham, 143
Saint Paul, 15

Saints, 97–98, 106
Saladin, *see* Salāh al-Dīn
Salāh al-Dīn, 111–112, 120
Samba, 69–70, 75
Samsāra, 35, 48
San Francisco Peaks, 151, 164
Sangha, 37, 48
Sanskrit, 19, 32
Santería, 68, 75
Sarabhai, Mallika, 23, 32
Sarah Silverman Program, The (television program), 89
Sarah, 108
Sarov, Russia, 93
Satori, 40, 48
Schlesinger, Rabbi Hanan, 87
Schumer, Amy, 89
Searchers, The (film), 160, 164
Secular Age, The, 14
Seiji, Ozawa, 59–60
Seinfeld (television program), 88
Seinfeld, Jerry, 88, 90
Seitō Manifesto, 174, 179
Seitō, 174, 179
Sermon on the Mount, 99–100
Seven Realized Ones, 53, 62
Seven Sages of the Bamboo Grove, 54, 55
Shadow puppet shows, 54, 62
Shaku, Soyen, 42, 48
Sheik, 115, 120
Shema, 77, 91
Shi'ite Muslims, 109–110, 120
Shintoism, 165–179
Shiva Tandava Stotram, 32 [it]
Shiva, 20, 22, 23, 25, 32
Shrine culture, 166ff.
Siddhartha Gautama, 35, 36, 48; *see also* Buddha
Sikhism, 137–150
Silverman, Sarah, 88–89, 91
Singh, Harbhajan, 147
Singh, Kirpal, 141–142, 149
Singh, Puran, 140, 149
Singh, Ranjit, 141, 149
Singh, Taru, 139
Singh, Vir, 141, 150
Sita, 22, 23, 32
Sita's Daughters (play), 23
Sivaraksa, Sulak, 38, 48
Slave trade, 68–69, 75
Snow Country, 175
Snyder, Gary, 43, 47
Sọfọla, *'Zulu*, 67–68, 75
Solomon, King, 85
Soul, 97, 106
Sound of the Mountain, The, 175
South Korea, 131–132
Soyinka, Wole, 71–73, 75
Spider Woman, 157, 164

Spirited Away (film), 176, 179
Sq'áh naagháí Bik'eh Hózhó, 152
St. Augustine, 97, 98, 102, 106
St. John of Damascus, 94
St. Peter's Basilica, 95, 106
St. Seraphim of Sarov, 93, 106
St. Teresa of Ávila, 97–98, 106
St. Tikhon, 101
Stagecoach (film), 160, 164
Studio Ghibli, 176, 179
Suffering, in Buddhism, 36ff.
Sufis, 112–113
Sugar Street, 114, 116
Sugawara no Michizane, 167, 179
Sultanpur, 137, 149
Sumar, Sabhia, 143–144
Sumo wrestling, 171–172
Sun Buer, 53, 62
Sun Qianli, 130, 135
Sundari, 141, 150
Sunni Muslims, 109–110, 120
Susanoo, 165, 179
Suzuki, Daisetz, 42, 43, 47
Suzuki, Shunryu, 43, 48
Sweet Trap, The (play), 67
Syncretism, 71, 75
Tai-Chi, 55–56, 62
Tales of Ise, The, 169, 179
Taliban, 118, 120
Talking God, 155
Talmud, 79, 91
Tamas (*Darkness*), 143, 150
Tambor, 69, 75
Tamil, 23, 28, 32
Tan, Amy, 129, 134
Tarkovsky, Andrei, 99, 104
Taylor, Charles, 14
Ten Commandments, 79, 80, 91
Tengboche Monastery, 43, 48
Tenjin Shrines, 167, 179
Terreiros, 69, 75
Theatre of the Absurd, 87, 91
Theodicy, 84, 91
Thich Nhat Hanh, 38, 39, 48
Thoa Khalsa, 143, 150
Tibet, 45
Tigris River, 112, 121
Tiruvalluvar, 28, 33
Tolstoy, Lev, 99–101, 105
Torah, 77–79, 91
Torii, 166, 179
Traditional Chinese medicine, 55–56, 62
Transcendence, 93ff.
Translation Movement, 110, 121
Treaty of Bosque Redondo, 156, 164
Treaty of Lahore, 141, 150
Trinity, 99, 106
Tripata, Mata, 145, 149
Tso, Hastiin, 160
Turban, 139–140, 150
University of al-Qarawiyyin, 79–80
Valmiki, 22, 23, 33
Varanasi, 23, 33
Vatican, 95, 106
Vaudeville, 87, 91
Vedas, 19, 33
Virgin Mary of Guadalupe, 95, 106
Vishnu, 19, 33
Vivekananda, Swami, 26, 33
Vodou, 70–71, 75
Voodoo, *see* Vodou
Vulture Peak, 40, 48
Wagon Master (film), 160
Wailing Wall, 86, 91
Waka, 173, 179
Walcott, Derek, 15
Wang Xizhi, 131, 135
Wang Zhe, 52
Waqfa document, 111, 121
Water Monster, 153
Wauneka, Annie, 155, 163
Way of the Dragon (film), 58, 62
"Way of the Intercepting Fist," 58, 62
Wayne, John, 159–160
"We Shall Overcome," 103, 106
Weaving, 157–158; carding, 157, 163; loom, 157, 164; shearing, 157, 164; spinning, 157, 164; warp, 157, 164; weft, 157, 164
Weber, Max, 13, 14, 102
What the Body Remembers, 145–146
White Wind, 151, 164
Wiesel, Elie, 84–85
Williams, Sunita, 22, 32
Winthrop, John, 102, 105
Wok, 128, 135
Women, in Buddhism, 37ff.
Women, in Yorubaland, 66–67
Words, and reality, 50
World War II, 158–159
Wu-wei, 58, 62
Xango, 14, 69, 75
Xi Kang, 55, 62
Xu Bing, 131, 135
Xunzi, 125
Yamabe no Akahito, 173, 179
Yellow Emperor's Classic of Medicine, The, 56
Yellow, Billy, 160
Yin and *yang*, 50–51, 56, 57, 62
Yoga Sutra, 21, 22, 33
Yoga, 21, 22, 24, 33
Yokozuna, 172, 179
Yom Kippur, 78–79, 91
Yoruba Andabo, 69, 75
Yoruba, 63–76

Yorubaland, 63ff.
You Bet Your Life (television program), 88
Yousafzai, Malala, 118, 120
Yu Dan, 123, 135
Yuan Mei, 129
Zaynab, 109–110, 121
Zazen, 48
Zeami, 167–170, 179

Zen Buddhism, 40–42, 48
Zero, 20
Zhu Xi, 124, 125, 135
Zhuangzi, 52
Zionism, 86, 91
Zionist Congress, First, 86, 90
Zither, 55
Zuanghi, 55, 62

www.ingramcontent.com/pod-product-compliance
Lightning Source LLC
Chambersburg PA
CBHW081409080526
44589CB00016B/2513